RESEARCH HIGHLIGHTS IN TECHNOLOGY AND TEACHER EDUCATION 2014

Senior Book Editors:

Leping Liu
David Gibson

Book Editors:

Victoria Brown
Terry Cavanaugh
John Lee
Cleborne Maddux
Marilyn Ochoa
Matthew Ohlson
David Slykhuis
Joke Voogt

Published by
AACE--Association for the Advancement of Computing in Education

Research Highlights in Technology and Teacher Education 2014
(ISBN: 978-1-939797-10-0) is published by
AACE, PO Box 719, Waynesville, NC USA
757-366-5606; Fax: 703-997-8760; E-mail: info@aace.org
© Copyright 2014 by AACE
www.aace.org
Available at http://www.aace.org/bookshelf.htm

Research Highlights in Technology and Teacher Education 2014

Forward...5
Preface..7

Articles

TPACK AND PRESERVICE EDUCATION

The Construct is in the Eye of the Beholder: School Districts' Appropriations and Reconceptualizations of TPACK..11
    Judi Harris and Mark Hofer (USA)

Preparing Special Education Teachers to Teach Mathematics and Science with Technology: A Study of Teachers' Surveys and Lesson Plans...19
    Irina Lyublinskaya and Nelly Tournaki (USA)

Mathematical Content, Pedagogy, and Technology: What It Can Mean to Practicing Teachers........................27
    Beth Bos and Kathryn Lee (USA)

Designing an Educational Technology Course for Preservice Social Studies Teachers Based on Technological Pedagogical Content Knowledge (TPACK) Survey Results......................................35
    Mark Hart and Swapna Kumar (USA)

Impact of Design Teams on Preservice Teachers' TPACK, Attitudes, & Skills..............................43
    Laurene Johnson (USA)

A Systems Approach for Integrating Multiple Technologies as Important Pedagogical Tools for TPACK............51
    Henry Gillow-Wiles and Margaret L. Niess (USA)

ASSESSMENT

Assessment-Talks and Talking about Assessment: Negotiations of Multimodal Texts at the Boundary...............59
    Anna-Lena Godhe and Berner Lindström (Sweden)

From Creation to Curation: Evolution of an Authentic 'Assessment *for* Learning' Task................69
    Peter R Albion (Australia)

RESEARCH ON LEARNING

Video Self Modeling via iPods: The Road to Independent Task Completion.............................79
    Julie Bucalos, Debra Bauder and Anne Bucalos (USA)

Using Digital Resources to Support Personalized Learning Experiences in K-12 Classrooms: The Evolution of Mobile Devices as Innovations in Schools...85
    Savilla Banister and Rachel Vannatta Reinhart (USA)

The Impact of a Digital Storytelling Assignment on Non-English-Major-Students' Motivation for Learning English in a Japanese University..91
    Naoko Kasami (Japan)

RESEARCH ON TEACHING

Psychosocial and Cognitive Dimensions of the 'Self' within Pre-service Teachers' Reflective Blogs................101
    Shaunna Smith and Rubén Garza (USA)

Patterns of Mathematics Teachers' Characteristics and Beliefs about Computer Use in Education: A Cluster Analytic Approach..111
    Onder KOKLU (Turkey), Elizabeth Jakubowski (USA), Tayfun SERVI(Turkey) and Jiajing Huang (USA)

Developing an Open Online Course for Teachers and Student Teachers...121
    Louise Mifsud, Tonje Hilde Giæver, Vibeke Bjarnø, Eli Gjølstad and Irene Beyer –Log (Norway)

Guiding Preservice Teacher Candidates to Implement Student-Centered Applications of Technology in the Classroom..131
    Christine J. Anderson and Laura Kieran (USA)

FOREWORD

Research Highlights in Technology and Teacher Education is now in its sixth year of publication, and has become one of the most important publications of the *Society for Information Technology and Teacher Education* (SITE). This series of books represent the best of the scholarship offered at the SITE international conference, this year held in Jacksonville, Florida and featuring about 1000 scholars and educators from nearly 60 countries.

Only a select set of articles, from the broad array of papers presented at the SITE conference, are accepted for publication in *Research Highlights*. To be considered for publication, a submission must first be accepted for presentation at the conference as a "full paper" and then designated for consideration as a potential article for the *Research Highlights* collection. At that point, an even more rigorous review commences. While still a relatively "new" publication, *Research Highlights* is already one of the most viewed in the extensive holdings of the *AACE* digital library (EdITLib).

The articles in this edition are guided and nurtured by a very strong team of editors. Articles in categories of TPACK, Assessment, Research and Teacher Education represent the four overarching themes of this year's offering. Notably, a third of the articles this year are authored by scholars outside the U.S.

In many ways, this publication reflects the healthy state of an organization that is increasingly recognized as an international leader in the intersecting fields of learning technologies and teacher education. As SITE celebrates its 25th anniversary, a publication representing such a rich and important scholarship is an important achievement.

This year's *Research Highlights in Technology and Teacher Education* is under the solid leadership of senior editors Leping Liu and David C. Gibson. I cannot thank them enough for their steadfastness and professional dedication. As an organization, SITE is notably strengthened by their unyielding commitment and rigorous standards. In addition to their outstanding professionalism, the *Research Highlights* collection would not be possible without the dedication of the numerous book editors and reviewers, who collectively did the tough editing and review work necessary to bring this collection to fruition.

As I conclude my tenure as SITE president, I wish to thank those who were instrumental in launching *Research Highlights in Technology and Teacher Education*, notably Ian Gibson, Gerald Knezek, and Cleborne Maddux. And I know that SITE's new president David Slykhuis is fully committed to the important academic role that SITE plays for an array of international scholars.

As you read this year's collection, I hope you consider ways that your voice can be represented in the future, first through a presentation at the SITE international conference and then through publication in *Research Highlights in Technology and Teacher Education*.

Sincerely,

Michael Searson, Ph.D.
President, SITE (2011-2014)
Executive Director, School for Global Education & Innovation, Kean University

PREFACE

Research Highlights in Technology and Teacher Education is now in its sixth year of publication. Collections in this book series have presented a growing body of research, highlighted with contemporary trends or issues, creative methods or innovative ideas, theory or practice-based models, and effective use of traditional or new tools in the field of information technology and teacher education. This year, fifteen chapters are organized into four themes: (a) TPACK and preservice education, (b) assessment, (c) research on learning, and (d) research on teaching.

TPACK AND PRESERVICE EDUCATION

Over the past nine years, TPACK (technology, pedagogy, and content knowledge) has been one of the most discussed themes in the literature on using information technology in teacher education. Theoretically and practically, it provides a framework for technology integration. Studies in this area have focused on exploring related issues (such as preservice teachers' perceptions of, attitudes towards, and knowledge about TPACK), and effective ways to use this framework to improve teaching and learning for teacher education students. This year, six chapters are included in this section.

In the first chapter "The Construct is in the Eye of the Beholder: School Districts' Appropriations and Reconceptualizations of TPACK," Judi Harris and Mark Hofer report a study of educational technology-related professional development in seven North American schools and districts in seven states/provinces. In this study, they found that educational leaders' discussion and operationalization of the TPACK construct differs from that of university-based researchers in intriguing and important ways. In these organizations, TPACK was both *appropriated* to reconnect curriculum and pedagogy with educational technology use after prior technocentric professional development was found to be lacking, and *reconceptualized* to focus more upon practice than knowledge. The authors also provide suggestions for further research.

Next, in "Preparing Special Education Teachers to Teach Mathematics and Science with Technology: A Study of Teachers' Surveys and Lesson Plans." Irina Lyublinskaya and Nelly Tournaki present a study that focuses on the development of Technological Pedagogical and Content Knowledge (TPACK) in mathematics and science for pre-service special education teachers. The TPACK development scores, measured through a survey (on teachers' perceptions of knowledge) and a TPACK levels rubric (on teachers' lesson plans), were significantly increased upon completion of the course requirements (n=167). A factor analysis of the survey was also conducted. The results raise questions about the domains of knowledge of the TPACK framework. Implications for teacher education programs are also discussed.

Authored by Beth Bos and Kathryn Lee, chapter three "Mathematical Content, Pedagogy, and Technology: What It Can Mean to Practicing Teachers" presents a study that explores how practicing teachers integrate technology-based instruction involving the study of number concepts, geometry, and statistics and probability. The authors examined 45 practicing teachers' attitudes toward using TPACK in mathematics teaching, and their progress in using TPACK in their lesson plans. Results indicated significant improvement.

In the fourth chapter, "Designing an Educational Technology Course for Preservice Social Studies Teachers Based on Technological Pedagogical Content Knowledge (TPACK) Survey Results," Mark Hart and Swapna Kumar introduce a study in which a required educational technology course was designed according to the TPACK framework and offered to 14 preservice social studies teachers. A modified TPACK survey was conducted to assess students' knowledge of TPACK, and the results were used to modify the design and curriculum of the course. This chapter also illustrates the use of the TPACK framework as well as instructional design techniques.

Laurene Johnson authored "Impact of Design Teams on Preservice Teachers' TPACK, Attitudes, & Skills." This chapter presents a quasi-experimental study that examines the effect of a design team's instructional approach on preservice teachers' attitudes toward technology, technology skills, and Technological Pedagogical Content Knowledge (TPACK). The researchers compared results with that obtained with a standard instructional approach.

In the last chapter of this section "A Systems Approach for Integrating Multiple Technologies as Important Pedagogical Tools for TPACK," Henry Gillow-Wiles and Margaret L. Niess describe the impact that a sequence of technology-based courses (as part of a 3-year online MS program) has on developing and extending teachers' technological pedagogical content knowledge (TPACK). Data from three representative courses in the program illustrate how engaging with systematically integrated multiple technologies supports teachers' development of TPACK. Implications for a systems approach of technology integration are discussed.

ASSESSMENT

Assessment is one of the most important emphases in the field of using technology in teacher education. Over the last decade, researchers and educators have systematically developed technology-standard-based assessment methods, produced valid and reliable instruments and measurements, and performed appropriate data analysis. In this book, two chapters are included in this section.

Chapter seven "Assessment-Talks and Talking about Assessment: Negotiations of Multimodal Texts at the Boundary" is authored by Anna-Lena Godhe and Berner Lindström from Sweden. The article focuses on how assessment is used in classrooms. In multimodal texts, the concept of literacy is expanded to more expressions, including images and sound. Excerpts from negotiations between teacher and students are introduced.

Authenticity is an important characteristic of learning experiences and contributes to transfer of learning into practice. However, maintaining authenticity as practice changes is challenging. In chapter eight "From Creation to Curation: Evolution of an Authentic 'Assessment *for* Learning' Task," Peter Albion from Australia presents a study that guides the evolution of an authentic assessment task in a teacher preparation course responding to changes in the program and the wider educational environment. Lessons learned through reflection during the evolutionary process and prospective developments are discussed.

RESEARCH ON LEARNING

Three chapters are included in this section, which explores the effective use and integration of mobile devices, video applications, and digital resources.

Chapter nine "The Impact of a Digital Storytelling Assignment on Non-English-Major-Students' Motivation for Learning English in a Japanese University" describes a study by Naoko Kasami from Japan. This study investigates how a digital storytelling assignment affected non-English-major-students' motivation for learning English. Sixty-five university students and a Faculty of Information and Communications participated. Keller's ARCS model was used to analyze the impact of the digital storytelling assignment. Findings indicated that the digital storytelling assignment could be a potential way to enhance non-English-major-students' motivation for learning English.

In chapter ten "Video Self Modeling via iPods: The Road to Independent Task Completion," Julie Bucalos, Debra Bauder and Anne Bucalos introduce their experiences to create video self-modeling scenarios with an iPod Touch ™ to help students with an autism spectrum disorder complete learning tasks independently. The iPod Touch™ promotes individualized instruction in an easily accessible format that can be generalized to a variety of environments. Procedures for developing a self-modeling video and integrating it into student learning are described. Advantages and challenges are also discussed.

The authors of chapter eleven "Using Digital Resources to Support Personalized Learning Experiences in K-12 Classrooms: The Evolution of Mobile Devices as Innovations in Schools," Savilla Banister and Rachel Vannatta Reinhart, present a study that examines the practice of adopting mobile devices in K-12 environments. The findings suggest that active learning environments, addressing personalized needs and providing evidence of student competencies, may be accomplished effectively by integrating mobile technologies more prominently in K-12 classrooms.

RESEARCH ON TEACHING

Four studies are included in this section. Chapter twelve, a study by Shaunna Smith and Rubén Garza entitled "Psychosocial and Cognitive Dimensions of the 'Self' within Pre-service Teachers' Reflective Blogs" begins this section. This study provides support for the importance of addressing the three blogging behaviors (write, read, and comment) as well as the psychosocial and cognitive dimensions that participants explore as they authentically represent the 'self'. Participants included 23 pre-service teachers from different content areas enrolled in an undergraduate field-based education course at a large southwestern university. Findings indicate that the use of reflective blogs can support the development of a community of practice extending beyond the walls of the classroom.

Chapter thirteen "Patterns of Mathematics Teachers' Characteristics and Beliefs about Computer Use in Education: A Cluster Analytic Approach" is a study conducted by Onder KOKLU, Elizabeth Jakubowski, Tayfun SERVI and Jiajing Huang. This study investigates the complex relationship between Turkish mathematics teachers' gender, computer experience, teaching experience, and beliefs about integrating computers in teaching mathematics. Participants are 312 secondary mathematics teachers in Turkey. The instrument is a 20-item beliefs scale. A confirmatory factor analysis confirmed the different factors in the scale. A cluster analysis determined homogeneous and well-discriminated classes of teachers with five clusters identified. Gender differences, teaching experience differences, and the resulting five clusters are analyzed by MANOVA.

Chapter fourteen "Developing an Open Online Course for Teachers and Student Teachers" describes a study by five authors from Norway: Louise Mifsud, Tonje Hilde Giæver, Vibeke Bjarnø, Eli Gjølstad, and Irene Beyer –Log. They describe and analyze the process of developing an open and flexible online course for teachers and student teachers, aiming at increasing and formalizing teachers' and student teachers' digital competence. Activity theories are used for organizational and pedagogical activity systems. The negotiation between different activity systems and areas are also discussed.

In the last chapter "Guiding Preservice Teacher Candidates to Implement Student-Centered Applications of Technology in the Classroom," Christine J. Anderson and Laura Kieran report a study that examines how to increase teacher candidates' implementation of student-centered technology applications in their lesson planning. A Technology Integration Matrix is used as an instructional guide to evaluate the degree of technology integration on multiple levels. Pre- and post-assessments were conducted, and significant difference found. The areas in which candidates made the greatest gains were collaborative and constructive technology applications.

Finally, we would like to take this opportunity to express our congratulations and our appreciation to the book review board, the other eight book editors, and the authors of all the manuscripts contributed to this book. We believe that this collection of papers will be a welcome addition to the literature in the field of information technology in teacher education.

May 1. 2014

Senior Book Editors
Leping Liu
David C. Gibson

SITE BOOK REVIEWERS 2014

Peter Albion, University of Southern Queensland, Australia
Sally Beisser, Drake University
Cindy Anderson, Roosevelt University, United States
Leanna Archambault, Arizona State University, United States
Youngkyun Baek, Boise State University, United States
Savilla Banister, Bowling Green State University, United States
Beth Bos, Texas State University, United States
Glen Bull, University of Virginia, United States
Livia D'Andrea, University of Nevada, Reno, United States
Aaron Doering, University of Minnesota, United States
Candace Figg, Brock University, United States
Penny Garcia, University of Wisconsin-Oshkosh, United States
Mark Hofer, College of William and Mary, United States
Natalie Johnson, Arkansas State University, United States
Kathryn Kennedy, International Association for K-12 Online Learning
Lin Lin, University of North Texas, United States
Chrystalla Mouza, University of Delaware, United States
Priscilla Norton, George Mason University, United States
Merryellen Schulz, College of Saint Mary, United States
Scott Slough, Texas A & M University, United States
Debra Sprague, George Mason University, United States
James Telese, University of Texas, Brownsville
Tandra Tyler-Wood, University of North Texas, United States
Roberta Weber, Florida Atlantic University, United States
Jana Willis, University of Houston-Clear Lake, United States
Thomas Winkler, Institute for Multimedia and Interactive Systems, Germany
Harrison Yang, State University of New York-Oswego, United States
Melda Yildiz, Kean University, United States
Hong Zhan, Embry-Riddle Aeronautical University
Linyan Song, Towson University
David Pugalee, University of North Ccarolina Charlotte
Hans van Bergen, Hogeschool Utrecht
Lawrence Walker, University of Canterbury
Lesia Lennex, Morehead State University
Jeremy Wendt, Tennessee Tech University
Niki Davis, University of Canterbury
Mahnaz Moallem, University of North Carolina Wilmington
Margaret Niess, Oregon State University
Mary Kayler, University of Mary Washington

The Construct is in the Eye of the Beholder:
School Districts' Appropriations and Reconceptualizations of TPACK

Judi Harris & Mark Hofer
College of William & Mary, USA
judi.harris@wm.edu   mark.hofer@wm.edu

Abstract: Despite debates about the specific parameters of its eight subcomponents, TPACK is generally understood within university-based teacher education communities as the knowledge needed to incorporate technologies—especially digital tools and resources—effectively in teaching and learning. How do professional development providers working within primary and secondary schools and districts conceptualize and operationalize TPACK? Our study of educational technology-related professional development in seven North American schools and districts in seven states/provinces found that educational leaders' discussion and operationalization of the TPACK construct differs from that of university-based researchers in intriguing and important ways. In these organizations, TPACK was both *appropriated* to reconnect curriculum and pedagogy with educational technology use after prior technocentric professional development was found to be lacking, and *reconceptualized* to focus more upon practice than knowledge.

Nine years have passed since the TPACK (technology, pedagogy, and content knowledge) theoretical construct (Thompson & Mishra, 2007) was introduced to the global educational technology community as technological pedagogical content knowledge (Koehler & Mishra, 2005; Mishra & Koehler, 2006). In less than a decade, university-based researchers have published approximately 800 articles, chapters, books, dissertations, and conference papers that examine, employ, and critique this way of understanding the knowledge that educators need to facilitate students' learning using educational technologies, especially digital tools and resources. The appearance of new TPACK-related scholarship over time shows no signs of slowing; during the last year alone, for example, the number of academic publications based in TPACK increased by approximately 25 percent (Harris & Hofer, 2013).

Yet as warmly as TPACK has been embraced in university-based teacher educators' work (Brantley-Dias & Ertmer, 2013), its diffusion in primary and secondary schools and districts has been considerably slower—and, as the results of this study showed, its K-12 conceptualizations and functions differ from how the construct has been understood and used in higher education. Extensive database and Web searches in early summer 2013 yielded approximately 60 elementary and secondary schools or school districts internationally (primarily within North America and Australia) that included mention of the TPACK construct in either organizational or professional development documents. Of those, online documents from 27 schools or districts showed that they had incorporated TPACK either frequently and/or in fundamental ways (e.g., using the construct in a district job title, such as "TPACK Coaches.")

Given TPACK's origins in higher education (Koehler & Mishra, 2005), its popularity with university-based researchers (Koehler, Mishra, Kereluik, Shin & Graham, 2014; Voogt, Fisser, Roblin, Tondeur, & van Braak, 2013), and an apparent intent for it to be used by researchers and postsecondary teacher educators (Brantley-Dias & Ertmer, 2013), we were curious about how it has made its way to school districts, why it was adopted there, and how it is understood and used in K-12 contexts for professional development purposes. To date, our work helping teachers to develop curriculum-specific TPACK in nine content areas (e.g., Harris & Hofer, 2009; Harris & Hofer, 2011), and assessing performance-based evidence of that knowledge (e.g., Harris, Grandgenett & Hofer, 2012; Hofer, Grandgenett, Harris & Swan, 2011), has focused upon a conscious process for TPACK-based professional development that works within teachers' everyday instructional planning processes and is taught by teacher educators. We became aware of K-12 schools and districts voluntarily appropriating these TPACK-based planning materials that we have developed, vetted, and made available via a Creative Commons license (http://activitytypes.wm.edu/). We were curious to see if and how the TPACK construct was being used in K-12 contexts in other ways as well. We began the study with no conscious beliefs or suppositions regarding how schools and districts understand and use TPACK for professional development beyond knowing that some K-12 organizations use our materials. We entered into this study, therefore, without expectations of either specific or general answers to our research questions.

Also, since relatively few schools and districts' online documents incorporated the TPACK construct in mid-2013, we thought that leaders within those organizations might find it helpful to consult with each other about the design and implementation of educational technology-related professional development that is informed, to some extent, by TPACK. To facilitate both professional networking among TPACK-using schools and districts, and the structured inquiry that we wished to initiate with a focused group of school- and district-based professional development providers, we organized and planned a two-day "TPACK Symposium."

The TPACK Symposium

It has long been acknowledged that sharing experiences in the form of stories is an engaging and effective way to share locally constructed, situated knowledge (Riessman, 1993). We reasoned that asking professional development providers in schools and districts that had voluntarily incorporated the TPACK construct to frame their TPACK-related work as stories to share and discuss with other professionals doing similar work in other educational organizations might facilitate an uncommon (and hopefully valuable) form of collaborative professional learning. Ideas shared by colleagues who are also helping K-12 teachers to develop and enact TPACK in other schools and districts could benefit home constituents indirectly, when symposium participants brought these ideas back home to try.

To form this group of professional development providers experienced with TPACK, we sent personalized email invitations to representatives from the 27 schools or districts that appeared to incorporate TPACK substantively within professional development plans and offerings, based upon documents located online with a series of exhaustive Web searches. We invited competitive application for 16 symposium seats, requesting two representatives participating from each of eight schools or districts. The Web-based application document requested contact and position information, plus answers to the following three requests for information:

- Please explain how TPACK frames professional development (PD) in your school or school district.
- Please describe one example of a PD session or other effort in your school/school district that is framed by TPACK.
- What might educators from other schools/districts/districts learn from your TPACK story?

In reviewing applicants' responses to these three questions, we sought to assemble a group of symposium participants whose schools and districts use TPACK in as diverse ways as possible. Fortunately, we had sufficient funding to invite representatives from all of the schools and districts that submitted applications.

Symposium Participants

During the symposium, representatives from seven schools or districts in five different U.S. states (plus the District of Columbia) and one Canadian province provided live, story-based presentations about how TPACK is used to shape and/or frame some of the professional development offered in their educational organizations. (Two schools were able to send only one representative each to the symposium, making the total number of attendees twelve, rather than fourteen.) Participants were provided with guidelines regarding the requested content of the presentations, and were asked to use a style and voice similar to a TEDTalk (http://www.ted.com/talks) *while telling their "TPACK Stories" at the symposium. The guidelines recommended that the following four topics be addressed during the presentations, which were videotaped with participants' schools' or district's permission:*

1. Focus:
   Your presentation should be primarily the *story* of how TPACK came to be used, and is used, to shape some of the professional development (PD) in your school/school district.

2. Background:
   How did you first learn about TPACK? How and why did TPACK seem to be a "good fit" for some of your school/school district's professional development?

3. Description:
Please describe the PD in your school/district that reflects TPACK; both the "big picture" (e.g., goals, how it fits with other school/district efforts, etc.) and (especially) how it works.

4. Reflection:
What are your most important realizations that have resulted from participating in this PD effort?

The presentations were shared live during the two-day meeting at a southeastern U.S. university in summer 2013. The symposium was designed to facilitate information-sharing and deep discussion about the genesis and nature of the TPACK-based professional development that had emerged in each participating school or district. Symposium participants discussed each TPACK Story in depth immediately following its presentation, and later small- and large-group exchanges identified and explored additional ideas and questions prompted by the presentations and discussions. Videorecorded, lightly edited and formatted versions of the seven TPACK Stories were posted to the TPACK Stories Web site after the edited footage was approved by the corresponding symposium participants. All meeting expenses, save travel to and from the host university, were paid using host university-based funds from a faculty award.

Study Data

Five types of data: applications (online documents) to participate in the symposium, video recordings of symposium presentations, audiorecordings of group discussions in response to the presentations, school- and district-based documents that illustrated use of the TPACK construct, and audiorecordings of post-symposium interviews were generated and analyzed by the researchers in this study. The videorecorded presentations and the audiorecorded discussions among school district representatives that followed each and all of the presentations formed both the basis of the symposium's agenda. Participants' online application materials, collected via a customized Web form, that described the TPACK-based professional learning happening in their school or district were the first type of data generated. The content of the participants' applications reflected a wide variety of ways of appropriating TPACK, which were shared and discussed during the symposium. The videorecorded presentations and the audiorecorded discussions of each of those presentations, plus a discussion-based examination of common themes emerging across presentations, formed two more types of data generated for the study. Each pair of symposium participants also provided an audiorecorded follow-up interview during the five months following the symposium. Documents available on the school/school districts' Web sites, plus additional documents supplied by symposium participants that demonstrate and/or address the ways in which TPACK is used as a way to frame professional learning in represented schools and districts, comprised the final type of data generated for this study.

Participants' applications, presentations, and school and district TPACK-related documents were first analyzed holistically and independently by the two researchers, with each separately noting emerging patterns and themes related to the study's two related foci: how TPACK is understood and enacted in the schools and districts that were represented at the symposium. After completing these individual holistic analyses of the first three types of data, the researchers deliberated to compare and combine their data analysis notes.

Audiorecorded group discussion data were analyzed by the researchers collaboratively during the symposium, immediately following each day's presentations and discussions. Audiorecorded interview data were transcribed verbatim by a transcription service. All interview transcripts (and audio files as needed) were then examined by each of the researchers independently to reveal within-case and across-case themes relative to the study's two foci. The researchers met to combine and compare their interview data analysis notes, then considered, discussed, and agreed upon the themes emerging across all five data types from the seven participating schools/districts.

We report the results of this study comprehensively elsewhere (Harris & Hofer, 2014). In this paper, we focus in particular upon how the TPACK construct was reinterpreted—specifically, appropriated and reconceptualized—by the twelve participating school- and district-based professional development providers to fit the meso-level contexts (Porras-Hernandez & Salinas-Amescua, 2013) within which they work.

Appropriating the TPACK Construct

In many ways, the schools and districts that were represented in the TPACK Symposium appropriated the TPACK construct in light of their particular school and district contexts and cultures. In fact, when one participant was discussing the importance of linking the construct with her district's current professional development emphasis upon building teacher leaders, she stated, "Culture trumps everything you do." Connecting and interpreting TPACK with and according to current and past curriculum and professional development initiatives determined, to a large degree, how the construct was described by each participant, and also how it was enacted within each educational organization.

We identified three primary themes related to this appropriation of the construct: TPACK as the solution to a professional development problem; as an organizational learning process; and as a way to connect previously isolated professional development initiatives. These themes are discussed in the three subsections that follow. While all of these themes were not reflected in every school or district's TPACK Story, considerable discussion and agreement emerged around each of these three organizing ideas following the presentations during which they were illustrated.

Learning from Past Professional Development Challenges

Participants reported that discovering and exploring the TPACK construct helped them to understand what had been missing in their prior educational technology initiatives and professional development efforts: more deliberate and clearly articulated connections among educational technologies, curriculum content and pedagogy. In many of the schools and districts represented, participants described a shift in professional development away from a "tool-centric" approach to a more holistic, TPACK-based approach. As one participant commented, "Technology should not be the focus. That was a hard lesson for us to learn."

This realization led the participants to be more intentional about connecting recommended uses of educational technology tools and resources to curriculum standards. In multiple districts, for example, participants identified curriculum-based tools and resources and mapped them directly to either the district's curriculum standards or recommended instructional strategies and learning activity types. In this way, educational technologies were introduced in the context of many teachers' primary professional focus: addressing students' curriculum-based learning needs. Participants described how TPACK helped to provide a "common language" for the teachers, IT coordinators, and curriculum specialists in schools or districts to use to facilitate this particular type of change. As will be explained below, however, this transition in focus for educational technology use takes considerable time and effort. During that transition, some professional development providers' understanding of the TPACK construct shifted as they used it as a conceptual tool.

TPACK is a Journey

As stated above, all participants realized that prior "technocentric" (Papert, 1987) educational technology professional development had not been successful in catalyzing the extent of educational change desired in the schools and districts that had sent representatives to the symposium. Participants clearly recognized and articulated this disconnect from curriculum and pedagogy within their prior educational technology professional development efforts, albeit in different ways and to different extents. In many instances, this is precisely what made TPACK so appealing. The construct, which attempts to illustrate and explain the interrelated and interdependent nature of curriculum content, pedagogy, and technology knowledge, highlighted a perceived (but previously not fully addressed) need felt by these K-12 teacher educators. However, moving away from focusing upon the affordances and constraints of technological tools and resources is a process that requires time. All of the participants described themselves as being in the process of fully implementing the TPACK construct in their schools and districts, rather than having already met this goal.

One participating district, for example, is shifting from a "tool-centric" approach to educational technology professional development to a "focus tools" approach. In an effort to both standardize the use of a common set of flexible digital tools (e.g., Google Drive, Explain Everything) and to limit the technology knowledge required of teachers, the district selected a discrete number of tools to include in their professional development initiatives. By narrowing the range of tools that would be supported, the district's instructional technologist was able to focus upon helping participating teachers to develop strong technological (TK) and technological pedagogical knowledge (TPK) (Mishra & Koehler, 2006). This knowledge then prepared them to connect pedagogically sound use of the tools to the district's curriculum. The participants from this district acknowledged that this professional development approach is structured around pedagogical use of selected tools, which might not seem like a TPACK-based effort. Yet, as one of the participants from the district commented, "If you can master the tools and master the process, you can be more creative [in addressing curriculum with technology]." To date, the educational technology-related professional development offered in this district does not address the development of teachers' TCK and TPACK nearly as much as their TK and TPK. The participants from this district acknowledged that structuring their work around "focus tools seems a bit counter-intuitive from what we started with: getting away from tool-centric thinking," and reported that their efforts in TPACK-based professional development are still evolving.

By contrast, representatives from another participating school district described how they had discovered the TPACK construct in 2008 and had been incorporating it systematically into their leadership and professional development initiatives ever since. The group was intentional in building awareness and buy-in with different layers of leadership in the district, including professional development providers, building-level administrators, and classroom teacher-leaders. Initially, they focused on TPACK-based professional development in literacy initiatives at multiple grade levels. They later embedded tools and resources into curriculum guides in a TPACK-based way as the district introduced content standards in ten different curriculum areas. Representatives from this district also presented a TPACK-based assessment system that included an observation instrument that helped administrators to assess the quality of technology integration during formal observations of classroom teachers. This systematic and phased approach to integrating TPACK into teacher professional learning in a district takes time to realize, and demonstrates the need for sustained commitment to such a process. It also suggests that successful TPACK-based work in schools and districts is probably best woven throughout multiple initiatives, as illustrated in the next section.

TPACK as a Connector

Several of the professional development providers at the symposium suggested that one of the key affordances of the TPACK construct for K-12 schools lies in the interconnected nature of the model's subdomains. The participants said that the graphical depiction of TPACK's interrelated components helped them to establish and strengthen connections among new and existing initiatives and programs in their schools and districts. In fact, multiple participants used the Venn diagram depiction of TPACK in their presentations during the symposium, superimposing text and images—representing multiple school or district initiatives—upon the construct's original diagram. These different versions of the TPACK diagram created by the symposium participants demonstrated how the construct was interpreted, implemented, and operationalized differently in different school and district contexts according to existing initiatives and emphases.

To many of the symposium's speakers, the TPACK construct became a way to connect seemingly disparate initiatives or projects in their school districts. Multiple participants characterized the construct as a "connector" or "glue." For example, prior to becoming aware of the construct, one large school division had developed a "skillful teacher" framework that guided professional development for the district. In this model, effective teaching incorporates knowledge and use of multiple skill sets, including technology integration. One of the participants from this district framed TPACK as "Find the right tool, at the right time, for the right learners." Another district had a strong, well-developed structure for instructional coaching as the primary vehicle for teacher professional development. A network of different types of coaches (e.g., literacy, math) was already in place to help the district realize its vision for personalized learning for each of its 56,000 students. Recognizing the complex teacher knowledge required to actualize this vision in the classroom, the district created a new type of coach – "TPACK Coaches" – to work with teachers and other coaches to help them connect the use of technology with curriculum and pedagogy. One participant from this district commented, "TPACK is a model that helps teachers see how it all fits," referring to new curriculum standards, technology initiatives, and more.

Reconceptualizing the TPACK Construct

While the examples presented above illustrate how the schools and districts represented at the symposium *appropriated* TPACK, we also found some evidence of their *reconceptualizations* of the construct. In some cases, these were comparatively minor adaptations of the construct; in other cases they seemed to alter key aspects of the construct itself. In the following three subsections, we share three themes and accompanying examples illustrating these reconceptualizations that emerged from analysis of the presentations and discussions at the symposium.

Well-Balanced Technology Integration

As explored by teacher educators and researchers to date, the TPACK construct represents interconnected domains of knowledge that teachers draw on to be able to effectively incorporate technologies within learning and teaching. Interestingly, *none* of the schools or districts participating in the TPACK Symposium characterized it in this way. To the symposium participants, *TPACK is not teachers' knowledge*. Rather, these educators seemed to see the construct as a way to describe *well-balanced technology integration in practice*. From this perspective, TPACK is somewhat external to the teacher. Participants characterized TPACK more as a leadership thinking tool; "a compass or guide" for ensuring that schools/districts are addressing curriculum content and pedagogy, in addition to technology, as they design, plan, and implement technology integration professional development for teachers. In this way, for the symposium participants, TPACK represents professional development that is not technocentric (Papert, 1987).

In two of the districts represented at the symposium, the TPACK construct guided the work of people other than teachers. In both of these organizations, these educators were instructional coaches, whose job it was to work with teachers, either individually or in small groups, as mentors. In essence, these coaches provided knowledge *for* the teachers about how and when to connect curriculum content, pedagogy, and technology tools and resources with whom they work. One of these two districts took this concept a step further in the formation of "instructional services teams" comprising teacher leaders with specific expertise (e.g., curriculum areas, technology, pedagogical approaches). These teams work with teachers who are organized into professional learning communities. The representatives from this district described the work as offering "professional learning, both embedded and after school, to support teacher learning to improve student understanding and…learning." Providing teachers with assistance in educational technology planning and implementation in these ways suggests that developing classroom teachers' independent TPACK has not necessarily been a focus in these two districts. A similar shift in focus for TPACK-based professional development is described next.

Focus on Practice Rather than Knowledge

While listening to the symposium participants' descriptions of how and why they incorporated the TPACK construct into their professional development efforts, we realized that they focused primarily on their teachers' technology integration *practice*, rather than on their TPACK *knowledge development*. This is quite different from the focus of much TPACK research with experienced teachers, which seeks to measure self-reported TPACK development, rather than its demonstration in the classroom. Even in the most curriculum-focused approach shared at the symposium, there seemed to be much more emphasis upon curriculum review and instructional planning processes (including plans for technology use) than upon developing the participating teachers' TPACK. Post-symposium interviews confirmed that growth in teachers' TPACK was assumed by the participants to occur naturally through multiple iterations of this collaborative professional development, but was not a specific aim of the work. Rather, the focus seemed to be on designing well-integrated, curriculum-based lessons, projects, and units for classroom implementation.

A majority of the symposium's participants looked to TPACK to assist with instructional planning. In the district that employed TPACK Coaches, coaches were charged with helping teachers plan in an integrated fashion. One of the participants from the district commented, "TPACK Coaches will … help teachers to plan with technology integration. What is the learning objective? What is the desired outcome? How can we help teachers to discern the appropriate tools to use?" Another school district integrated the use of TPACK-based learning activity types taxonomies (Harris & Hofer, 2009) to assist teachers in their planning of curriculum-based learning experiences for their students. Similar to the collaborative planning process and coaching model discussed above, the focus of this work seemed to be on the instructional planning process, rather than on targeted efforts to help teachers develop their TPACK. It seems reasonable to assume that as teachers engage in these experiences, they will develop their TPACK organically. However, the symposium participants were far less interested in tracking this knowledge development than they were with focusing on teachers' practice.

TPACK as Distributed Knowledge?

One surprising finding from the study relates to how participants viewed the nature of the knowledge described in the TPACK construct. One of the participants, for example, used TPACK repeatedly as a verb. He conceptualized "TPACKing" as the process by which a team of teachers collaboratively develop their TPACK through a curriculum design, implementation, and review process. He characterized this process as a means for individuals with different expertise (e.g., classroom teacher, curriculum experts, instructional technologists, library media specialists) to incorporate their unique perspectives and knowledge into this curriculum review process. For example, as a teacher would discuss her approach to an upcoming unit on the solar system, the instructional technologist might share Web-based resources to provide students with multiple representations of the ways in which the planets revolve around the sun. The library media specialist might then offer a research strategy to help the students engage in collaborative research about the sun and planets. By each collaborating member sharing her knowledge, all of the members contribute their particular expertise "for the good of the group." In this case, it would seem that this participant views TPACK as a more *distributed* form of knowledge rather than an individual teacher's *integrated* knowledge. After the participant presented and explained this idea, several other school/district representatives echoed and expanded upon it, sharing their own strategies for "helping their teachers TPACK" in similar ways.

Other symposium participants seemed to hold quite different conceptions of TPACK's "location"—specifically, that it is interactively and collaboratively *built,* but *held* individually. In the schools and districts in which the primary approach to professional development is coaching—four of the seven school districts represented at the symposium—TPACK-building was a goal for interactions among collaborating teachers (e.g., same grade-level or content-area teachers), and especially between professional development coaches and their teacher-clients, but seemed to be assumed to be something held and used independently by individual teachers (and their coaches). We suspect that contextual conditions dictated these particular interpretations of the locus of TPACK, since instructional and curriculum planning in the two schools in which TPACK seemed to be distributed, rather than held individually by teachers and coaches, were "bottom-up," generative, collaborative, and professional learning community (PLC)-based.

Recommendations for Future Inquiry

Given the rather dramatic differences revealed in this study between conceptualizations and applications of the TPACK construct described by participating school- and school district-based educators, contrasted with those represented in the voluminous scholarly TPACK literature, further investigation of schools' and districts' appropriation and reconceptualization of TPACK could constitute an interesting and useful new line of educational technology research. Complementary recommendations for further investigation of the contextual aspects of and influences upon TPACK *(Porras-Hernandez & Salinas-Amescua, 2013) and the possibility of differing conceptions of the construct as it is held and enacted by instructors working in elementary, secondary and higher education (Cox & Graham, 2009)* suggest, along with the results of this study, that additional examination of the ways in which TPACK is built, held, and enacted in elementary and secondary schools and districts is warranted.

References

Brantley-Dias, L., & Ertmer, P. (2013). Goldilocks and TPACK: Is the construct "just right?" *Journal of Research on Technology in Education, 46*(2), 103-128.

Cox, S., & Graham, C. R. (2009). Diagramming TPACK in practice: Using an elaborated model of the TPACK framework to analyze and depict teacher knowledge. *TechTrends, 53*(5), 60-69.

Harris, J., Grandgenett, N., & Hofer, M. (2012). Testing an instrument using structured interviews to assess experienced teachers' TPACK. In C. D. Maddux, D. Gibson, & R. Rose (Eds.), *Research highlights in technology and teacher education 2012* (pp. 15-22). Chesapeake, VA: Society for Information Technology & Teacher Education (SITE).

Harris, J., & Hofer, M. (2013, March). *got research? TPACK eNewsletter update.* Presentation at the Society for Information Technology and Teacher Education (SITE) Annual Conference, New Orleans, LA.

Harris, J., & Hofer, M. (2009). Instructional planning activity types as vehicles for curriculum-based TPACK development. In Association for the Advancement of Computing in Education (Eds.). *Research highlights in technology and teacher education 2009* (pp. 99-108). Chesapeake, VA: AACE.

Harris, J. B., & Hofer, M. J. (2011). Technological Pedagogical Content Knowledge (TPACK) in action: A descriptive study of secondary teachers' curriculum-based, technology-related instructional planning. *Journal of Research on Technology and Education, 43*(3), 211-229.

Harris, J., & Hofer, M. (2014, April). *"TPACK stories:" Schools and school districts repurposing a theoretical construct for technology-related professional development.* Paper session presented at the American Educational Research Association Annual Meeting, Philadelphia, PA.

Hofer, M., Grandgenett, N., Harris, J., & Swan, K. (2011). Testing a TPACK-based technology integration observation instrument. In C. D. Maddux (Ed.), *Research highlights in technology and teacher education 2011* (pp. 39-46). Chesapeake, VA: Society for Information Technology & Teacher Education (SITE).

Koehler, M. J., & Mishra, P. (2005). Teachers learning technology by design. *Journal of Computing in Teacher Education, 21*(3), 94-102.

Koehler, M. J., Mishra, P., Kereluik, K., Shin, T. S., & Graham, C. R. (2014). The technological pedagogical content knowledge framework. In J. M. Spector, M. D. Merrill, J. Elen, & M. J. Bishop (Eds.), *Handbook of research on educational communications in technology* (pp. 101-111). New York: Springer.

Mishra, P., & Koehler, M. J. (2006). Technological pedagogical content knowledge: A framework for teacher knowledge. *Teachers College Record, 108*(6), 1017-1054.

Papert, S. (1987). *A critique of technocentrism in thinking about the school of the future.* Retrieved from http://www.papert.org/articles/ACritiqueofTechnocentrism.html

Porras-Hernandez, L. H. & Salinas-Amescua, B. (2013). Strengthening TPACK: A broader notion of context and the use of teachers' narratives to reveal knowledge construction. Journal of Educational Computing Research, 48, 223-244. doi: 10.2190/EC.48.2.f

Riessman, C. K. (1993). *Narrative analysis.* Newbury Park, CA: Sage Publications.

Thompson, A. D., & Mishra, P. (2007). Breaking news: TPCK becomes TPACK!. *Journal of Computing in Teacher Education, 24*(2), 38.

Voogt, J., Fisser, P., Roblin, N. P., Tondeur, J., & van Braak, J. (2013). Technological pedagogical content knowledge – A review of the literature. *Journal of Computer Assisted Learning, 29*(2), 109-121. doi: 10.1111/j.1365-2729.2012.00487.x

Preparing Special Education Teachers to Teach Mathematics and Science with Technology: A Study of Teachers' Surveys and Lesson Plans

Irina Lyublinskaya
Nelly Tournaki
College of Staten Island – The City University of New York, USA
irina.lyublinskaya@csi.cuny.edu
nelly.tournaki@csi.cuny.edu

Abstract: This study focuses on the development of Technological Pedagogical and Content Knowledge (TPACK) in mathematics and science of pre-service special education teachers via one course. TPACK development is measured through a survey (teachers' perceptions of knowledge) and lesson plans (teachers' artifacts). Paired samples *t*-test revealed that upon completion of the course requirements, the participants' TPACK scores increased significantly in regards to their perceptions as well as their lesson plans. Correlations between the two measures were not significant leading to a discussion about assessing constructs through measures of self–perception and teaching artifacts. Factor analysis of the survey raises questions about the domains of knowledge of the TPACK framework. Implications for teacher education programs are discussed.

Purpose

Teacher preparation programs have long recognized that teachers need to be knowledgeable of the effective use of educational technologies. This study focuses on the development of Technological Pedagogical and Content Knowledge (TPACK) in mathematics and science of pre-service special education teachers via one course. In the last decade, the TPACK framework has significantly influenced teacher education professionals. As a result it led to re-thinking and re-designing of teacher preparation programs nationally and internationally (Burns 2007; Chai, Koh, & Tsai 2010; Niess 2005, 2007; Shoffner 2007) but so far only two studies (Lyublinskaya & Tournaki in press; Lyublinskaya & Tournaki 2013; Tournaki & Lyublinskaya 2014) have been applied to programs preparing special education teachers; the focus has been on general education.

The College of Staten Island's graduate program in elementary special education requires the completion of a course that focuses on integrating technology into teaching mathematics and science in special education and inclusive classrooms. This course introduces strategies and techniques for using instructional technology in teaching concepts in science and mathematics to children with learning and behavior problems. The purpose of the current study is to assess whether the completion of this course is associated with significant gains in pre-service special education teachers' TPACK in mathematics and science as measured by a) self-reports: completion of the Survey of Pre-service Teachers' Knowledge of Teaching and Technology, (SPTKTT; Schmidt et al. 2009) and b) teaching artifacts: scoring of lesson plans with the TPACK Levels Rubric (Lyublinskaya & Tournaki 2011). In addition, the relationship between the survey and lesson plan scores is examined.

Theoretical Framework

Traditionally universities prepare teachers to teach with technology by delivering a single technology course. These courses used to be, and in some cases still are, independent of content or pedagogy courses (Graham, Culatta, Pratt, & West 2004; Hsu & Sharma 2006). However, offering one such course is not enough to prepare teachers to teach with technology (Hsu & Sharma 2006; Mishra, Koehler, & Kereluik 2009; Steketee 2005). We need courses that integrate the teaching of all the components of teacher knowledge: content knowledge on a subject matter, pedagogy skills, and technology skills (Angeli & Valanides 2005; Chai, Koh, & Tsai 2010; Jonassen, Howland, Marra, & Crismond 2008; Mishra & Khoeler 2006). Mishra and Khoeler (2006) have clearly articulated a theoretical framework of teacher knowledge and refer to this integrated form of contextualized knowledge as TPACK.

Using the conceptual domains of the professional knowledge base – Content Knowledge (CK), Pedagogical Knowledge (PK), and Pedagogical Content Knowledge (PCK) as a framework (Shulman 1987), teachers integrate technology with their professional knowledge yielding four types of knowledge related to technology: Technological Knowledge (TK), Technological Pedagogical Knowledge (TPK), Technological Content knowledge (TCK) and

Technological Pedagogical and Content Knowledge (TPACK). TPACK describes the body of knowledge that teachers need for teaching with technology in their assigned subject areas and grade levels (Hughes 2005; Hughes & Scharber 2008). TPACK is identified with knowledge that relies on the interconnection and intersection of content, pedagogy, and technology (Mishra & Koehler 2006; Niess 2008).

Methods

Context

The study took place at the College of Staten Island, in New York City. Two sections of the course, in which data were collected, were taught in four consecutive semesters. Each section of the course met weekly for 15 two-hour sessions with the same instructor who used TPACK as the organizing framework for developing the course content and the activities. The first four sessions focused on the theoretical aspects of the TPACK framework – they were dedicated to the analysis of models and strategies for technology-infused lessons with special emphasis on the analysis of the principles for the effective use of technology (Goldenberg 2000). During this time, pre-service teachers developed the drafts of their first lesson plan and received feedback. By the fifth session, they submitted their first lesson plans. The following eight sessions were devoted to the use of specific technology tools (for example, interactive whiteboards, data collection technology, calculators, web 2.0 tools, spreadsheets, presentation software, mathematics and science educational software) in teaching and learning. The pre-service teachers developed their own standards-based mathematics or science activities that utilized specific technology tool and instructional notes on how to use the activity in inclusion classrooms with description of objectives, assessment, and adaptations for learners with special needs. Discussions addressing adaptations of technology to students with special needs, differentiated instruction and assessment with technology continued throughout the course. Thus, these assignments and course discussions addressed TPK.

To develop TCK, all pre-made technology-based activities focused on key mathematics or science concepts. Completion of these activities in class followed by small group or whole class discussions of the topic in the context of using technology intended to help students develop conceptual understanding of key ideas of each subject. At the same time, pre-service teachers developed their second lesson plan, following the same procedure: they first developed drafts that received feedback, and submitted the final plan by the 12th session. The course included 20 hours of fieldwork observations and teaching of two developed lessons to students with disabilities. Last three sessions focused on the importance of teachers evaluating and reflecting on their own teaching.

CK, PK, TK, and PCK were not specifically targeted in this course, as all pre-service special education teachers completed initial teaching certification requirements in general education, which included general education courses on pedagogy, content-based courses in mathematics and science, a basic technology education course, as well as science and mathematics methods courses.

Participants

The 167 participants were students enrolled in a required 3-credit graduate course titled *Integrating Technology in Math and Science Instruction in Special Education and Inclusive Classrooms.* Females comprised 74% of the sample. 65% were between the ages of 23 and 26 years old, 7% were between 18 and 22, 17% between 26 and 32, 14% were 33 years old or older. The majority (43%) of the participants held a childhood teaching license, 38% - adolescent Social Studies license, 15% - early childhood license, 2% - adolescent English license, and 1% - adolescent mathematics license.

Materials

SPTKTT (Schmidt et al. 2009) was used to measure pre-service teachers' perception of TPACK. This survey was developed for pre-service general education teachers through content validation by national experts; it has a Cronbach's alpha of 0.80 indicating good internal reliability, and has construct validity for each knowledge domain subscale investigated through principal components factor analysis. The original scale includes 47 items on a 5-point Likert scale addressing seven domains of teachers' knowledge with CK in four core subject areas. Since the course in the present study focused only on mathematics and science, the items addressing literacy and social studies were omitted, resulting in a 37-item survey. All participants completed the survey twice – during the first and the last sessions of the course.

The TPACK Levels Rubric (Lyublinskaya & Tournaki 2011) was used to assess lesson plans developed by the pre-service teachers. The structure of the rubric is based on the TPACK framework for assessing the development of teachers' classroom technology integration across five progressive levels [*Recognizing* (1), *Accepting* (2), *Adapting* (3), *Exploring* (4), *and Advancing* (5)] in each of the four components of TPACK as identified by Niess (2011): (1) *An overarching conception about the purposes for incorporating technology.* (2) *Knowledge of student understanding, thinking, and learning in subject matter topics with technology.* (3) *Knowledge of curriculum and curricular materials that integrate technology.* (4) *Knowledge of instructional strategies and representations for teaching and learning with technologies.* The rubric was tested for reliability and validity with in-service mathematics teachers using TI-Nspire technology (Lyublinskaya & Tournaki 2011). In this study, we completed a Factor Analysis using varimax rotation with Kaiser normalization to confirm the construct validity of the rubric when applied to pre-service special education teachers. The procedure was performed on two sets of 167 lesson plans. For this sample size, Stevens (2002) suggests to consider loadings greater than 0.6, thus, all loadings less than 0.6 were suppressed. The procedure confirmed that four factors of TPACK corresponded to the four components of PCK for each set of lesson plans (Tab. 1).

	Lesson Plan 1				Lesson Plan 2			
	1	2	3	4	1	2	3	4
Curriculum	.810						.785	
Instruction		.780			.813			
Students			.740			.804		
Conception				.696				.717

Table 1. Results of Factor Analysis of the TPACK Levels Rubric with Four Factors.

Results/Conclusions

To evaluate whether pre-service special education teachers' perceptions of teacher knowledge changed over the course of a semester as a result of a completion of a TPACK related course, a paired samples *t*-test was used to compare the mean scores for all domains of knowledge between the initial and final administration of the SPTKTT survey (Tab. 2).

	Initial Administration of SPTKTT		Final Administration of SPTKTT				
	M	SD	M	SD	N	T	Cohen's *d*
TK	3.59	.84	3.64	.64	164	-1.001	n/a
CK Math	3.75	.73	3.88	.60	165	-2.526*	.209
CK Science	3.47	.72	3.69	.61	165	-4.044*	.317
PK	4.01	.42	4.09	.39	163	-2.260*	.190
PCK	3.64	.51	3.97	.92	163	-4.409**	.442
TCK	3.14	.76	3.85	.53	163	-10.286**	1.089
TPK	3.80	.72	4.17	.41	163	-6.185**	.640
TPACK	3.56	.63	3.99	.46	163	-7.722**	.786

* $p < .05$ ** $p < .001$

Table 2. Descriptive Statistics and Results of Paired Samples t-Test of SPTTPK Survey

	Initial Administration of SPTKTT								Final Administration of SPTKTT							
	1	2	3	4	5	6	7	8	1	2	3	4	5	6	7	8
TK1			.743						.751							
TK2			.810						.805							
TK3			.806						.772							
TK4								.477	.808							
TK5			.700						.767							
TK6			.754						.812							
TK7			.543						.553							
CKMath8				.848												.804
CKMath9				.857												.790
CKMath10				.830												.763
CKScience11					.779										.615	
CKScience12					.833										.839	
CKScience13					.831										.768	
PK14		.813									.494		.410			
PK15		.867									.806					
PK16		.788									.818					
PK17		.764									.601					
PK18		.617									.798					
PK19		.427					.443				.478					
PK20		.557									.400			.481		
PCK21				.514								.734				
PCK22						.763						.759				
PCK23				.410		.476										
PCK24						.812						.770				
TCK25	.483							.516						.762		
TCK26	.614							.484						.756		
TPK27	.675									.455				.630		
TPK28										.464				.630		
TPK29						.774								.758		
TPK30						.803								.752		
TPK31	.426					.582				.462				.465		
TPACK32	.675									.790						
TPACK33	.726									.726						
TPACK34	.782									.721						
TPACK35	.737									.656						
TPACK36	.736									.491						
TPACK37	.809									.645						

Table 3. Results of Factor Analysis of Eight Factors on SPTTPK Survey (all loading below 0.4 are suppressed)

The *t*-test revealed that upon completion of the course requirements, students perceived to have significant gains in each domain of teacher knowledge except for TK - with small effect sizes in CK Mathematics and PK, moderate effect sizes in CK Science and PCK, and large effect sizes in TCK, TPK and TPACK. In fact, the domains of CK, PK, TK, and PCK were not specifically targeted in this course still, teachers' perceptions indicated that they gained in CK, PK, and PCK - possibly the lesson plans and other activities helped students re-process and further master knowledge of content and pedagogy. The largest effect sizes were obtained for the domains of TCK, TPK and TPACK. Such gains might be an indication of the success of the course. Further, confirmatory Factor Analysis with varimax rotation within each knowledge domain and Kaiser normalization was conducted on the two sets of survey to confirm the construct validity when applied to pre-service special education teachers (Tab. 3).

The following domains loaded as factors in both pre and post surveys: TK, CK Science, CK Math and PK, and in the rest of the factors, the loadings were not as clear cut as presented in the Schmidt et al. (2009) factor analysis. That might be the result of unclear boundaries among overlapping domains. These results are consistent with the study by Fisser et al. (2012) that reported even less definitive boundaries among domains when they factor analyzed the same survey with 287 Dutch pre-service early childhood and elementary education teachers. Therefore, further examination is necessary to substantiate the domains of teacher knowledge. The results of this part of the study should be viewed in relation to its limitation - the survey is a self-assessment that measures participants' perceptions of teacher knowledge not their actual knowledge observed in the classroom as they teach. Since teachers' interactions with students in inclusive classrooms may not be congruent with their responses to the surveys (Fang 1996) we also examined changes in teacher knowledge through scoring two lesson plans developed during the course, with the TPACK Levels Rubric (Lyublinskaya & Tournaki 2011). Results of a paired samples t-test indicated that scores significantly improved for all the components measured by the TPACK rubric with large effect sizes (Tab. 4) indicating that the course objectives of effectively integrating technology into teaching and learning mathematics and science were met.

	Lesson Plan 1		Lesson Plan 2		N	t	Sig (2-tailed)	Cohen's d
	Mean	SD	Mean	SD				
Conception	2.36	.86	2.91	.75	169	-6.84	<.001	0.69
Students	2.28	.76	2.75	.69	131	-6.69	<.001	0.65
Curriculum	2.75	.67	3.13	.59	131	-5.96	<.001	0.61
Instruction	2.53	.87	3.03	.68	131	-6.50	<.001	0.64
Total	2.15	.79	2.67	.70	131	-7.41	<.001	0.70

Table 4. Descriptive Statistics and Paired t-Test Results for All Levels of TPACK Scores of the Lesson Plans

Finally, a correlation was performed to evaluate whether there was a relationship between self-perception TPACK (SPTKTT) and external TPACK (lesson plans). It indicated no significant correlations between scores on pre-survey and first lesson plan as well as between scores on post-survey and second lesson plan. This result empirically confirms earlier claims that self-perceptions of teachers might not relate to the quality of teaching artifacts (Fang 1996).

As with any single group design, this study has limitations. Since all participants were graduate students taking a required course, the control group design was not possible. Thus, the observed gains in pre-service teachers' TPACK scores could have been explained by other factors that were not controlled. The attrition rate over the four semesters of the study was 13%. The study analyzed data only for students who completed the course. This might have indicated larger effect of the course on the TPACK development. While prior content knowledge of students was controlled by diagnostics science and mathematics tests, their prior PK, TK and PCK were not assessed. Although, there were several uncontrolled variables that might have affected participants' performance before or during the study, results of the study suggest that the course completion contributed to the TPACK development of pre-service teachers.

Significance

Based on the results of this study we encourage the educational community to adopt similar courses in their special education teacher preparation programs in which TPACK is built in and taught in a systematic way to better prepare pre-service teachers for teaching students with special needs in a technology-infused school environment. At the same time, the construct of TPACK needs to be further examined since studies using factor analysis do not seem to confirm all the domains presented in the model by Mishra and Koehler (2006). Finally, empirical evidence is provided that self-reports of teachers on their TPACK do not correlate with TPACK demonstrated through teaching artifacts developed by the teachers.

References

Angeli, C. & Valanides, N. (2005). Preservice elementary teachers as information and communication technology designers: an instructional systems design model based on an expanded view of pedagogical content knowledge. *Journal of Computer Assisted Learning, 21*(4), 292-302.

Burns, K. (2007). Technology, content and pedagogy: United in pre-service teacher instruction. *Technology and Teacher Education Annual, 18*(4), 2177.

Chai, C. S., Koh, J. H. L., & Tsai, C-C. (2010). Facilitating preservice teachers' development of Technological, Pedagogical, and Content Knowledge (TPACK). *Educational Technology & Society, 13*(4), 63-73.

Cohen, J. (1969). *Statistical power analysis for the behavioral sciences*. New York, NY: Academic Press.

Fang, Z. (1996). A review of research on teacher beliefs and practices. *Educational Research, 38*(1), 47-65.

Fisser, P., Voogt, J., Agyei, D., Kafyulilo, A., Alayyar, G., Schmidt-Crawford, D., Thompson, A., Gibson, D., Knezek, G. & Tondeur, J. (2012). Developing TPACK around the world: Probing the framework even as we apply it. In P. Resta (Ed.), *Proceedings of Society for Information Technology & Teacher Education International Conference 2012* (pp. 1129-1131). Chesapeake, VA: AACE.

Graham, C. R., Culatta, R., Pratt, M., & West, R. (2004). Redesigning the teacher education technology course to emphasize integration. *Computers in the Schools, 21*(1/2), 127-148.

Hsu, P. S. & Sharma, P. (2006). A systemic plan to technology integration. *Educational Technology & Society, 9*(4), 173-184.

Hughes, J. E. (2005). The role of teacher knowledge and learning experiences in forming technology-integrated pedagogy. *Journal of Technology and Teacher Education, 13*(2), 277-302.

Hughes, J. E. & Scharber, C. (2008). Leveraging the development of English TPCK within the deictic nature of literacy. In AACTE's Committee on Innovation and Technology (Eds.), *Handbook of Technological Pedagogical Content Knowledge (TPCK) for Educators* (pp.87-106). Mahwah, NJ: Routledge.

Jonassen, D., Howland, J. Marra, R., & Crismond, D. (2008). *Meaningful learning with technology* (3rd ed.). Upper Saddle River, NJ: Pearson.

Lyublinskaya, I. & Tournaki, E. (2011). The effects of teacher content authoring on TPACK and on student achievement in algebra: Research on instruction with the TI-Nspire handheld. In R. Ronau, C. Rakes, & M. Niess (Eds.), *Educational Technology, Teacher Knowledge, and Classroom Impact: A Research Handbook on Frameworks and Approaches*. Hershey, PA: IGI Global.

Lyublinskaya, I. & Tournaki, N. (in press). Preparing special education teachers for teaching mathematics and science with technology by integrating the TPACK framework into the curriculum: A study of teachers' TPACK development through assessment of lesson plans. *Journal of Technology and Teacher Education*.

Lyublinskaya, I. & Tournaki, N. (2013). Integrating TPACK framework into coursework and its effect on changes in TPACK of pre-service special education teachers. In R. McBride & M. Searson (Eds.), *Proceedings of Society for Information Technology & Teacher Education International Conference 2013* (pp. 5006-5011). Chesapeake, VA: AACE.

Mishra, P. & Koehler, M. J. (2006). Technological pedagogical content knowledge: A framework for teacher knowledge. *Teachers College Record, 108*(6), 1017–1054.

Mishra, P., Koehler, M. J., & Kereluik, K. (2009). The song remains the same: Looking back to the future of educational technology. *Techtrends, 53*(5), 48-53.

Niess, M. L. (2005). Preparing teachers to teach science and mathematics with technology: Developing a technology pedagogical content knowledge. *Teaching and Teacher Education, 21*(5), 509-523.

Niess, M. L. (2007). Developing teacher's TPCK for teaching mathematics with spreadsheets. *Technology and Teacher Education Annual, 18*(4), 2238-2245.

Niess, M. L. (2008). Knowledge needed for teaching with technologies – Call it TPACK. *AMTE Connections*, 17(2), 9–10.

Niess, M. L. (2011). Investigating TPACK: Knowledge growth in teaching with technology. *Journal of Educational Computing Research, 44*(3), 299-317.

Schmidt, D. A., Baran, E., Thompson, A. D., Mishra, P., Koehler, M. J., & Shin, T. S. (2009). Technological Pedagogical Content Knowledge (TPCK): The development and validation of an assessment instrument for preservice teachers. *Journal of Research on Technology in Education, 42*(2), 83-87.

Shoffner, M. (2007). The PT3 Crossroads Project: Searching for Technology-PCK and results. In R. Carlsen et al. (Eds.), *Proceedings of Society for Information Technology & Teacher Education International Conference 2007* (pp. 2636-2640). Chesapeake, VA: AACE.

Shulman, L. (1987). Knowledge and teaching: Foundations of the new reform. *Harvard Educational Review, 57*(1), 1-22.

Steketee, C. (2005). Integrating ICT as an integral teaching and learning tool into pre-service teacher training courses. *Issues in Educational Research, 15*(1), 101-113.

Tournaki, N. & Lyublinskaya, I. (2014). Preparing special education teachers for teaching mathematics and science with technology by integrating the TPACK framework into the curriculum: A study of teachers' perceptions. *Journal of Technology and Teacher Education, 22*(2), 243-259

Mathematical Content, Pedagogy, and Technology:
What It Can Mean to Practicing Teachers

Beth Bos
Curriculum & Instruction
Texas State University, USA
bb33@txstate.edu

Kathryn Lee
Curriculum & Instruction
Texas State University, USA
kl10@txstate.edu

Abstract: The purpose of this study is to look at how practicing teachers integrate technology-based instruction involving the study of number concepts, geometry, and statistic and probability, during their Master's program. Though results show significant improvement, there is a need for district support in the form of one-to-one technology for all students if technology is to become a seamless student tool. The program's courses produced a positive attitude about technology, pedagogy, and content (mathematics) knowledge (TPACK) that lasted a year after the program was completed.

Introduction

Technology has a natural drawing power for today's youth. It stimulates their interest, curiosity, and creativity. To harness this energy and direct it towards learning mathematics teachers embrace information computer technology (ICT) as a formative power. Teachers need experiences in using technology to go deeper into the mathematics, to direct student interest toward exploring mathematics to problem-solve, reason and prove, strengthen communication and transform a student's view of mathematics. The following study takes a longitudinal look at the results of a professional development program focused on elementary teachers and their development of a deeper understanding of mathematics through the use of technology and the design of instructionally sound mathematics lessons.

Literature Review

Moyer, Bolyard and Spikell (2002) define "an interactive, Web- based visual representation of a dynamic object that presents opportunities for constructing mathematical knowledge" (p. 373). Many virtual manipulatives (or dynamic objects) called applets (in Java) or apps (for the IPad), commonly used for mathematics today, are movable pictorial representations and are commonly used for mathematics today. In addition to virtual manipulatives, which are based on physical objects, some computational media have created new representational forms (e.g., dynamic geometry programs, graphing applets) (Kaput & Roschelle, 1998) The National Council of Teachers of Mathematics (2000) reports that "work with virtual manipulatives can allow young children to extend physical experience and to develop an initial understanding of sophisticated ideas like the use of algorithms" (NCTM, 2000, p. 26-27). Sarama and Clements (2009) report this statement as follows "computer manipulatives provide unique affordances for the development of integrated- concrete knowledge" (p. 147). Sarama and Clements (2009) note, "What gives integrated- concrete thinking its strength is the combination of separate ideas in an interconnected structure of knowledge. For students with this type of interconnected knowledge, knowledge of physical objects, actions performed on them, and symbolic representations are all inter-related in a strong mental structure" (p. 146).

We know that adequate *pedagogical integration* of digital technologies is a critical factor for instructional success in integrating technology. Technology will not reach its potential in maximizing teaching and learning without pedagogical integration (Conlon & Simpson, 2003; Cuban, Kirkpatrick, & Peck, 2001; Niess, 2007). Additionally, in order to pedagogically integrate a technology, teachers must first perceive and understand the affordances of the specific technology and then relate the affordances to their instructional goals during lesson planning (Angeli & Valanides, 2009). The challenge for mathematics teachers is to leverage technology affordances of digital tools in their classroom. Leveraging begins with *cognitively* integrating these affordances with teachers' knowledge of specific mathematical tasks and instructional guidance. Technology affordances that teachers construct or activate are important for planning the use of technology in class within a problem-based instructional learning model. Problem-based instruction creates an atmosphere for reasoning and critical thinking and teamed with technology can be very powerful (Donnelly, 2010).

Conceptual Model

TPACK, a conceptual model used to help teachers understand the relationship between technology, pedagogy and content (mathematical) knowledge, assists in holistically viewing the relationships involved in integrating technology into learning and instruction (Mishra and Koehler, 2006).

Many researchers, beginning with Koehler and Mishra (2005), advocate that one way to learn about the complexities of teaching with technology is to engage in the design process (Koehler, et al., 2011). As Koehler et al. (2011) explain, "through the design process, learners must constantly work at the nexus of content (what to teach), pedagogy (how to teach it), and technology (using what tools)" (p. 151).

Theoretical Framework

In the past few decades, a constructivist discourse has emerged as a powerful model for explaining how knowledge is produced in the world, as well as how students learn. For constructivists like Kincheloe (2000) and Thayer-Bacon (1999), knowledge about the world does not simply exist out there, waiting to be discovered, but is rather constructed by human beings in their interaction with the world. "The angle from which an entity is seen, the values of the researcher that shape the questions he or she asks about it, and what the researcher considers important are all factors in the *construction* of knowledge about the phenomenon in question" (Kincheloe, 2000, p. 342). Thayer-Bacon (1999) invokes a quilting bee metaphor to highlight the fact that people are socially and culturally embedded, rather than isolated individuals constructing knowledge. To assert that knowledge is constructed, rather than discovered, implies that it is neither independent of human knowing nor value free. Indeed, constructivists believe that what is deemed knowledge is always informed by a particular perspective and shaped by various implicit value judgments (Gordon, 2009).

According to Windschitl (1999), constructivism is based on the assertion that learners actively create, interpret, and reorganize knowledge in individual ways. "These fluid intellectual transformations," he maintains, "occur when students reconcile formal instructional experiences with their existing knowledge, with the cultural and social contexts in which ideas occur, and with a host of other influences that serve to mediate understanding" (p.752).

Methods

A quasi-experimental design was used for the modified TPACK Survey by Schmidt, Baran, Thompson, Koehler, and Shin (2009), and a qualitative method, Lyublinskaya and Tournaki's (2011) TPACK Levels Rubric, was used to assess use of technology as found in the teachers' lesson plans. The study addressed the following research questions:

1. What effects are noticed about teachers' attitude toward the use of technological, pedagogical, and content (mathematical) knowledge and the integration of technology before, directly following participation in a mathematics content class enhanced with technology, and a year after the courses were completed? H1: Teachers' attitude toward the integration of technology using TPACK will improve over the period of treatment and will be maintained over an extended period of time.
2. What effects emerged in comparing teachers' lesson plans over a series of three semesters using Lyublinskaya and Tournaki's (2011) TPACK Levels Rubric? H2: Lesson plans will show advancement in the TPACK Levels and improved use of best practices.

Participants

The population studied included 45 practicing teachers enrolled in a professional development program with an emphasis on elementary mathematics. The teachers ranged in age from 22 to 60 years old and taught in five different school districts having at least 50% or more students as identified as at-risk for dropping out of school by Texas Education Agency. The cohort's ethnicity was 3% Asian, 10% Black, 27% Hispanic, and 60% White; and gender 7% male, 93% female. Teachers taught in urban, suburban and rural areas of Central Texas.

Treatment

The study's focus centered on three semesters where number theory, geometry, and probability and statistics were taught using various forms of computer related technology. Students were taught about mathematical fidelity and analyzed elementary interactive, Web- based visual representation of a dynamic object that presents opportunities for constructing mathematical knowledge for both mathematical and pedagogical fidelity (Bos, 2011). The practicing teachers were asked to identify a Web-based visual representation and ask the following questions and then enter their response in a digital discussion. Did the application appear to be procedural or did it increase their awareness of the patterning and logic involved? Did the application only serve as motivational or did it engage the participant as learners and doers of the mathematics through exploring rich word problems? Was it used to replace pencil and paper tasks or was it used to get students to think and reflect on past mathematical knowledge structures? Is the application related to a mathematical concept and does the action on the object make sense of the mathematics? After the dynamic Web-based visual representation was examined teachers were asked to find applications they could use in their classroom to strengthen the teaching of mathematics. This proved to be more difficult than they thought and participants came to the conclusion that using technology effectively in teaching mathematics was more difficult than they realized. Semester by semester the participants looked at dynamic Web-based visual representations to answer the above questions and evaluate the interactive representations for mathematical and pedalogical fidelity.

The first semester on number concepts participants complied problem based instructional units with connections to web-based interactive visual representation they felt were high in mathematical and pedagogical fidelity. (See www.//ci5303.pbworks.com). Over the course of the second semester on geometry, GeoGebra, graphing calculators, Google Sketch Up, and sites from Library of Virtual Manipulates were used to explore basic constructions, transformations, rotations, dilations, and three dimensional shape manipulations. The interactive Web-based visual representations were evaluated for mathematical and pedagogical fidelity and the participants made problem based instruction units based on geometry topics with the dyanamic Web-based visual representations. In the third semester *TinkerPlots® Dynamic Data™ Exploration* software was used along with other interactive visual representation found on the Web to examine statistical relationships. The teachers planned lessons from measuring climate change to designing a successful school carnival. The searches for dynamic Web-based visual representations continued throughout the program and were then applied to instructional units with a wide range of mathematical concepts.

Data Sources

The TPACK Survey by Schmidt, Baran, Thompson, Mishra, Koehler, and Shin (2009) was used to obtain data. The self-reported survey was designed for pre-service teachers and has been used by both pre-service and in-service teachers. Though the survey claims to determine technology knowledge, pedagogical knowledge, and content knowledge, because the data is self-reported the researchers have used it as indicating participant attitude toward the indicators. In the original test all core subject areas are represented. Because our focus was only on mathematical knowledge content the other subject areas' content were omitted. The TPACK Survey was administered during the teachers' first semester of the program, their last semester of the 36-hour mathematics specialist program, and one year after completion of the program.

Lyublinskaya and Tournaki's (2011) TPACK Levels Rubric was developed based on the TPACK framework for technology integration in the classroom where teachers progress through five progressive levels in each of four components of TPACK as identified by Niess, van Zee, & Gillow-Wilese (2010). The developers organized the rubric as a matrix where each cell represented a specific TPACK level (one of the four components of TPACK). Thus, each row of the rubric represented a specific component of TPACK and each column of the rubric represented a specific level of TPACK. For each cell of the matrix Lyublinskaya and Tournaki developed two specific performance indicators that were consistent with qualitative descriptors developed by Niess, van Zee, & Gillow-Wilese (2010) and the principles for a practical application of technology developed by Dick and Burrill (2009). The relationship between TPACK components and the TPACK levels rubric is highlighted in Table 1.

Table 1.
TPACK Components and TPACK Level Rubric

TPACK Components	Component Descriptor	TPACK Levels Rubric
Technology knowledge (TK)	Understanding of technology tools	
Content knowledge (CK)	What is known about a specific subject (mathematics) – Number Concepts, Geometry, Probability and Statistics?	
Technological content knowledge (TCK)	What is known about the affordances to represent or enhance content?	
Pedagogical knowledge (PK)	Teaching methods and processes. (i.e. problem-based, inquiry-oriented, concept attainment, and situated cognition)	Knowledge of instructional strategies and representations for teaching and learning subject matter topics with technologies
Pedagogical content knowledge (PCK)	Pedagogy specific to a particular subject area.	Knowledge of curriculum and curricular materials that integrate technology in learning and teaching mathematics;
Technology pedagogical knowledge (TPK)	Understanding how technology supports particular teaching approach	An overarching conception about the purposes for incorporating technology in teaching subject matter topics.
Technology Pedagogical Content Knowledge		Knowledge of students' understandings, thinking, and learning in subject matter topics with technology

The purpose of the TPACK Levels Rubric is to assess teachers' TPACK level based on qualitative data collected from teachers, such as lesson plans. The instrument is not intended for direct data collection. The following scoring procedure is applied when using the rubric. The possible range of scores for each component is 0 – 5, where the component score can be an integer (both performance indicators are met) or half-integer (one out of two performance indicators are met). The score is assigned for each component independently.

The TPACK Levels Rubric, used in this study for evaluating lesson plans, was tested for reliability and validity. Content validity was addressed by employing two TPACK experts. The experts were both researchers who were involved in the initial development of the TPACK conceptual framework for mathematics educators. They reviewed the rubric and provided written comments in response to three specific free-response questions about the rubric. The developers revised some of the rubric's items according to the experts' comments. In order to test for inter-rater reliability, two different experts in the field used the revised rubric to score the 45 documents (13 lesson plans with supplemental TI-Nspire documents, 13 narratives of lesson presentations during professional development, and 19 narratives of classroom teaching observations). Each expert was provided with specific instructions and explanations on using the rubric. Both experts found the rubric to be easy to use with all artifacts provided to them for scoring. The range of correlations between the scores of the two experts on the same components was from $r = 0.613$ to $r = 0.679$ $p < .01$. Correlations that examined whether there was a relationship among the four components of the rubric for each expert were also found statistically significant, i.e., the range of correlations for Expert 1 was from $r = .85$ to $r = .94$ $p < .01$ and for Expert 2 was from $r = .93$ to $.97$ $p < .01$. The significant correlations between the four components of TPACK could mean that teachers move to a higher TPACK level only after they achieve the previous level on all components (Lyublinksaya & Tournaki, 2011). The rubric was modified to work with Web 2.0 and other computer related technologies as stated in this paper.

Results

To measure attitude about knowledge in the TPACK domains the researcher administered the TPACK survey (Schmidt, et al., 2009) three times by way of a web-based survey once at the beginning of the program (pretest), at the end of the program (posttest), and a year after the program ended (posttest 2).

Table 2.
Paired t-test

Categories	Pre		Post		Post2		ANOVA for Pre Post		
	M	SD	M	SD	M	SD	t	df	D
TK	3.67	.73	4.00	.72	3.91	.81	2.91*	89	.41
MK	3.57	.72	4.10	.69	4.22	.67	3.46*	44	.73
PK	3.99	.95	4.61	.49	4.60	.54	5.65**	89	.82
PCK	3.80	.61	4.63	.61	4.47	.50	2.71*	29	1.36
TPK	3.68	.68	4.22	.52	4.35	.59	3.21*	59	.90
TPCK	3.70	.84	4.24	.80	4.24	.80	5.47**	41	.66

Note. TK = Technology Knowledge, MK = Mathematical Knowledge, PK = Pedagogical Knowledge, PCK = Pedagogical Content Knowledge, TPK = Technology Pedagogical Knowledge, Technology Pedagogical Content Knowledge.
* Significant at $p < .01$, ** Significant at $p < .001$

As shown in Table 2, results of matched-pairs *t*-test yield a statistically significant improvement in all knowledge areas of the matched-pairs t-test for technological pedagogical content (mathematical) knowledge and TPACK domains. A year after the program ended, the participants were surveyed for a third time (Post2 data). The results were very similar to the Post Test data used to calculate the ANOVA *t* value.

TPACK Levels Rubric

A qualitative analysis of 155 lesson plans written by the teachers in the program was conducted with four coders rating the use of technology using Lyublinskaya and Tournaki's TPACK Levels Rubric (2011). The results showed teacher growth in the use of technology (TPACK) over the three-semester sequence (mean first semester .98, second semester 2.25, and third semester 3.74 out of a total of 5). An ANOVA was conducted yielding an F score of 21.41 and a $p < .001$.

According to the modified Lyublinskaya and Tournaki's rubric (2011) during the first semester technology was used for motivation, rather than actual subject matter development. This would be considered the *Recognizing Level*. Technology was not used for inquiry tasks. During the first semester of the professional development program in-service teachers were taught about technology in terms of mathematical and pedagogical fidelity and the role of technology as a tool to develop concepts. Class assignments included critiquing the interactive activities found at the National Library of Virtual Manipulatives, Mathplayground, and' Illuminations. These first semester students were hesitant to try concept related technology and were under no pressure to add technology to their lesson, opting out for using it to motivate students. During the second semester the technology activities included inquiry tasks; the teachers focused on students' thinking while students were using technology on their own (*Adapting Level*). During this level technology was used as a replacement for non-technology based tasks with traditional representations and was used for learning new knowledge by students. In their lesson plans, the teachers focused on students' thinking of mathematics and other multidisciplinary topics including science, while students themselves were using technology–both for learning new knowledge and reviewing prior knowledge. In the third semester of the professional development program curriculum, the larger part of technology use was by students to explore and experiment with the technology for new knowledge and for practice (*Exploring Level*). The teacher served as a guide for student learning focusing on students' mathematics and conceptual understanding. Technology activities were built around learning objects that explicitly promote student reflection – especially the posing of questions for sense making. In this same semester inservice teachers reviewed the teaching of statistics, practicing with *Tinkerplots* and graphing calculators with their cohorts in the program. In their subsequent lesson plans, the teachers had the students use technology to explore and experiment to gain new knowledge by making connections through doing inquiry activities. The third semester coding indicated that the inservice teachers advanced to the beginning of the Exploring Level. The inter-rater reliability was 85% using four raters – two practicing teachers and two Associate Professors.

Data Analysis

After the internal consistency and reliability were checked on the TPACK survey a paired t-test was run using SPSS and the results were examined. The post-test experienced increases that lead to the use of a ANOVA to determine the t score to assess whether the means of two groups were *statistically* different from each other and d score, the effect size, were noteworthy. In using the TPACK Levels Rubric to determine the level of advancement in integrating TPACK into lesson plans an ANOVA was used. All indicators showed statistical significance.

The results of the study address the research questions. The first research question was "What effects are noticed about teachers' attitude toward the use of technological, pedagogical, and mathematical knowledge and the integration of technology before, directly following participation in a mathematics content class enhanced with technology, and a year after the class was completed?" The results show improvement in teacher's attitude toward technology knowledge, mathematical knowledge, pedagogical knowledge, pedagogical content knowledge, technological content knowledge, and technological pedagogical content (mathematical) knowledge even a year after the completion of the MMT program. The significant t scores and effect sizes indicate improvement. The design of the TPACK model is to have all the contributing parts (TK, MK, PK, PCK, TPK) lead to an improvement in TPCK. The significant gains indicate a transformation of positive attitudes toward the use of TPACK rejecting the null hypothesis allowing us to accept hypothesis one. Teachers' attitude toward the integration of technology using TPACK improved through the use of the treatment and this growth appeared to be consistent to the survey responses a year after the program's completion.

The second research question asked, "What effects emerged in comparing the lesson plans over a series of three semesters using Lyublinskaya and Tournaki's (2011) TPACK Levels Rubric?" The lesson plan rubric results confirm that participants progressed in the use of TPACK in their lesson plans and also learned to apply correct pedagogies, including the use of best practices and processes to use technology to enhance learning. Lesson plans were examined and the results indicate advancement from Recognize to the Exploration Stage in use of the TPACK model. Rejecting the null hypothesis, the lesson plans show advancement in the TPACK Levels and show improved use of best practices.

Limitations

The study is limited by the broad approach taken to describe the integration of technology using the TPACK model. Yet it is because of the broad spectrum of knowledge bases that makes TPACK a universal and powerful framework.
Within the TPACK survey instrument the TCK domains relied on one question to provide evidence of this domains; therefore, the reliability and internal consistency could not be determined creating threats to reliability and internal validity. Since data from the TPACK survey were self-reported the researcher used the results to determine the teacher's attitude about the nature of the TPACK domain. The TPACK Levels Rubric was used to support the overall design of the study and counter threats to reliability and internal validity by providing another indicator of the use of the TPACK domains by the target sample. However the objectivity of raters may have posed a threat to

validity due to their own experience and expectations.

The TPACK Levels Rubric showed significant change in the teachers understanding and use of technology, but the ratings also indicate teachers had significant room to improve to the Advance Level. This could be related to the lack of one-to-one technology in the teachers' classrooms.

Discussion

The research in this study confirmed the findings of Desimone (2011) and Darling-Hammond and McLaughlin (2011) that professional development should be ongoing and intensive. "Professional development needs to be content focused, require active learning, and should be coherent and fit in with other goals within the school environment" (Desimone, 2011, p. 69). "It must be connected to and derived from teachers' work with their students. It must be sustained, ongoing, intensive, and supported by modeling, coaching, and the collective solving of specific problems of practice" (Darling-Hammond & McLaughlin, 2011, p. 82). Teacher professional development is undergoing a paradigmatic shift that suggests the benefits of an intensive and sustained training program similar to the university-school district partnership addressed in this study.

The problem-based approach to studying mathematics set the stage for the teachers' critical thinking. Teachers were required to communicate in their groups, look for connections, and build on each other's thinking. The teachers in the masters program learned that mathematics is messy, noisy, and that persistence and flexibility are essential to mathematical pursuits as they struggled with challenging questions in class. The teachers' problem-based approach to learning that they experienced in the program transferred to their own classes as one teacher reported, "I let my students answer other students' questions now and I watch. I let them know they are capable to think through problems without me interrupting their thought process."

Conclusion

Evidence supports the belief that technology, pedagogy, and mathematical content can be taught to elementary teachers in ways that (a) support their understanding of students' learning and thinking about mathematical concepts with technology; (b) change their conception of how technology tools and representations support mathematical thinking; (c) provide instructional strategies for developing lessons with technology. Though technology may not be the complete solution to developing student's mathematical understanding, it can change the way teachers teach, provide visual models, and encourage students' active construction of their mathematical understanding. This is accomplished through fostering the use of various representations within mathematics, making connections, communicating cognitive processes, and supporting problem solving and reasoning. Additionally, adequate time is essential to preparing instructional lessons with appropriate pedagogy and based on conceptually and flexible procedural oriented technology.

Experienced teachers have a level of conceptual knowledge and experience that pre-service teachers do not, but, as noted in this study, it took time and more experience with technology tools in mathematically rich environments for the experienced teachers to trust and feel comfortable with the mathematical power of technology. Discussion and constant self-evaluation helped. Developing the instructional strategies for cultivating lessons with technology required modeling and using the technology in their own classrooms before they felt comfortable integrating the technology in their instructional units. The more exploratory the teachers were in their own classrooms the more comfortable they became in relinquishing some control and trusting their students to ask better questions, explore, and make connections through the use of technology. Also of importance is the lasting change to teachers' pedagogy and technology as shown in the results of the administration of the TPACK survey a year after their completion of the program.

References

Angeli, C., & Valanides, N. (2009). Epistemological and methodological issues for the conceptualization, development, and assessment of ICT-TPCK: Advances in technological pedagogical content knowledge (TPCK). *Computers & Education, 52*(1), 154-168.

Bos, B. (2011). Teachers preparation using TPACK when fidelity of treatment is defined. *Contemporary Issues in Technology and Teacher Education, 11*(2), 167-183.

Conlon, T., & Simpson, M. (2003). Silicon Valley versus Silicon Glen: The impact of computers upon teaching and learning: A comparative study. *British Journal of Educational Technology, 34*(2), 137-150.

Cuban, L., Kirkpatrick, H., & Peck, C. (2001). High access and low use of technologies in high school classrooms: Explaining an apparent paradox. *American Educational Research Journal, 38*(4), 813-834.

Darling-Hammond, L., & McLaughlin, M. W. (2011). Policies that support professional development in an era of reform. *Phi Delta Kappan, 92*(6), 81-92.

Desimone, L. M. (2011). A primer on effective professional development. *Phi Delta Kappan, 92*(6), 68-71.

Dick, T., & Burrill, G. (2009). *Technology and teaching and learning mathematics at the secondary level: Implications for teacher preparation and development.* Paper presented at the Annual Meeting of Association of Mathematics Teacher Educators, Orlando FL.

Donnelly, R. (2010). Harmonizing technology with interaction in blended problem-based learning. *Computers & Education, 54*(2), 350-359.

Gordon, M. (2009). Toward a pragmatic discourse of constructivism: Reflections on lessons from practice, *Educational Studies, 45*(1), 39-58.

Kaput, J. J., & Roschelle, J. (1998). The mathematics of change and variation from a millennial prespective: New content, new context. In C. Hoyles, C. Morgan, & G. Woodhouse (Eds.), *Rethinking the mathematics* (pp. 155–170). London: Springer Verlag.

Kincheloe, J. (2000). From positivism to an epistemology of complexity: Grounding rigorous teaching. In J. Kincheloe & D. Weil (Eds.), *Standards and Schooling in the United States, An Encyclopedia, Volume Two*, pp. 325-396. Santa Barbara, CA: ABC-CLIO.

Koehler, M. J. & Mishra, P. (2005). What happens when teachers design educational technology? The development of Technological Pedagogical Content Knowledge. *Journal of Educational Computing Research. 32*(2), 131-152.

Koehler, M. J., Mishra, P., Bouck, E. C., DeSchryver, M., Kereluik, K., Shin, T. S., & Wolf, L. G. (2011). Deep play: developing TPACK for 21st century teachers. *International Journal of Learning Technology, 6*(2), 146-163.

Lyublinksaya, I., & Tournaki, N. (2011). The effects of teacher content authoring on TPACK and on student achievement in algebra: Research on instruction with the TI-Nspire handheld. In R. N. Ronau, C. R. Rakes, & M. L. Niess (Eds.), *Educational technology, teacher knowledge, and classroom impact: A research handbook on frameworks and approaches* (pp. 295-322). Hershey, PA: IGI Global. doi:10.4018/978-1-60960-750-0.ch013

Mishra, P., & Koehler, M. H. (2006). Technological pedagogical content knowledge: A framework for teacher knowledge. *Teachers College Record, 108*(6), 1017-1054.

Moyer, P. S., Bolyard, J. J., & Spikell, M. A. (2002). What are virtual manipulatives? *Teaching Children Mathematics, 8*(6), 372–377.

Moyer-Packenham, P. S., & Suh, J. M., (2012). Learning mathematics with technology: The influence of virtual manipulatives on different achievement groups. *Journal of Computers in Mathematics and Science Teaching, 31*(1), 39-59.

National Council of Teachers of Mathematics. (2000). *Principles and standards of for school mathematics.* Reston, VA: Author.

Niess, M. (2007). Reflections on the state and trends in research on mathematics teaching and learning: From here to Utopia. In F. Lester (Ed.), *Second handbook of research on mathematics teaching and learning*, (pp. 1293-1311). Greenwich, CT: Information Age Publishing.

Niess, M. L., van Zee, E., & Gillow-Wilese, H. (2010-11). Knowledge growth in teaching mathematics/science with spreadsheets: Moving PCK to TPACK through online professional development. *Journal of Digital Learning in Teacher Education, 27*(2), 42-52.

Sarama, J., & Clements, D. H. (2009). "Concrete" computer manipulatives in mathematics education. *Child Development Perspectives, 3*(3), 145–150. doi:10.1111/j.1750-8606.2009.00095

Schmidt, D. A., Baran, E., Thompson, A. D., Mishra, P., Koehler, M. J., & Shin, T. S. (2009).Technological pedagogical content knowledge (TPACK): The development and validation of an assessment instrument for pre-service teachers. *Journal of Research on Technology in Education, 42*(2), 123-149.

Thayer-Bacon, B. (1999). The thinker versus a quilting bee: Contrasting images. *Educational Foundations, 13*(4), 47-65.

Windschitl, M. (1999). The challenges of sustaining a constructivist classroom culture. *Phi Delta Kappan, 80*, (10), 751-755.

Designing an Educational Technology Course for Preservice Social Studies Teachers Based on Technological Pedagogical Content Knowledge (TPACK) Survey Results

Mark Hart
College of Public Health and Health Professions
University of Florida, USA
kramtrah@phhp.ufl.edu

Swapna Kumar
School of Teaching and Learning, College of Education
University of Florida, USA
swapnak@ufl.edu

Abstract: An educational technology course for preservice social studies teachers was created based on technological pedagogical content knowledge (TPACK) (Mishra & Koehler, 2006) and refined based on the results of a TPACK-survey completed by students before the course began. The instructor was able to eliminate aspects correlating with high self-assessed knowledge and focus on areas which showed a perceived lack of knowledge. Results of this survey provide a snapshot of students' perceived knowledge, according to TPACK components, prior to entering the teaching field. This paper demonstrates how course design can quickly be modified if the class curriculum has a TPACK foundation connected with a TPACK pre-class survey.

Introduction

The technological pedagogical content knowledge (TPACK) framework (Koehler & Mishra, 2005; Mishra & Koehler, 2006) centers on measuring how content, pedagogy, and technology depend on one another to lead towards effective teaching. Although it is a relatively recently constructed framework, numerous studies have used this model to make connections between teacher knowledge and successful technology integration (Koehler, Shin, & Mishra, 2012). The framework contends that Technical Knowledge (TK), Content Knowledge (CK), and Pedagogical Knowledge (PK) are needed for effective teaching (Koehler & Mishra, 2009). Recent studies have focused on the use of TPACK in specific content areas, as well as the use of the framework to gauge the knowledge of preservice instructors (Koehler, Shin, & Mishra, 2012). Common findings, related to preservice teachers, show that many surveyed preservice teachers are frequent technology users in their personal life, but often lack the ability to best integrate technology with their content and instruction as teachers (McCormick & Scrimshaw, 2001).

In this study a required educational technology course was designed according to the TPACK framework, following which the preservice social studies teachers (n=14) who enrolled completed a modified TPACK survey to gauge their knowledge prior to the start of the class. The results were then integrated into the course design to modify the curriculum, allowing for the instructor to customize the class to address areas which the students self-identified as potentially needing improvement. This paper thus illustrates the use of the TPACK framework as well as instructional design techniques that used a validated survey from the research to design a preservice educational technology course for a specific content area. Furthermore, it provides a snapshot into the perceived knowledge and skills of preservice teachers who have grown up surrounded by technology and will soon be entering the teaching profession.

Theoretical Framework

Technological Pedagogical Content Knowledge (TPCK) was first introduced as a framework to help researchers better understand the teacher knowledge needed for successful technology integration (Koehler & Mishra, 2005; Mishra & Koehler, 2006). Seven components are included in the later renamed TPACK framework, defined as:

- *Technology knowledge (TK):* knowledge about various technologies
- *Content knowledge (CK):* knowledge about subject matter
- *Pedagogical knowledge (PK):* knowledge referring to the methods and process of teaching
- *Pedagogical content knowledge (PCK):* content knowledge that deals with the teaching process
- *Technological content knowledge (TCK)*: knowledge of how technology can create new representations of content
- *Technological pedagogical knowledge (TPK):* knowledge of how various technologies can be used in teaching
- *Technological pedagogical content knowledge (TPACK):* knowledge required by teachers for integrating technology into their teaching in any content area (Mishra & Koehler, 2006)

The foundations of TPACK allow for the simultaneous ability to examine individual components of the model while also studying overlapping aspects. Abbitt (2011) identified 22 studies that attempted to assess preservice teachers' understanding of TPACK components using quantitative and qualitative methodologies. The Survey of Preservice Teacher's Knowledge of Teaching and Technology (Schmidt et al., 2009) used in this study is described by Abbitt as "among the more mature tools" (2011, p 290) designed to collect data on teachers' self-assessment of the seven knowledge domains within TPACK.

Teacher Technology Preparation in Social Studies

In the last decade, research involving teacher training and technology has placed a greater emphasis on promoting content-specific instruction for technology integration (Koy & Divaharan, 2011). This push away from content-neutral instruction is congruent with the foundations of TPACK that stresses the interconnectedness of technology with content and pedagogy (Mishra & Koehler, 2006). The specific content area of social studies has long been guided by the National Council of Social Studies (NCSS) mission "to help young people make informed and reasoned decisions for the public good as citizens of a culturally diverse, democratic society in an interdependent world" (NCSS, 2010). A recent update to the standards has placed greater emphasis on purposes, knowledge, processes, and products, which demonstrate understanding (NCSS, 2010). Traditional social studies classrooms have long been considered teacher-centered using lectures to transfer knowledge of events and themes in history from instructor to student (Koy & Divaharan, 2011). This model has perpetuated a system where future social studies teachers are trained in this format and often begin teaching in the same style (Hammerness et al., 2005). More recent efforts, however, have been made to move away from the memorization of who, what, where, and when facts and towards more constructivist models which allow students to focus more on using those facts to collaborate on critical thinking problems and inquiry (Shin et al., 2009). To help guide these efforts to prepare social studies teachers for using technology appropriately and effectively, a recent study proposed a model for social studies education that specifically integrates the TPACK model in its design. Hammond & Manfra (2009) advocate the Giving-Prompting-Making method that responds to Mishra and Koehler's (2006) observation that technology training for teachers tends to only look at the tools themselves and not at how to use them. For example this model would advocate teachers showing a film to share factual information (Giving), then using other selected video clips as guides for writing and discussion (Prompting) and finally allowing the students to apply the material in a corresponding video they created (Making) (Hammond & Manfra, 2009). In this model the technology does not come before the content, and technology is only considered once the pedagogical content is decided.

Social Studies Teacher Education Course

The context for this research is a required course in Educational Technology for social studies preservice teachers in a Master of Education program. The course explores a number of different Web applications that can be used to teach Social Studies with the primary focus on the proactive application of digital literacy from a teaching and learning perspective. This includes the incorporation of emerging technologies to foster a mindset of 21st century learning principles and how they can best be facilitated in the social studies classroom.

The course, Integrating Technology in Social Studies Curriculum, is delivered in a blended format over 16 weeks with the class meeting in a three hour weekly face-to-face session for 13 weeks and additionally completing online requirements through the learning management system. The main topics covered in the course include: digital literacy for inquiry learning in social studies, primary sources in digital resources, personal learning environments and networks, service learning and technology in social studies, and bridging the digital divide.

Previously the course was designed with specific goals and objectives towards better facilitating students' TPACK. Specifically four modules were integrated into the course to develop students' PK, TPK, and TPACK. The first module, to enhance PK, focused on introducing students to the idea of inquiry-based learning through an online discussion that worked to connect this approach with various social studies disciplines (Leeman, 2013). The second module worked to bridge the gap between personal technology knowledge and TPK. In this lesson students took on the role of a student who was completing a group project on Jamestown through a wiki page. At the conclusion of this lesson students held a roundtable discussion on the assignment. They discussed aspects that were difficult from the student perspective and what could be explained or done by an instructor to eliminate these problems (Leeman, 2013). The third and fourth modules were TPACK-specific and involved designing a guided historical inquiry lesson and finally sharing and reflecting on lesson choices. The third module had students complete an online training through the Library of Congress that highlights locations for teachers to get resources specific to their field and location. Students were then instructed to use this information and a wiki space to develop a lesson plan through historical inquiry. The final module built on the third - students completed their peers' lessons and the process culminated in a reflective journal piece where they summarized what they learned from the lesson they created and completed (Leeman, 2013).

Methodology

While this course has been successfully offered in previous years, the new instructor sought to revise the course and use data generated from a TPACK survey with the intention of further grounding the instructional efforts in the TPACK framework. The first step in obtaining baseline information from the students was to find, and use, a validated TPACK instrument. The Survey of Preservice Teacher's Knowledge of Teaching and Technology was chosen because it has a specific focus on preservice teachers similar to those enrolled in the course. This survey included an initial pool of 44 items based on the seven components of TPACK developed by six researchers and evaluated by three nationally known researchers for validity (Schmidt et al., 2009). Ultimately the instrument was refined and expanded to 75 items measuring self-assessments of preservice teachers' knowledge of the seven TPACK domains: 8 TK items, 17 CK items, 10 PK items, 8 PCK items, 15 TPK items, and 9 TPACK items (Schmidt et al., 2009). Each item requests participants to answer the questions using a five-point Likert-scale (Strongly Disagree, Disagree, Neither Agree nor Disagree, Agree, Strongly Agree). The internal consistency of each domain subscale using Cronbach's alpha reliability technique of the Survey of Preservice Teacher's Knowledge of Teaching and Technology according to Schmidt et al. (2009) was: TK (.82), CK-social studies (.84), PK (.84), PCK (.85), TCK (.80), TPK (.86) and TPACK (.92). Construct validity for each domain subscale was also investigated by Schmidt et al. (2009) using principal components factor analysis with varimax rotation within each knowledge domain and Kaiser normalization.

For the purpose of this study, changes made to the instrument involved the removal of content questions not related to social studies. Open-ended questions were added at the end to allow the instructor to learn more about tools the students were already familiar with and used at the time. Considering factor loadings were calculated for each subscale and internal consistency was labeled for each content area, the reliability of the survey remained intact. After finalizing the changes to the survey, the questions were entered in an online survey tool and distributed to the 14 students who had enrolled in the course, prior to the start of the course. Students were given a week to complete the survey. When the survey results were received, the data were analyzed by computing the percentages of answers according to the Likert-scale responses. The mean ratings for each question were calculated with Strongly Agree being assigned a value of 5 and Strongly Disagree 1. The mean for each TPACK component was also calculated.

Findings

Fourteen preservice teachers (F=9, M=5) in the final year of their teacher education program enrolled in the course completed the survey. Ten of the students were 21 or 22 years old, two students were between 22-25 and two students between 25-32. Three of the students had previously taken an educational technology course.

Table 1: Technology Knowledge (TK), Content Knowledge (CK – Social Studies) and Pedagogical Knowledge (PK)

Question	Strongly Disagree	Disagree	Neither Agree or Disagree	Agree	Strongly Agree
Technology Knowledge (TK)					
I know how to solve my own technical problems.	7.1% (1)	21.4% (3)	7.1% (1)	**64.3% (9)**	0% (0)
I can learn technology easily.	0% (0)	7.1% (1)	14.3% (2)	**57.1% (8)**	21.4% (3)
I keep up with important new technologies.	14.3% (2)	14.3% (2)	28.6% (4)	**35.7% (5)**	7.1% (1)
I frequently play around with technology.	7.1% (1)	14.3% (2)	**42.9% (6)**	28.6% (4)	7.1% (1)
I know a lot of different technologies.	7.1% (1)	21.4% (3)	21.4% (3)	**42.9% (6)**	7.1% (1)
I have the technical skills I need to use technology.	0% (0)	14.3% (2)	14.3% (2)	**57.1% (8)**	14.3% (2)
Content Knowledge (CK) Social Studies					
I have sufficient knowledge about social studies.	0% (1)	0% (0)	7.1% (1)	**85.7% (12)**	7.1% (1)
I can use a historical way of thinking.	0% (0)	0% (0)	28.6% (4)	**42.9% (6)**	28.6% (4)
I have various ways and strategies of developing my understanding of social studies.	0% (0)	0% (0)	21.4% (3)	**57.1% (8)**	21.4% (3)
Pedagogical Knowledge (PK)					
I know how to assess student performance in a classroom.	0% (1)	35.7% (5)	**35.7% (5)**	28.6% (4)	0% (0)
I can adapt my teaching based upon what students currently understand or do not understand.	0% (0)	14.3% (2)	**42.9% (6)**	**42.9% (6)**	0% (0)
I can adapt my teaching style to different learners.	0.0% (0)	14.3% (2)	35.7% (5)	**50.0 (7)**	0% (0)
I can assess student learning in multiple ways.	0% (0)	7.1% (10)	**50.0% (7)**	42.9% (6)	0% (0)
I can use a wide range of teaching approaches in a classroom setting.	0% (0)	14.3% (2)	**50.0% (7)**	35.7% (5)	0% (0)
I am familiar with common student understandings and misconceptions.	0% (0)	28.6% (4)	**35.7% (5)**	**35.7% (5)**	0% (0)
I know how to organize and maintain classroom management.	0% (0)	**42.9% (6)**	**42.9% (6)**	14.3% (2)	0% (0)

In terms of technology knowledge (Table 1), students' highest ratings were for the item "I can learn technology easily" and "I have the technical skills I need to use technology" and their lowest ratings were for the item "I keep up with important new technologies." Students' content knowledge ratings were high (Table 1) but for pedagogical knowledge, students did not rate any item as strongly agree (Table 1). The item "I am thinking critically about how to use technology in my classroom" had the highest rating among the items for technological pedagogical knowledge in Social studies (Table 2) as did "My professors appropriately model combining content, technologies, and teaching approaches in their teaching" for technological pedagogical and content knowledge (Table 3). The responses indicate that the students feel they are receiving proper modeling of technology usage in their classes and have begun the process of internalizing these lessons and applying them to their own future lessons.

Table 2: Technological Pedagogical Knowledge (TPK) (Social studies)

Question	Strongly Disagree	Disagree	Neither Agree or Disagree	Agree	Strongly Agree
I can choose technologies that enhance teaching approaches for a lesson.	0% (1)	14.3% (2)	**50.0% (7)**	35.7% (5)	0% (0)
I can choose technologies that enhance students' learning for a lesson.	0% (0)	14.3% (2)	**50.0% (7)**	35.7% (5)	0% (0)
My teacher education program has caused me to think more deeply about how technology could influence the teaching approaches I use in my classroom.	0% (0)	0% (0)	**35.7% (5)**	35.7% (5)	28.6% (4)
I am thinking critically about how to use technology in my classroom.	0% (0)	0% (10)	21.4% (3)	**57.1% (8)**	21.4% (3)
I can adapt the use of the technologies that I am learning about to different teaching activities.	0% (0)	14.3% (2)	**42.9% (6)**	35.7% (5)	7.1% (1)
I can select technologies to use in my classroom that enhance what I teach, how I teach, and what students learn.	0% (0)	21.4% (3)	28.6% (4)	**50.0% (7)**	0% (0)
I can use strategies that combine content, technologies, and teaching approaches that I learned about in my coursework in my classroom.	0% (0)	21.4% (3)	**42.9% (6)**	35.7% (5)	0% (0)
I can provide leadership in helping others to coordinate the use of content, technologies and teaching approaches at my school and/or district.	7.1% (1)	21.4% (3)	**50.0% (7)**	21.4% (3)	0% (0)
I can choose technologies that enhance the content for a lesson.	0% (0)	14.3% (2)	28.6% (4)	**57.1% (8)**	0% (0)

Table 3: Technological Pedagogical and Content Knowledge (TPACK) (Social studies)

Question	Strongly Disagree	Disagree	Neither Agree or Disagree	Agree	Strongly Agree
I can select effective teaching approaches to guide student thinking and learning in social studies	0% (1)	14.3% (2)	**50.0% (7)**	35.7% (5)	0% (0)
I know about technologies that I can use for understanding and doing social studies.	0% (0)	21.4% (3)	28.6% (4)	**50.0% (5)**	0% (0)
I can teach lessons that appropriately combine social studies, technologies and teaching approaches.	0% (0)	21.4% (3)	**50.0% (7)**	28.6% (4)	0% (4)
My professors appropriately model combining content, technologies, and teaching approaches in their teaching.	0% (0)	7.1% (1)	21.4% (3)	**64.3% (9)**	7.1% (1)

Mean ratings for all items in each category (see Table 4) indicated that students' rated their content knowledge as highest among the different components with a mean of 4.0 out of 5. Their pedagogical knowledge was rated as lowest, with a mean of 3.19 out of 5 with technological pedagogical content knowledge following at 3.32 out of 5. Students were also asked to list all of the technologies that they are knowledgeable in using and want to use in their social studies classroom. The six most listed known technologies, in order of highest frequency, were PowerPoint, Microsoft Office Tools, YouTube, Google Earth, Smartboards, and blogs.

Course Design

The survey revealed self-assessments similar to the findings of McCormick & Scrimshaw (2001) where students were familiar with technology in their personal life but did not feel knowledgeable to use the new technologies teaching. This survey also revealed that this group of students was comfortable with their content knowledge, so the focus should be on how to blend together technical and content knowledge with better pedagogical approaches. As previously stated, the course focused on technology integration into social studies curriculum had previously been designed and offered according to the TPACK framework (Leeman, 2013). The instructor thus modified the existing curriculum and syllabus based on the data from the student survey, between the time the survey responses were received and the beginning of classes. The course was previously built with a foundation in TPACK, therefore much of the class was kept intact including the four major modules to enhance TPACK. Changes to the course based on the survey involved making changes to the specific content, examples, or time spent on items based on the feedback from the survey. For example, aspects of the course that was primarily social studies content-specific were reduced further from the course because students had rated themselves as comfortable with content knowledge. Second, the number of technologies which were to be covered was also reviewed, reduced, changed and taught from different perspectives. The short-response portion of the survey about new technologies revealed that students were already familiar with many of the technologies that were going to be covered in class. With this in mind, a shift was made to add different tools and to not teach the included technologies from the perspective of their features and abilities but rather only from how they can be used by teachers and students. A foundation of Strengths – Weaknesses – Opportunities – Threats (SWOT) analysis is being used for each technology introduced, but the preservice teachers are encouraged to answer these questions with considerations of classroom use and how their Social studies students in K-12 classrooms will use the application or technology. Another change made to the course, in addition to reducing the number of technologies taught, was to also introduce a mobile device (iPads) and investigate and learn more about the content of each week of the term.

While the focus of this study was to design curriculum based on the pre-course survey, a post-course survey was administered to students to assess their TPACK at the end of the course. Initial analysis of the post-course data shows growth in all areas based on the means for each section. Since various factors, including the general knowledge learned from the technology course as well as information learned in other courses, can explain an increase in self-evaluated TPACK components, a more thorough analysis of the responses to each individual question will better pinpoint reasons for learning gains. The means for all sections were higher in the post-survey compared to the pre-survey (see Table 4), reinforcing the choices made in curriculum changes based on the pre-course survey.

Table 4: Means for TPACK categories (pre-test versus post-test)

Category	Mean rating for all items: Pre-survey / Post-survey	
Technology Knowledge (TK)	3.39	4.20
Content Knowledge (CK)-social studies	4.00	4.53
Pedagogical Knowledge (PK)	3.13	4.13
Technological Pedagogical Knowledge (TPK)	3.38	4.38
Technological Pedagogical Content Knowledge (TPACK)	3.32	4.20

Beyond the Likert-scale based responses for the survey, other analysis to determine reasons for learning gains will be examined through the course evaluations and responses to the open-ended questions on the survey. An initial examination of these resources show strong support for two areas of the course which were changed based on the pre-course survey. Various students remarked that they appreciated the approach of learning how to properly evaluate tools versus just being taught how various tools work. This is supported by the responses to the specific question which showed the most growth between surveys "I can provide leadership in helping others to coordinate the use of content, technologies and teaching approached at my school and / or district". In the pre-survey this question was scored as a mean of 2.86 among students, whereas the mean on the post-survey was 3.80. Another area which was singled out by students was the in-depth examination of iPads. Students seemed to appreciate the depth of study on one specific tool, which they felt taught them to apply this approach to other and future tools.

To get students more comfortable with thinking how they will use technology tools in their classrooms, changes were also made for the preservice teachers themselves to do more of the introducing and using of the tools in class versus the instructor introducing the tools. To further develop the preservice students' ability to select proper tools according to the task, a scenario was presented each week where a specific topic and environment was presented in class and the preservice teachers had to come to a consensus in small groups on which technology, or strategy, they would select for this lesson. All groups then made their presentations, and explained why they chose that specific technology or strategy to the rest of the class, followed by a larger discussion that resulted in a full-class decision. This approach allowed for intense conversation and for students to consider various approaches to the same task.

Conclusion

Often teachers are forced to create curriculum in the summer time, or the beginning of the term, prior to even meeting and assessing their students. Data collected from students, even in the form of self-reports, can assist teacher educators in assessing students' incoming knowledge and designing learning experiences for that specific group. In this study, the instructor used the TPACK framework to design the course and then used data from a TPACK-based survey to select which areas of the curriculum needed more or less attention for that group of students. This approach also intended to help students apply specific strategies in their learning of new technologies and in the ways they apply them in their teaching. Technologies are constantly changing and new technologies and resources that can be used to teach Social studies are emerging constantly. Focusing on strategies to analyze new technologies and how they can be applied in the classroom will help preservice teachers transfer these strategies to other technologies in their future teaching career.

References

Abbitt, J. (2011). Measuring Technological Pedagogical Content Knowledge in Preservice Teacher Education: A Review of Current Methods and Instruments. *Journal of Research in Teacher Education, 43*(4) 281-200-

Hammerness, K., Darling-Hammond, L., Bransford, J., Berliner, D., Cochran-Smith, M., McDonald, M., & Zeichner, K. (2005). How teachers learn and develop. *Preparing teachers for a changing world: What teachers should learn and be able to do*, 358-389.

Hammond, T. C., & Manfra, M. M. (2009). Giving, prompting, making: Aligning technology and pedagogy within TPACK for social studies instruction. *Contemporary Issues in Technology and Teacher Education*

Koehler, M., & Mishra, P. (2005). What happens when teachers design educational technology? The development of technological pedagogical content knowledge. *Journal of Educational Computing Research, 32*(2), 131–152.

Koehler, M., & Mishra, P. (2009). What is technological pedagogical content knowledge (TPACK)?. *Contemporary Issues in Technology and Teacher Education, 9*(1), 60-70.

Koehler, M. J., Shin, T. S., & Mishra, P. (2011). How do we measure TPACK? Let me count the ways. *Educational technology, teacher knowledge, and classroom impact: A research handbook on frameworks and approaches*, 16-31.

Koehler, M. J., Mishra, P., Kereluik, K., Shin, T. S., & Graham, C. R. (2014). The technological pedagogical content knowledge framework. In *Handbook of Research on Educational Communications and Technology* (pp. 101-111). Springer New York.

Koh, J. H., & Divaharan, S. (2011). Developing pre-service teachers' technology integration expertise through the TPACK-developing instructional model. *Journal of Educational Computing Research, 44*(1), 35-58.

Leeman, J. (2013). Guiding Pre-service Teachers Toward Technology Supported Learner-Centered Instruction: Using the TPACK Literature to Inform Teacher Educator Pedagogy. In R. McBride & M. Searson (Eds.), *Proceedings of Society for Information Technology & Teacher Education International Conference 2013* (pp. 4983-4988). Chesapeake, VA: AACE. Retrieved from http://www.editlib.org/p/48918

McCormick, R., & Scrimshaw, P. (2001). Information and communications technology, knowledge and pedagogy. *Education, Communication & Information, 1*(1), 37-57.

Mishra, P., & Koehler, M.(2006). Technological pedagogical content knowledge: A framework for teacher knowledge. *The Teachers College Record, 108*(6), 1017-1054.

National Council for the Social Studies (2010). *National curriculum standards for social studies: A framework for teaching, learning, and assessment.* Silver Spring, MD: Author.

Schmidt, D. A., Baran, E., Thompson, A. D., Mishra, P., Koehler, M. J., & Shin, T. S. (2009). Technological pedagogical content knowledge (TPACK): The development and validation of an assessment instrument for preservice teachers. *Journal of Research on Computing in Education, 42*(2), 123.

Shin, T., Koehler, M., Mishra, P., Schmidt, D., Baran, E., & Thompson, A. (2009). Changing technological pedagogical content knowledge (TPACK) through course experiences. In G. Ian, W. Roberta, M. Karen, C. Roger & W. Dee Anna (Eds.), *Proceedings of the Society for Information Technology & Teacher Education International Conference 2009* (pp. 4152– 4159). Chesapeake, VA: AACE.

Impact of Design Teams on Preservice Teachers' TPACK, Attitudes, & Skills

Laurene Johnson
Hezel Associates, USA,
Laurene@hezel.com

Abstract: This study examined the effect of a design team's instructional approach on preservice teachers' attitudes toward technology, technology skills, and Technological Pedagogical Content Knowledge (TPACK). In a design teams approach, participants work in collaborative teams to design solutions to real-world problems. This quasi-experimental study explored the efficacy of an educational technology course implemented with a design team's approach compared to the same course utilizing a standard instructional approach. Findings indicated significant differences between the treatment and comparison groups on TPACK when measured with evidence from lesson plans. No significant differences were found between groups on survey-measured attitudes, technology skills, or TPACK, though both groups had significant growth on these measures. These results suggested that the design teams approach was appropriate for use in preservice teacher technology education, but additional research is necessary to determine in which contexts and with what specific learning outcomes it is most effective.

Introduction

In the approximately 30 years since technology first appeared in schools it has become an integral part of the educational experience as educators have transitioned to more technological solutions to everyday tasks. Technology has a role in almost all aspects of school functioning—communicating, teaching, learning, and ultimately preparing students to be productive members of the future workforce. Where technology was once a scarce commodity, almost every school in the United States now has Internet access, and approximately one computer for every three students (National Center for Education Statistics 2010). While there have been heavy investments over the past 15 years in improving technology infrastructure, access to technological tools, and educators' technology skills in K-12 schools to promote the ubiquitous use of these tools in educational settings (Lawless & Pellegrino 2007; U.S. Department of Education 2010), technology has never been incorporated into the regular instructional practices of all teachers (Cuban 2001; Mueller, Wood, Willoughby, Ross, & Specht 2008; Project Tomorrow 2011).

Our teachers are responsible for preparing students for an increasingly technological world. Teachers who are unable to use technology to enhance student learning will potentially leave students unprepared to function in our technological society. All teachers therefore, including those new to the profession, should be ready to integrate technology into instruction. Surveys of teachers and students suggest that technology use in classrooms has increased over the past 10 years, but use of technology in classrooms is neither ubiquitous nor taking advantage of the unique affordances that technology tools offer to promote student learning (Ertmer & Ottenbreit-Leftwich 2010; Gray, Thomas, & Lewis 2010; Jonassen 2006; Steeves 2012). While it has been suggested that it was predominantly "digital immigrant" teachers (Prensky 2001) who struggled with technology integration, new teachers have also consistently reported over time that they felt unprepared to use technology effectively in the classroom (Dawson & Norris 2000; Evans & Gunter 2004; Gray, et al. 2010).

There has been a substantial focus on determining what knowledge preservice teachers need with respect to technology integration and the types of instruction that are most likely to produce teachers who can effectively use technology with students. Much of this prior research has examined single instructional approaches, single outcomes, or used highly contextualized instruments with limited generalizability to other teacher education programs (Kay 2006). Research that explores multiple factors that impact teachers' technology integration abilities and compares approaches is essential to developing a better understanding of what instruction is most effective in educating future teachers to be effective technology integrators (Hofer, Grandgenett, Harris, & Richardson 2010; Kay 2006).

In addition, the importance of exploring these factors in realistic instructional contexts has been emphasized by many experts in the field (Koehler & Mishra 2005a; Shulman 1986; Zhao, Pugh, Sheldon, & Byers 2002). While conducting research *in situ* inevitably results in variables that are difficult to control, studying realistic contexts is essential to adequately account for the demands, complexities, and overall messiness inherent in real-world educational environments (Shulman 1986; Zhao, et al. 2002). Research that intends to inform educational practice in preservice teacher education must occur in these contexts in order to provide sufficient guidance to add to the knowledge base regarding what instructional approaches and techniques will be effective in teacher preparation (Koehler, Mishra, Yahya, & Yadav 2004; Polly, Mims, Shepherd, & Inan 2010).

Figure 1 presents this study's theoretical framework. The framework depicts how the existing research in the field suggests that the traditional components of preservice teacher technology integration education (shown on the left), combined with the inclusion of the design teams approach as described in the literature, should result in increased attitudes toward technology, technology skills, and TPACK. This research study focused on testing the center section of the theoretical model, to determine whether the addition of the design teams approach to the existing instruction produced significant changes in the intermediate outcomes of attitudes, skills, and TPACK. This research sought to answer the following question: What effect does the integration of a design teams approach into an existing technology integration course have on preservice teachers' attitudes toward technology, technology skills, and TPACK?

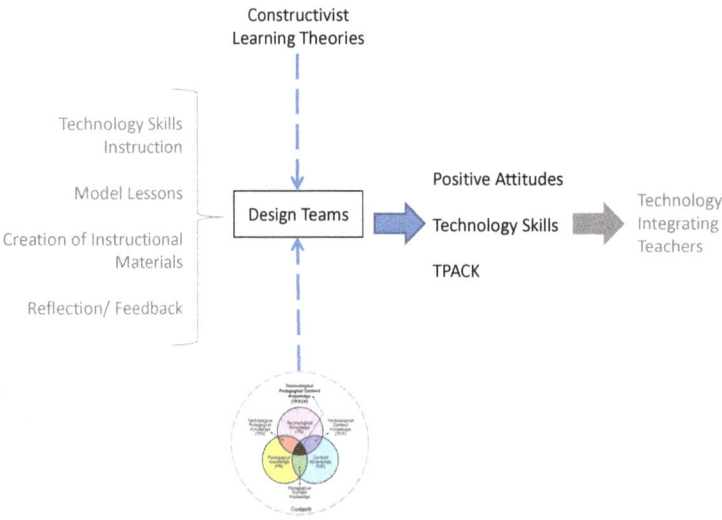

Figure 1: Theoretical Framework

Design Teams for Preservice Teacher Technology Integration Instruction

In proposing their TPACK framework, Koehler and Mishra (2005a) suggested Learning By Design (LBD) (Kolodner, et al. 2003) as an appropriate approach for helping teachers develop their understandings of the TPACK components. Design teams were initially conceived for the teaching of science (Kolodner, et al. 2003), but in the Learning Technology by Design approach (Koehler, Mishra, & Yahya 2007), teachers worked in collaborative groups called design teams, "over extended periods of time" (p. 744) to "develop technological solutions to authentic problems" (p. 741). Teachers enhanced their TPACK understandings through engaging in and solving real-world, ill-structured problems that provided context for learning about instructional technology (Koehler & Mishra 2005b).

To apply a design teams approach to a technology integration course with preservice teachers, the essential components and structures must be identified. Descriptions of the implementations of design teams approaches in the literature were used to inform this implementation. Researchers who have used design teams approaches agreed that they comprise two primary components: small group activities and whole group activities. While small group activities were focused on investigating, exploring, justifying decisions, and developing artifacts; whole group activities were for learning from each other's successes and failures, providing and receiving feedback, and refining participants' understandings of key concepts essential for problem solving (Koehler, Mishra, Hershey, & Peruski 2004; Kolodner, et al. 2003). The instructor has a facilitative role, providing (a) guidance for the collaborative process, (b) instruction on necessary content or skills, and (c) expert feedback and resources as needed (Kolodner, et al. 2003).

The design teams approach should include specific elements to guide participants through both the design and learning processes (Kolodner, et al. 2003). While the research on the use of design teams approaches in education includes settings from eighth grade to university faculty, the major elements of the overall approach were primarily the same across these examples:
1. Presentation of a design challenge
2. Whole group instruction on essential content
3. Brainstorming potential solutions, refining ideas, and developing potential solutions or artifacts
4. Sharing solutions and testing of artifacts
5. Feedback from the whole class and within teams, and team and personal reflection
6. Focus on implementation through refining, redesigning, and testing
7. Sharing with the whole class, and team and personal reflections

Iteration was essential in the implementation process: These steps were repeated until the teams developed an artifact that they considered their final product. In terms of work with preservice and inservice teachers, this artifact was often the learning materials that were implemented with students (Fessakis, Tatsis, & Dimitracopoulou 2008; Koehler & Mishra 2005b; Kolodner, et al. 2003).

In the literature, implementations consisted of two primary class structures: community (the whole class) and design teams (groups of 3 or 4 people), each with a specific function within the process (Alayyar 2011; Kolodner, et al. 2003). The community had three functions: (a) setting expectations and goals, (b) poster sessions for sharing drafts and receiving input, and (c) testing and feedback to assess functioning and plan modifications (Alayyar, Fisser, & Voogt 2010; Koehler, Mishra, Hershey, et al. 2004; Kolodner, et al. 2003). There were six primary functions for the design teams: (a) clarifying the problem or task, (b) assigning team members' roles, (c) implementation, and (f) debriefing to reflect on the process (Alayyar, et al. 2010; Koehler, Mishra, Hershey, et al. 2004; Kolodner, et al. 2003).

Each of these community and design teams' functions represented an essential component in the design teams' approach. These components were organized and sequenced by the instructors to provide the scaffolding and iteration necessary for learning to take place (Kolodner 2002). The steps in the approach built upon each other, fostering the relationships and thinking processes required for authentic problem solving, thus the appropriate sequencing of the components is essential in ultimately promoting learning (Hawkes & Romiszowski 2001; Koehler, Mishra, Hershey, et al. 2004). The iterative sequence of the components presented above, synthesized from the approaches presented in the literature, is included in Figure 2.

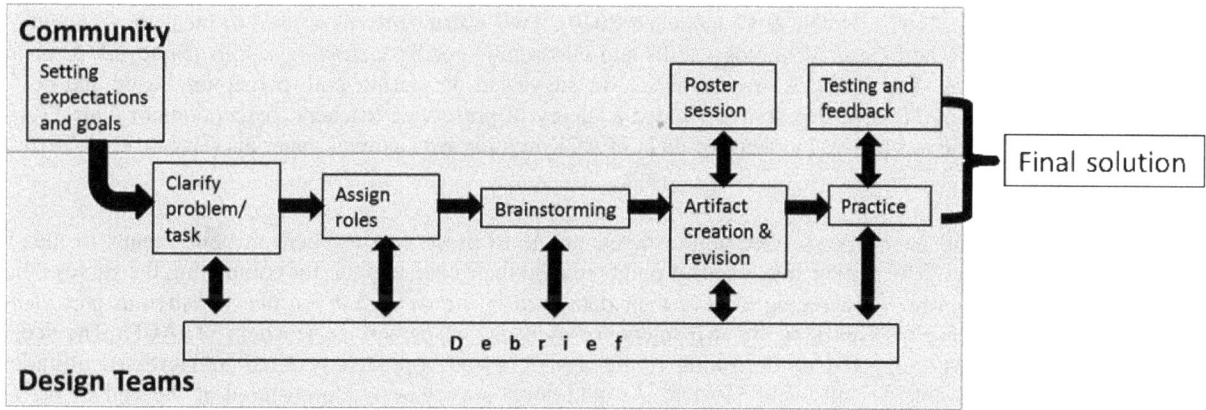

Figure 2: Sequence of components in the design team's approach.

Methods

A medium-sized university in the northeast region of the United States required students majoring in either early childhood or elementary education to take three one-credit courses on integrating technology into teaching. The course that was the focus of this research was the second in the three-course series. The first course introduced preservice teachers to the concept of technology integration, the use of basic technologies, and provided classroom-appropriate, hands-on technology-based activities. The second course focused on exposing students to emerging technologies and required preservice teachers to write and implement a technology-infused lesson in their field placement (Lei, Lu, & Gilliard-Cook 2010).

This second course consisted of six 2 hr 15 min sessions during the semester: three during the first 3 weeks of the semester, 2 in the middle of the semester, and 1 during the final week. The preservice teachers spent six weeks in field placement classrooms, three weeks at a time, during the semester that they were enrolled in this course. The class met during the weeks that students were not at their field placement schools.

A quasi-experimental design, approved by the institutional review board, was used to compare the efficacy of two different instructional approaches implemented with two different groups of preservice teachers. The comparison group received instruction which included the basic components suggested in the literature for preservice technology education—practice with technology skills, exposure to exemplary models of technology integrated into instruction to support student learning, practice designing instruction that integrates technology to enhance learning, opportunities to reflect on their experiences, and an emphasis on positive attitudes toward technology (Adamy & Boulmetis 2005; Alayyar, et al. 2010; Hur, Cullen, & Brush 2010; Kay 2007; Koehler & Mishra 2005b; Pope, Hare, & Howard 2002; Williams, Foulger, & Wetzel 2009). This was accomplished in this version of the course through (a) practice using technology tools, (b) model lessons to provide examples of effective technology integration for classroom contexts, (c) creation of technology-based instructional materials, and (d) reflection and feedback. The treatment group received instruction which included a design teams approach.

The participants in this study were a convenience sample of 53 preservice teachers enrolled in the technology integration course during the fall and spring semesters in the 2011-2012 school year. The 31 students enrolled in the two Fall 2011 semester sections served as the comparison group (receiving the standard instruction), while the 22 students enrolled in the two Spring 2012 semester sections served as the treatment group (receiving the design teams approach). The primary researcher served as both researcher and course instructor.

Five instruments were used to measure the three outcome variables: *attitudes toward technology*, *technology skills*, and *TPACK*: Teachers' Attitudes Toward Computers Questionnaire (TAC) version 5.1 (Christensen & Knezek 2000a), Technology in Education Competency Survey (TECS; Christensen & Knezek 2000b, 2001), Technology Proficiency Self-Assessment (TPSA; Ropp 1999), Survey of Teachers' Knowledge of Teaching and Technology (TPACK Survey; Schmidt, et al. 2009), and Technology Integration Assessment Rubric (TPACK Rubric; Harris, Hofer, & Grandgenett 2010). Two instruments were used to measure *technology skills* in order to measure both basic technology skills and classroom-specific technology skills (Snoeyink & Ertmer 2001; Zhao, Kendall, & Tan 2003). As researchers have suggested measuring both perception-based and performance-based evidence of TPACK, this study included a survey of preservice teachers' perceptions of their TPACK and a lesson plan rubric to measure evidence of their TPACK in their instructional materials (Harris, et al. 2010; Schmidt, et al. 2009).

Pre- and post-surveys were administered online to preservice teachers in both groups to measure these desired outcomes. The participants received points toward their course grade for completing the surveys, but did not receive any incentive for agreeing to have their data used in the study. Lesson plans written as part of the course requirements were also assessed by two raters for evidence of preservice teachers' TPACK. The scores on all instruments were compared to determine if the design teams approach resulted in increased attitudes toward technology, technology skills, and TPACK. An additional survey was administered at the end of the course on preservice teachers' perceptions of the quality of the course instruction to assess any differences which may have impacted the outcomes. This six-question instrument assessed the instructor's (1) knowledge, (2) preparation, (3) presentation skills, (4) encouragement of participation, (5) enthusiasm, and (6) whether the student would recommend the instructor. An additional researcher performed a manipulation check by conducting four classroom observations each semester to ensure the instructional approaches were implemented as intended.

Analysis

The analysis focused on comparing the two conditions (treatment and comparison) on the three outcome variables to determine if the treatment group showed significantly more growth on these variables than the comparison group. This would suggest that the design teams approach was effective in improving these outcomes in preservice teachers.

Scales or subscales were calculated as appropriate for each instrument based on the instructions provided by the instrument's author. Overall scores were calculated for each rater for each lesson plan by summing each rater's four criteria scores, as suggested by the rubric's authors, and used in subsequent analyses.

Three MANCOVAs were planned, one for each of the three outcome variables: attitudes toward technology, technology skills, and TPACK. The pre-survey scores were used as covariates to control for preexisting differences between the groups on these variables when appropriate, with the grouping as the independent variable and the post-survey scores as the dependent variables. If pre-survey scores were not appropriate for use as covariates, t-tests were conducted on pre-survey scores to assess for pre-existing differences between groups prior to conducting a MANOVA to test for differences in the outcome variables. To ensure that the overall chance of making a Type I error was less than .05 in these analyses, the Bonferroni correction was applied to lower the alpha level to accommodate multiple tests.

A bivariate correlation was calculated for the two overall lesson plan scores to check for adequate agreement between the two raters. The mean of the two raters' scores was calculated for use in the analysis. A t-test was used to compare the mean scores of the treatment and comparison groups to determine if the intervention had a significant effect on TPACK as measured by the rubric.

It was hypothesized that the treatment group would show significantly greater scores on all measures, indicating that the design teams approach was effective in promoting preservice teachers' positive attitudes toward technology, technology skills, and TPACK.

Findings

Instructor Effects and Reliability

In order to control for the potential of the instructor's actions impacting the results, t-tests were used to compare the mean scores for each of the six questions from the course evaluation for the two groups. There were significant differences with large effects between the comparison and treatment groups for three of these comparisons, with the comparison group having significantly higher means on these three variables. These variables were included to control for the potential of the instructor being better with the treatment group (consciously or unconsciously), and it was expected that there would be no significant differences between the two groups. In reality the opposite occurred, with the comparison group scoring the instructor significantly higher than the treatment group on three questions. This finding was likely the result of the comparison group having known the instructor prior to the course under study, thus this pre-existing relationship resulting in higher scores.

Reliability for all scales and subscales of the five outcome measures was assessed using Cronbach's alpha. All scales and/or subscales indicated alpha values at or greater than .7, which is generally considered acceptable reliability (Leech, Barrett, & Morgan 2008) and appropriate for the planned analysis in terms of reliability.

Changes in Attitudes, Skills, and TPACK

MANOVA was used to test for post-survey differences between the two groups on attitudes toward technology and TPACK, as correlations indicated pre-survey scores were not appropriate covariates and t-tests found no significant differences on the pre-surveys between the two groups on these variables. MANCOVA was used to test for differences between the two groups on technology skills. The Bonferroni correction was applied in all cases to accommodate the multiple comparisons. There were no significant differences found between the two groups for attitudes toward technology (Wilk's $\Lambda = .82$, $F(9,43) = 1.03$, $p = .435$, partial $\eta^2 = .18$), technology skills (Wilk's $\Lambda = .94$, $F(2,43) = 1.43$, $p = .251$, partial $\eta^2 = .06$), or the TPACK Survey (Pillai's trace $= .09$, $F(7,45) = .67$, $p = .698$, partial $\eta^2 = .09$). These results suggested that the treatment and comparison groups were not different with respect to the outcome variables, potentially indicating that the design teams approach did not have the desired effect.

The t-test of the lesson plan rubric scores indicated there were significant differences between the two groups, $t(51) = -3.20$, $p = .002$, $d = .90$. This suggests that the treatment did make a difference, with a large effect, on preservice teachers' TPACK as reflected in their written lesson plans. These differences suggest that the treatment group's lesson plans showed significantly more evidence of the TPACK components than did the comparison group's as measured by the TPACK Rubric. The design teams approach improved preservice teachers' TPACK as evidenced in written lesson plans. This conflicts with the results found in the TPACK Survey analysis, providing mixed results with respect to the effect of design teams on preservice teachers' TPACK.

Exploring the Findings

While there were not significant differences based on survey data, the post-survey means on almost every variable were higher for both groups than the pre-survey means. Further exploration was done to determine if there were significant differences pre- to post-survey for both groups combined, which would provide additional information about the effectiveness of the instructional approaches in increasing attitudes toward technology, technology skills, and TPACK.

After adjusting the alpha level for multiple comparisons, group means were compared for all subscales on the four survey instruments using a paired t-test. Contrary to results in the literature, this analysis found no significant differences in attitudes toward technology. Statistically significant differences with medium to large effects were found with respect to technology skills on both measures and for six of the seven TPACK subscales: CK, PK, PCK, TCK, TPK, and TPACK. These findings indicate that both groups' technology skills and TPACK increased as a result of taking the course.

Discussion

These results partially supported the hypothesis that preservice teachers participating in the design teams approach would show significantly greater increases in their TPACK than a group of preservice teachers who participated in the same course using the standard instructional approach, as there were significant differences found between the two groups' TPACK Rubric scores but no differences in TPACK Survey scores. The results did not support the hypothesis in terms of preservice teachers' attitudes toward technology and technology skills, as no differences were found between the two groups on these variables. Prior research had suggested that design teams was a potentially preferable approach for improving these outcomes and suggested additional research was needed (Koehler & Mishra 2005a). These mixed results provide important information about this approach, in that it was not universally more effective than a standard approach in improving scores on these variables in this research.

As follow-up analyses found significant differences on technology skills and TPACK between pre- and post-surveys for the entire sample of preservice teachers, the findings suggested that the design teams approach was not more effective in producing the desired outcomes, but both instructional approaches improved preservice teachers' technology skills and self-reported TPACK. Neither approach was successful in improving attitudes toward technology.

The design teams approach did significantly improve preservice teachers' TPACK as evidenced in lesson plans. Evidence from other research suggests that preservice teachers tend to over-estimate their TPACK on self-report measures, and that improvements on self-report measures were often inconsistent with preservice teachers' abilities to apply their TPACK in instructional contexts. Including additional measures that are more closely related to teaching practice could produce a more complete picture of preservice teachers' technology integration knowledge (Alayyar, et al. 2010; Archambault & Barnett 2010; Harris, et al. 2010; Hofer, et al. 2010; Shin, et al. 2009).

Where prior research looked only at the effectiveness of the design teams approach in improving factors related to preservice teachers' technology integration abilities, this study compared instructional approaches in an attempt to determine if the design teams approach was more effective in promoting improvements in the technology integration knowledge and skills of preservice teachers. The findings of this study suggest that a design teams approach can be effective, and perhaps raises the questions of when, with whom, and for what purposes? Both approaches worked well at improving technology skills and TPACK, while a design teams approach worked better than the standard approach for improving TPACK related specifically to lesson planning. It is still unclear, however, whether these lesson planning results transfer into implementation, or if these results have long-term impacts. It is likely there is not one universally effective instructional approach, but appropriate approaches for particular contexts.

References

Adamy, P., & Boulmetis, J. (2005). The impact of modeling on pre-service teachers' technology confidence. *Journal of Computing in Higher Education, 17*(2), 100-120.

Alayyar, G. (2011). *Developing preservice teacher competenices for ICT integration through design teams.* Doctoral Dissertation, University of Twente, Enschede, The Netherlands.

Alayyar, G., Fisser, P., & Voogt, J. (2010). *Technology integration in the science teachers' preparation program in Kuwait: Becoming TPACK competent through design teams.* Paper presented at the Society for Information Technology & Teacher Education, San Diego, CA.

Archambault, L. M., & Barnett, J. H. (2010). Revisiting Technological Pedagogical Content Knowledge: Exploring the TPACK framework. *Computers & Education, 55*(4), 1656-1662.

Christensen, R., & Knezek, G. (2000a). Internal consistency reliabilities for 14 computer attitude scales. *Journal of Technology and Teacher Education, 8*(4), 327-336.

Christensen, R., & Knezek, G. (2000b). *Internal consistency reliability for the Technology in Education Competency Survey.* Paper presented at the Preparing Tomorrow's Teachers Evaluator's Workshop, American Educational Research Association Annual Meeting, New Orleans, LA.

Christensen, R., & Knezek, G. (2001). *The Technology in Education Competency Survey (TECS): A self-appraisal Instrument for NCATE standards.* Paper presented at the Society for Information Technology & Teacher Education International Conference, Orlando, Florida.

Cuban, L. (2001). *Oversold and underused: Computers in the classroom.* Cambridge, MA: Harvard University Press.

Dawson, K., & Norris, A. (2000). Pre-service teachers' experiences in a K-12/university technology-based field initiative: Benefits, facilitators, constraints, and implications for teacher educators. *Journal of Computing in Teacher Education, 17*(1), 4-12.

Ertmer, P. A., & Ottenbreit-Leftwich, A. T. (2010). Teacher technology change: How knowledge, confidence, beliefs, and culture intersect. *Journal of Research on Technology in Education, 42*(3), 255-284.

Evans, B. P., & Gunter, G. A. (2004). A catalyst for change: Influencing preservice teacher technology proficiency. *Journal of Educational Media and Library Sciences, 41*(3), 325-336.

Fessakis, G., Tatsis, K., & Dimitracopoulou, A. (2008). Supporting "learning by design" activities using group blogs. *Educational Technology & Society, 11*(4), 199-212.

Gray, L., Thomas, N., & Lewis, L. (2010). Teachers' use of educational technology in U.S. public schools: 2009. Washington, DC: U.S. Department of Education, National Center for Education Statistics.

Harris, J., Hofer, M. J., & Grandgenett, N. (2010). *Testing a TPACK-based technology integration assessment rubric.* Paper presented at the Society for Information Technology & Teacher Education (SITE), Chesapeake, VA.

Hawkes, M., & Romiszowski, A. (2001). Examining the reflective outcomes of asynchronous computer-mediated communication on inservice teacher development. *Journal of Technology and Teacher Education, 9*(2), 285-308.

Hofer, M. J., Grandgenett, N., Harris, J., & Richardson, K. (2010). *Preservice teachers' technologically integrated planning: Contrasting quality and instructional variety by development approach.* Paper presented at the American Educational Research Association, Denver, Colorado.

Hur, J. W., Cullen, T., & Brush, T. (2010). Teaching for application: A model for assisting pre-service teachers with technology integration. *Journal of Technology and Teacher Education, 18*(1), 161-182.

Jonassen, D. H. (2006). *Modeling with technology: Mindtools for conceptual change.* Upper Saddle River, NJ: Pearson Education, Inc.

Kay, R. H. (2006). Evaluating strategies used to incorporate technology into preservice education: A review of the literature. *Journal of Research on Technology in Education, 38*(4), 383-408.

Kay, R. H. (2007). A formative analysis of how preservice teachers learn to use technology. *Journal of Computer Assisted Learning, 23*(5), 366-383. doi: 10.1111/j.1365-2729.2007.00222.x

Koehler, M., & Mishra, P. (2005a). Teachers learning technology by design. *Journal of Computing in Teacher Education, 21*(3), 94-102.

Koehler, M., & Mishra, P. (2005b). What happens when teachers design educational technology? The development of Technological Pedagogical Content Knowledge. *Journal of Educational Computing Research, 32*(2), 131-152.

Koehler, M., Mishra, P., Hershey, K., & Peruski, L. (2004). With a little help from your students: A new model for faculty development and online course design. *Journal of Technology and Teacher Education, 12*(1), 25-55.

Koehler, M., Mishra, P., & Yahya, K. (2007). Tracing the development of teacher knowledge in a design seminar: Integrating content, pedagogy and technology. *Computers & Education, 49*(3), 740-762. doi: doi:10.1016/j.compedu.2005.11.012

Koehler, M., Mishra, P., Yahya, K., & Yadav, A. (2004). *Successful teaching with technology: The complex interplay of content, pedagogy, and technology.* Paper presented at the Society for Information Technology & Teacher Education International Conference 2004, Atlanta, GA, USA.

Kolodner, J. L. (2002). Facilitating the learning of design practices: Lessons learned from an inquiry into science education. *Journal of Industrial Teacher Education, 39*(3), 9-40.

Kolodner, J. L., Camp, P. J., Crismond, D., Fasse, B., Gray, J., Holbrook, J., et al. (2003). Problem Based Learning meets Case-Based Reasoning in the middle-school science classroom: Putting Learning by Design™ into practice. *The Journal of the Learning Sciences, 12*(4), 495-547.

Lawless, K. A., & Pellegrino, J. W. (2007). Professional development in integrating technology into teaching and learning: Knowns, unknowns, and ways to pursue better questions and answers. *Review of Educational Research, 77*(4), 575-614.

Leech, N. L., Barrett, K. C., & Morgan, G. A. (2008). *SPSS for intermediate statistics: Use and interpretation.* New York: Psychology Press.

Lei, J., Lu, L., & Gilliard-Cook, T. (2010). *IDE 300: Integrating Technology into Instruction II Syllabus.* Syracuse University.

Mueller, J., Wood, E., Willoughby, T., Ross, C., & Specht, J. (2008). Identifying discriminating variables between teachers who fully integrate computers and teachers with limited integration. *Computers & Education, 51*(4), 1523-1537.

National Center for Education Statistics. (2010). Educational technology in U.S. Public Schools: Fall 2008. Washington, D. C.: U.S. Department of Education.

Polly, D., Mims, C., Shepherd, C. E., & Inan, F. (2010). Evidence of impact: Transforming teacher education with Preparing Tomorrow's Teachers to Teach with Technology (PT3) grants. *Teaching and Teacher Education, 26*(4), 863-870.

Pope, M., Hare, D., & Howard, E. (2002). Technology integration: Closing the gap between what preservice teachers are taught to do and what they can do. *Journal of Technology and Teacher Education, 10*(2), 191-203.

Prensky, M. (2001). Digital natives, digital imigrants. *On the Horizon, 9*(5), 1-6.

Project Tomorrow. (2011). The new 3 E's of education: Enabled, Engaged, Empowered: How today's educators are advancing a new vision of teaching and learning. Irvine, CA: Project Tomorrow.

Ropp, M. M. (1999). Exploring individual characteristics associated with learning to use computers in preservice teacher preparation. *Journal of Research on Computing in Education, 31*(4), 402-424.

Schmidt, D. A., Baran, E., Thompson, A. D., Mishra, P., Koehler, M., & Shin, T. S. (2009). Technological Pedagogical Content Knowledge (TPACK): The development and validation of an assessment instrument for preservice teachers. *Journal of Research on Technology in Education, 42*(2), 123-149.

Shin, T. S., Koehler, M., Mishra, P., Schmidt, D. A., Baran, E., & Thompson, A. D. (2009). *Changing Technological Pedagogical Content Knowledge (TPACK) through course experiences.* Paper presented at the Society for Information and Teacher Education International Conference, Chesapeake, VA.

Shulman, L. S. (1986). Those who understand: Knowledge growth in teaching. *Educational Researcher, 15*(2), 4-14.

Snoeyink, R., & Ertmer, P. A. (2001). Thrust into technology: How veteran teachers respond. *Journal of Educational Technology Systems, 30*(1), 85-111.

Steeves, V. (2012). Young Canadians in a wired world: Teachers' perspectives. Retrieved from http://beta.images.theglobeandmail.com/archive/01374/Young_Canadians_in_1374384a.pdf

U.S. Department of Education. (2010). National Education Technology Plan 2010. Retrieved from http://www.ed.gov/technology/netp-2010

Williams, M. K., Foulger, T. S., & Wetzel, K. (2009). Preparing preservice teachers for 21st century classrooms: Transforming attitudes and behaviors about innovative technology. *Journal of Technology and Teacher Education, 17*(3), 393-418.

Zhao, Y., Kendall, C., & Tan, S. H. (2003). Educational technology standards for teachers. In Y. Zhao (Ed.), *What should teachers know about technology? Perspectives and practices* (pp. 31-44). Greenwich, CT: Information Age Publishing.

Zhao, Y., Pugh, K., Sheldon, S., & Byers, J. L. (2002). Conditions for classroom technology innovations. *Educational Administration Abstracts, 38*(2), 147-282.

A Systems Approach for Integrating Multiple Technologies as Important Pedagogical Tools for TPACK

Henry Gillow-Wiles
Oregon State University, USA
gillowwh@onid.orst.edu

Margaret L. Niess
Oregon State University, USA
niessm@onid.orst.edu

Abstract: This research presents a description of the impact a sequence of technology-based courses (as part of a 3-year online MS program) using a 'systems of technologies' approach has on developing and extending teachers' technological pedagogical content knowledge (TPACK). Data collected from a representative course in the program illustrate how engaging with systematically integrated multiple technologies supports teachers' development of their TPACK and extends their thinking of how students learn with technology. Implications for how taking a systems approach to technology integration can support teaching and learning with technology are discussed.

Introduction and Purpose

In the 1990s, teacher educators considered teacher knowledge development for teaching with technology as an accumulation of knowledge about technologies - the features, affordances, and constraints for teaching with the technologies. Since the turn of the century, teacher knowledge development programs recognized the importance of integrating instruction about digital technologies with instruction about the content and pedagogical methods for teaching the content; this adjustment recognizes that teachers' knowledge for teaching with technologies is "complex, multifaceted, and situated" (Mishra & Koehler, 2006, p. 1017).

Teaching with technology is no longer an option or an afterthought. The central position technology has in the lives of today's students requires teachers to construct learning experiences where technology plays a central role in the resulting effectiveness. While technologies are designed and optimized for a particular use or function, teachers are challenged to integrate multiple technologies in concert in ways that support particular learning goals and objectives (Gillow-Wiles & Niess, 2013). For example, technology designed for enhancing inquiry-based learning (e.g., graphing calculators) can be paired with technology best suited for sharing student thinking (e.g., computer/projector or document camera) to support collaboration and reflection, leading toward deeper, higher level thinking. Since each of these technologies supports only part of the learning experience, knowing how they interact and how best to integrate them is an important pedagogical aspect of a teachers' technological pedagogical content knowledge (TPACK) (Niess & Gillow-Wiles, 2013).

The burgeoning landscape of available technologies for use in the classroom creates another aspect of TPACK development that must be considered, how to chose the "best" technology(ies) for a given educational experience. Teachers must develop the knowledge needed to choose the most appropriate technology for a particular aspect of a learning experience and how best to holistically integrate multiple technologies into a dynamic and complete package where each aspect of learning is attended to and completely supported (Niess & Gillow-Wiles, 2013). Responding to emerging learning perspectives where technology is becoming an essential component to teaching and learning rather than an 'add-on', taking an integrated, systems approach to making technology choices is one way to make sense of a complex environment. To understand how teachers develop this systems thinking about teaching with multiple technologies, the primary question guiding our investigation was: What is the impact of incorporating a selection of complementary technologies as a technology system in a collaborative learning environment on teachers' thinking about TPACK development?

Perspectives

The TPACK theoretical framework presents a transformation of teachers' knowledge, highlighting the knowledge inputs that must be rearranged, merged, organized, assimilated and integrated to no longer be individually discernible in their thinking and reasoning for teaching with technologies. Niess (2005) describes four components of this transformed knowledge to include teachers': (1) overarching conception of what it means to teach specific content with technologies; (2) knowledge of students' thinking and understandings of content with technologies; (3) knowledge of curricular materials incorporating technologies; and (4) knowledge of instructional strategies and representations for teaching specific topics with technologies. Further, Niess, Sardi and Lee (2007) hypothesized a TPACK developmental process in five levels: recognizing, accepting, adapting, exploring and advancing. Additional research provided more detailed descriptors for the four TPACK components at each level (Niess, 2013).

Interaction and engagement with technology are critical in the development and enhancement of teachers' TPACK in the context of integrating mathematics, science, and technology (Kim, Kim, Lee, Spector, & DeMeester, 2013). TPACK is more than a set of multiple domains of knowledge and skills of content, pedagogy, and technology and their intersections (pedagogical content knowledge, technological content knowledge, technological pedagogical knowledge, and TPACK) (Mishra & Koehler, 2006; Niess, 2008). TPACK requires strategic thinking for knowing when, where, and how to use domain-specific knowledge and strategies, such as planning and problem solving along with monitoring progress towards specific instructional goals (Shavelson, Ruiz-Primo, Li, & Ayala, 2003). TPACK relies on "an understanding of how technology can be integrated with subject matter and the technology itself" (Keating & Evans, 2001, p. 2).

The framework for designing the courses in this study was in part developed to help the participants learn how to learn with technologies. The dynamic interplay, illustrated in Figure 1, between the different technologies provided participants with tools they needed for inquiry, communication/sharing, and collaboration. When the participants were able to smoothly transition from one technology use category to another, they were best able to direct their own learning, engage with the online community of learners, and develop shared and individual knowledge (Akyol & Garrison, 2008). It is in the intersection of these use categories where the greatest impact exists for developing the participants' systems knowledge for teaching and learning with multiple technologies (Kim, Kim, Lee, Spector, & DeMeester, 2013).

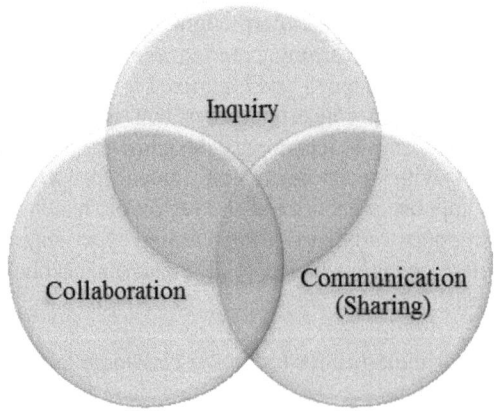

Figure 1. Researcher conjectured technology usage categories.

In this framework, the interactive relationship between technology usage categories is developed through a systematically-conceptualized holistic integration of multiple technologies, each supporting a specific instructional goal. The culmination of instructor technology choices focusing on backing the educational goals lies at the intersection of the technology usage categories, where the different technologies merge into a system of technologies. In this context, we refer to the definition of the word system as "a regularly interacting or interdependent group of items forming a unified whole or a group of interacting bodies under the influence of related forces" (*Merriam-Webster's online dictionary,* n.d). This group of interacting items (different technologies) is under the influence of related forces (the needs of the educational context) where each technology provides support for part of the instructional strategy choices and/or educational goals. When technologies are used in concert (a unified whole), they become a system of technologies where the whole is greater than the sum of the parts. It is at the intersection of the three technology use categories (Figure 1) that individual technologies transform to become a pedagogical tool, a meaningful component of the technological pedagogical knowledge (TPK) dimension of TPACK (Niess, 2005).

When technology is integrated into teaching and learning as a technology system, the system becomes a pedagogical tool, here characterized as "a tool that mediates a teacher's action, providing clear and detailed principles regarding learning that can be easily translated into teaching practice. Pedagogical tools, therefore, not only make links between theory and practice, they help teachers move from the potentially abstract to the concrete" (Seale & Cooper, 2010, p.1110). These technology system based pedagogical tools are at the foundation of a learning trajectory where technology plays an essential role (Niess & Gillow-Wiles, 2013).

The complexity of integrating technology into teaching and learning, let alone integrating multiple technologies as a systematically organized package, requires a framework to be a manageable concept to communicate (Niess & Gillow-Wiles, 2013). To provide a possible framing structure, Sztajn, Confrey, Wilson, & Edgington (2012) described a learning trajectory as a concept through which learning experiences could be framed, suggesting that such a learning trajectory provides an "ordered network of experiences…to move from informal ideas, through successive refinements of representation, articulation, and reflection, towards increasingly complex concepts over time" (p. 968). The trajectory consistently engaged them in thinking and reflecting about the dynamic interactions among content, pedagogy and technology emerging from the tasks in which they are engaged (Roberts, 2002; Wheatley, 1992). In essence, the emphasis was on pedagogies supportive of learning with technologies - learner-centered, inquiry-based, engaging participants in collaborative learning, reflection, and understanding the value of including shared and individual knowledge development.

Data Sources and Methodology

In the MS Interdisciplinary Mathematics. Science and Technology Education program, three specific technology courses (SED 520, SED 521, and SED 522) emphasized the systems pedagogical approach.

- **SED 520** This course merges multiple technologies including Web 2.0 collaboration technologies, such as Google Docs, Skype, video and image capture applications, as tools that teachers explore for enhancing student learning in authentic, integrated ways that engage the in thinking critically, solving problems and making decisions, communicating and collaborating. Additional technologies focus more on content knowledge creation and development. These technologies include data collection devices such as Vernier temperature probes and the attending LoggerLite data collection applications, as well as investigative technologies like web inquiries, where the information gathering potential of the Internet is presented as a key component of the learning experience. Leveraging these educational tools in the presentation and completion of projects, conducting research and using data and information gathering tools, and, in essence, using the technologies effectively, creatively and productively in ways that support students in extending and enhancing their knowledge, skills and abilities (International Society for Technology in Education (ISTE), National Educational Technology Standards for Students (NETS-S), 2007).

- **SED 521** This course develops and extends knowledge of digital technologies, primarily video and image technologies, to focus on shared and individual knowledge creation and extension. The participants' TCK and TPK are further developed through learning to use digital image technologies to support student-directed inquiry as well as in developing and extending community-centered shared knowledge.

- **SED 522** This course focuses on the integration of spreadsheets as algebraic reasoning tools in science and mathematics. SED 522 supports participants in extending their TCK and TPK as they learn about Excel spreadsheets as learning tools for student inquiry. This course emphasizes the development of a portfolio of lessons where spreadsheets play an integral role in student algebraic reasoning and thinking as they are learning specific mathematics and science content.

Because of the scope of the course and number of technologies utilized, SED 520 was selected as representative of the three-course sequence. Overall, 10 in-service teacher program participants assented to participate in this ethics-approved research project as required to be in compliance with our institutional policies, federal and state laws and regulations. These teachers were between 28 and 42 years old, with eight females and two males. With their approval, we gathered data for describing their coursework, in particular: course syllabi and their enactments in Blackboard (our online course management system); all participant products and interactions (including Discussion Board interactions and discussions, unit/weekly products, unit/weekly reflective essays and reflective learning community essays); and multiple interviews upon course and program completion. These data sources supported the identification of rich descriptions of their learning experiences within the social meta-cognitive constructivist learning environment.

The social meta-constructivist (Chiu, 2008; Chiu & Kuo, 2010) context throughout the learning trajectory engaged participants in a community, where they collaborated about their explorations, research, and reflections about their own thinking and their students' thinking when learning mathematics/science with digital and video technologies. The researcher-designed learning trajectory interwove digital data collection (Vernier temperature probes), digital image and video technologies, instructional approaches, and science/mathematics topics over a 10-week period. Multiple threads were used to integrate the participants' engagement in the four TPACK components: their (1) overarching conceptions of what it means to teach science/mathematics with these technologies along with their (2) knowledge of students' thinking and understandings, (3) knowledge of curricular materials, and (4) knowledge of instructional strategies.

We used electronic case course portfolios (Meyers, Chappell, Elder, Geist, & Schwidder, 2003) to track the participants' interactions and progressions. Analysis of multiple participant reflections provided the knowledge and community of learners' engagements while examining the impact of the shared knowledge of the community and its impact on their emerging individual knowledge as they participated in the instructional activities (Puntambekar, 2006). Interviews supplied their reflective thinking about their learning with specific identification of the tasks and resources influential in their thinking as well as their reflections on the impact of the community of learners on their knowledge growth (Wheately, 1992; Yukawa, 2006). Each of these learning products (probe activities, videos, forum postings, essays, and collaborative documents) were collected and examined from a phenomenology perspective (Husserl, 1976).

A multiple case study was chosen to frame the analysis of the various data collected because this analysis methodology provides for the development of "analytic generalizations" (Curtis, Gessler, Smith, & Washburn, 2000, p. 1002), where a careful analysis, driven by theory, revealed an underlying commonality of participant perceptions across the cases. Throughout this qualitative study (Patton, 2002), we identified common themes in their uses of various digital technologies. Electronic case portfolios captured their progressions, focusing on the development of their TPACK in the course (Meyers, Chappell, Elder, Geist, & Schwidder, 2003). Aspects of inter-rater reliability were addressed through both researchers individually reviewing the data and discussing their perceptions. These discussions continued until the researchers agreed on the emerging results of the data analysis.

Results and/or Substantiated Conclusions

Using the research question as a guide, the data analysis focused on the connection between taking a systems approach to integrating technology and the development of the teacher's TPACK. This connection took different forms, illustrated by the themes emerging from the data. Overall, there was no correlation between individual technology usage categories described in Figure 1 and individual TPACK concepts. However, it became apparent that there were three primary ways the teachers thought about using multiple technologies together as a system, where each technology played a specific role.

Alignment of Student Thinking with Technologies and Teacher Use of Technology Tools

As a whole, the participants described their personal (in class) experiences as students using multiple technologies in an integrated, holistic fashion. Recognizing how students used technology helped the participants conceptualize the need for teachers to introduce the technology into the classroom for use in a similar fashion, as an integrated system rather than as individual technologies for singular purposes. Additionally, their narratives illustrated how, through their experiences in the course, they gained a better understanding of how they might integrate multiple technologies as pedagogical tools where the different technologies are part of a system of technology. This systems approach was recognized to be much more in alignment with how students natively use technology, thus providing an easier technology learning curve for enhancing student engagement.

Relating her thinking about how students use technology in their lives, LC wrote, "Thinking about my own students, they are very impatient and I can't help but think it is because of social networking, smart phones, and other personal technology devices. Students have access to an infinite amount of information at the touch of a button." Continuing to connect her thoughts with how teachers need to respond, she added, "Teachers have to be prepared for this shift. Not only do teachers have a tougher time keeping the attention of their students, but they also must be able to keep up with the technologies and programs students are using."

Reinforcing this perspective, LH connected how students learn with how she viewed that teachers need to respond in their pedagogical choices: "21st century students are digital natives and learn more naturally with the use of technology. While educators may be considered digital immigrants and view technology as a threat in the classroom due to lack of experience, we must try to expose ourselves and our students to different forms of technology and help advance our students' learning. I have discovered that there are many different forms of technology that can be used in the classroom to benefit student learning."

These representative comments illustrate how the course participants came to think about student technology use and how these uses impacted their TPACK needs, specifically developing their knowledge of students' thinking and understandings of content with technologies. Their comments suggested they made the connection between how students think about technology and how teachers might best use technologies as thinking and learning tools.

Multiple Technologies in a Systems Approach Supports Individual and Group Knowledge Development

Collectively, the participants described their use of collaborative applications, like Google Docs, in concert with Blackboard discussion forums to support the creation of, and engagement in, a community of learners. Their discussions indicated they used Google Docs for collaborative activities and Blackboard forums for sharing and review, sometimes creating and sharing videos to better illustrate their thinking. The individual knowledge developed through giving and receiving personal feedback in the forums/videos supported the development of shared knowledge resulted from their interaction when collaboratively creating Google documents for explaining their ideas. The participants recognized that through this integrated communication, each technology (asynchronous discussion forums/videos and real-time collaborative platforms) played a critical, but distinct role in their knowledge development.

From their experiences in the course, the participants developed and extended their understanding of how engaging multiple technologies as learning tools potentially supported students in developing shared (collaboration) and individual knowledge (reflection). In detailing her experiences in the course, RK explained, "Throughout this course and the Masters program, I have been exposed to many digital learning environments and have become familiar with their strengths and weaknesses, opportunities and threats. Tools such as blackboard, Google docs and Skype have provided me with many opportunities to engage my peers in collaborative and cooperative experiences which helped me to develop knowledge." She continued to comment and connect collaboration with developing shared knowledge. "One of the most insightful concepts learned was the differences and similarities between the construction of individual and shared knowledge. Though individual knowledge can be developed in a variety of ways within the classroom, the use of collaboration is an effective method for the development of shared knowledge."

LH wrote of her understanding concerning how technology can support both individual knowledge through reflection and shared knowledge through engagement in a learning community. "Technology applications such as Google Docs or Blackboard provide a learning community environment that provides a safe environment to share individual knowledge while working towards a common understanding. These applications also facilitate instant feedback to the responder, which allows students to reflect on their own individual knowledge and redefine their knowledge and understanding."

"Collaborative software helps to support a structure of cooperation as students seek to develop shared knowledge," wrote AH, in describing her perspective of the role collaborative software plays in student learning. She continued to illustrate how she thought of collaborative learning, "In the process of learning together, students add to their existing knowledge while creating an understanding that belongs to the group."

These representative comments illustrate the participants' thinking about collaborative learning and the role technology plays in the reflection/sharing cycle. Their comments suggest their experiences learning to integrate technologies into a system helped them understand the importance of knowing how different technologies can be used to support different educational goals. In this case, they were making technology choices that would align with a collaborative learning instructional strategy. The data analysis suggested the teachers thought deeply about what elements of this learning strategy would be best supported by various technologies and what characteristics a technology must have to provide support for each element. Additionally, the teachers thought deeply about how using several technologies together potentially affects student learning.

Course Experiences Developed and Extended Their TPACK

By design, the experiences of the participants in the course put them into the role of teacher-as-student, where they were learning through using a system of different technologies, each used for a distinct pedagogical purpose. Furthermore, the participants reflected on these educational experiences from a teacher-as-teacher perspective to describe how they extended their TPACK for using systems of technologies as pedagogical tools. The comments of the participants illustrated how this dual role of both student and teacher supported them in connecting their individual learning with their community to create a shared understanding of TPACK and student learning. JB described how his experiences in the course influenced his thinking about technology as a pedagogical tool, "The influence of my expanded shared knowledge of Web 2.0 technologies and student learning on my own TPACK was that Web 2.0 technology needs to be carefully selected to support all levels of ability." He also recognized that each technology has a preferred use saying, "These technologies are specific for certain learning processes. They need to be researched before the beginning of a math or science unit to encourage the process of inquiry and develop higher order thinking skills. Web 2.0 technologies need to be carefully selected for their capability to enhance and help achieve learning outcomes." Additionally, he connected his course experiences using technology with his thinking about individual and shared knowledge development, "This understanding was a significant influence on my learning as I reflected on the difference between individual knowledge and shared knowledge."

CA recognized the critical nature of purposeful decision making when it came to bringing technology into the classroom. She wrote, "There are currently many programs online that can aid in the collaborative process and many more come out every day. No matter what programs or software educators use it is important that it is analyzed thoroughly. After this is done educators can decide if this program is suitable for their students." She continued by discussing how in choosing technology, there must remain an awareness of the importance of collaborative learning and how a system of chosen technologies can support that pedagogy, "Then educators can integrate the appropriate technology for students to use in order to work collaboratively with others. No matter what programs we use it is important that educators expose their students to technology and allow them to work collaboratively. This exposure by educators will prepare their students for the 21st century."

Echoing the thinking of CA, AF wrote, "Through my recent experiences in this course, I have started thinking more along the lines of how I can use the technology to support the concepts and teaching strategies I am targeting. After completing a SWOT analysis for Google Docs, I realized the importance of looking at the different aspects of particular technologies prior to integrating them into the curriculum." She recognized the impact the course had on her thinking of technology as a pedagogical tool and how she needs to make technology decisions.

CF summarized the thinking of the participants as a group when she wrote, "Advances in technology are rapidly increasing the availability of digital technologies designed to advance collaborative and cooperative learning." Commenting on the importance of teacher preparation for teaching with technology as well as returning to recognizing how students use technology in their own lives, she continued with, "It is important that the education community support teachers in implementing these technologies into the classroom. Not only are web applications like Google applications, powerful learning tools in their own right but digital technologies are becoming more fundamental in our work and daily lives and education must endeavor to model the society that the students live in."

These comments illustrated the impact the teachers' experiences in the program had on both their TPACK and how they thought about integrating technologies into systems of technologies. They were able to put all the pieces together (i.e. TPACK, systems of technologies, collaborative learning strategies) to create holistic learning experiences where separate technologies were integrated into a system that supported an inquiry based collaborative learning environment. Leveraging their developing knowledge of the four TPACK components, the teachers created both individual and group knowledge about teaching with technology.

Significance and Implications

There is agreement on the critical nature of the need to integrate technology into the classroom as teaching and learning tools, but there are many perspectives of how best to accomplish this important goal. Analysis of existing teacher pre-service and in-service programs indicates a predominance of programs where educational technology is presented in a single (or a few) courses where the manipulation of the technology is the focus of instruction. This study, as a continuation of previous research (Gillow-Wiles & Niess, 2013; Niess & Gillow-Wiles, 2013), proposes that how technology can be used to support a particular pedagogical choice, in this case collaborative learning, should be the instructional focus in teacher preparation programs. The results of this research imply that when participants have learning experiences where they engage with technology systems as learning tools through social, metacognitive (Chiu, 2008; Chiu & Kuo, 2010) pedagogical experiences that include reflection and collaboration, they are able to transition these experiences into developing and extending their TPACK and their thinking of student learning with systems of technologies.

As with any teacher educational experience, the hoped for result is that teachers will take their new knowledge into their classrooms to help support student learning. Although this study did not track the teachers beyond their program experiences, the changes in their thinking about how to best integrate technology into their classrooms strongly suggested they will include this new perspective in their lessons.

Teacher education that simulates actual teaching experiences are typically successful in supporting the transfer of skills and perspectives (Putnam & Borko, 2002). Having the teachers in this study take on the role of a student provides them with an understanding of how students think and learn with technology. Having them take on the role of teacher provides them with an understanding of how they might think about technology as a thinking and learning tool that results in student learning. Together, these perspectives create an experience that is authentic and much like what they will experience in the classroom, supporting them bringing their new knowledge into action. Like all educational research, this project asks a new set of questions. Further research might investigate (1) the transference of the teachers' TPACK into classroom action, (2) the impact of technology as a system on student achievement and (3) the connection between instructional strategy choices and how technologies are integrated into a system.

References

Akyol, Z., & Garrison, D. (2008). Development of a community of inquiry over time in an online course: Understanding the progression and integration of social, cognitive and teaching presence. *Journal of Asynchronous Learning Networks, 12*(3-4), 3-22.

Chiu, M. M. (2008). Flowing toward correct contributions during group problem solving: A statistical discourse analysis. *Journal of the Learning Sciences, 17*(3), 415-463.

Chiu, M. M., & Kuo, S. W. (2010). From metacognition to social metacognition: Similarities, differences and learning. *Journal of Education Research, 3*(4), 321–338.

Curtis, S., Gesler, W., Smith, G., & Washburn, S. (2000). Approaches to sampling and case selection in qualitative research: examples in the geography of health. *Social Science & Medicine (1982), 50*(7-8), 1001–14.

Gillow-Wiles, H., & Niess, M. (2013, March). Using multiple digital technologies in an online ms program to develop TPACK. In *Society for Information Technology & Teacher Education International Conference* (Vol. 2013, No. 1, pp. 3892-3899).

Husserl, E. (1976). *The crisis of European sciences and transcendental phenomenology*, An Introduction to Phenomenology, 1–116.

International Society for Technology in Education. (2007). National educational technology standards and performance indicators for students. Eugene, OR: International Society for Technology in Education.

Keating, T., & Evans, E. (2001). *Three computers in the back of the classroom: Pre-service teachers' conceptions of technology integration.* Paper presented at the American Educational Research Association Conference.

Kim, C., Kim, M. K., Lee, C., Spector, J. M., & DeMeester, K. (2013). Teacher beliefs and technology integration. *Teaching and Teacher Education, 29*, 76–85.

Meyers, J. D., Chappell, A., Elder, M., Geist, A., & Schwidder, L. (2003). Re-Integrating the research record. *Computing in Science and Engineering, 5*(3), 44-50.

Mishra, P., & Koehler, M. J. (2006) Technological pedagogical content knowledge: A framework for teacher knowledge. *Teachers College Record, 108*, 1017-1054.

Niess, M. L. (2013). Central component descriptors for levels of technological pedagogical content knowledge. Special issue on Technological Pedagogical Content Knowledge. *Journal of Educational Computer Research, 48*(2), 173-198.

Niess, M. L. (2008). Knowledge needed for teaching with technologies – Call it TPACK, *AMTE Connections*, Spring, 9-10.

Niess, M. L. (2005). Preparing teachers to teach science and mathematics with technology: Developing a technology pedagogical content knowledge. *Teaching and Teacher Education, 21*(5), 509 - 523.

Niess, M., & Gillow-Wiles, H. (2013). Advancing K-8 teachers' STEM education for teaching interdisciplinary science and mathematics with technologies. *Journal of Computers in Mathematics and Science Teaching, 32*(2), 219-245.

Niess, M.L., Sadri, P., & Lee, K. (April 9-13, 2007). Dynamic spreadsheets as learning technology tools: Developing teachers' technology pedagogical content knowledge (TPCK). Paper presentation for the American Education Research Association Annual Conference, Chicago, IL.

Patton, M. Q. (2002). *Qualitative research and evaluation methods* (3rd Ed.). Thousand Oaks, CA: Sage.

Putnam, R., & Borko, H. (2002). What do new views of knowledge and thinking have to say about research on teacher learning. *Teaching, Learning and the Curriculum in ..., 29*(1), 4–15.

Puntambekar, S. (2006). Analyzing collaborative interactions: divergence, shared understanding and construction of knowledge. *Computers & Education, 47*(3), 332-351.

Roberts, B. (2002). Interaction, reflection and learning at a distance. *Open Learning, 17*(1).

Seale, J., & Cooper, M., (2010). E-learning and accessibility: An exploration of the potential of generic pedagogical tools. *Computers & Education.54*, 1107-1116.

Shavelson, R., Ruiz-Primo, A., Li, M., & Ayala, C. (2003). Evaluating new approaches to assessing learning (CSE Report 604). Los Angeles, CA: University of California, National Center for Research on Evaluation.

Sztajn, P., Confrey, J., Wilson, P. H., & Edgington, C. (2012). Learning trajectory based instruction: toward a theory of teaching. *Educational Researcher, 41*(5), 147–156.

System. (n.d.). In *Merriam-Webster's online dictionary* (11th ed.). Retrieved from http://www.m-w.com/dictionary/system

Wheatley, G. H. (1992). The role of reflection in mathematics learning. *Educational Studies in Mathematics, 23*(5), 529-541.

Yukawa, J. (2006). Co-reflection in online learning: Collaborative critical thinking as narrative. *Computer-Supported Collaborative Learning, 1*, 203-228.

Assessment-Talks and Talking about Assessment: Negotiations of Multimodal Texts at the Boundary

Anna-Lena Godhe
University of Gothenburg, Sweden
anna-lena.godhe@ait.gu.se

Berner Lindström
University of Gothenburg, Sweden
berner.lindstrom@ait.gu.se

Abstract: This article focuses on how assessment is enacted in the classroom, in terms of negotiations of what assessing multimodal texts mean and imply. The concepts of literacy and assessment have both undergone recent changes where they are now conceived of as social actions which are influenced by their situatedness in different settings. In multimodal texts the concept of literacy is expanded since they include several expressions, such as images and sound. Excerpts from negotiations between teacher and students is in the article presented in order to explore what assessing multimodal texts entail in an educational setting. Studying the negotiations between students and teachers may give insights into tensions between established and emerging practices and contribute to an understanding of which aspects enable and restrain changes in educational settings.

Introduction

Writing essays has, for a long time, been the conventional way to express meaning and to show your skills in handling the written language in the language classroom. Being able to read and write typographical texts, on paper or on screen, is a vital part of education (e.g., Lankshear and Knobel, 2008). However, with the use of computers in the classroom it is now possible to create texts consisting of several ways of expressing meaning such as images, sound, written and spoken language. Considering the presence and abundance of multimodal texts in different media today, being able to communicate and express meaning using several forms of expression is a skill which is becoming increasingly important (Jewitt and Kress, 2004). Hung et al. (2013, p. 400) write that use of digital technologies has led to a re-conceptualization of literacy. Likewise, Cope et al. (2011, p. 84) conclude that what is measured in literacy assignments has not caught up with changes that mean that it is no longer enough to use words alone for representation.

Literacy has traditionally been associated with the ability to read and write typographical text, but several attempts to expand the concept have been made during the last few decades. An expansion of the concept of literacy has been argued for, based on literacy being viewed as a social practice (e.g., Barton and Hamilton, 1998) as well as referring to aspects of multiplicity in contemporary societies (e.g., The New London Group, 1996). Moreover, the concept of literacy has been challenged by a multimodal approach where the claim is that all modes are meaning-making devices which in turn mean that language, spoken or written, can no longer be seen as central but as one way amongst others to express meaning (Jewitt and Kress, 2004). Lastly, an expansion of literacy in relation to the use of digital technology has been argued for since these technologies facilitate new ways of creating texts as well as receiving and sharing them electronically (Lankshear and Knobel, 2008, p. 25). Older media, such as TV, fostered consumers and spectators, but new media, such as the Internet and social media, encourages participation as well as production. By offering diverse forms of interactive engagement and participation, new media thereby alters the notion of literacy (Livingstone, et al., 2005). In order to engage in what

Jenkins et al. (2006) has termed participatory cultures, it is necessary to be able to read and write but also to use several modes when producing media, since new media literacies involve social skills developed through collaboration and networking. Those who engage in these participatory cultures are encouraged to share material which they have created themselves but also to comment on what others have written (ibid.). The creation of texts thereby becomes increasingly collaborative. In contrast, texts written in classrooms are mainly created individually and addressed to the teacher (e.g., Lankshear and Knobel, 2008). Multimodal texts, which are easily shared digitally, may therefore address a larger audience than the teacher. They may also respond to similar texts which the students have encountered outside the classroom.

With the emergence of tasks, often related to the use of ICT, which in many ways challenges the traditional meaning of school tasks, negotiations of the nature of the task as well as the assessment of it are needed. Commonly used assessment criteria do not recognize multimodal outcomes (Jewitt and Kress, 2004). How to assess literacy objects such as multimodal texts therefore have to be negotiated. The multimodal texts are at the boundary as they incorporate several kinds of expressions which are not conventionally used when creating texts in language education. Moreover, the multimodal texts are at the boundary in another sense as they relate to activities outside of school and references from the outside will need to be negotiated when incorporated in a school task. As written and spoken words are the primary focus in language education, both students and teachers are used to creating and assessing written or spoken language (e.g., Jewitt and Kress, 2004). When texts also contain other ways of expressing meaning it may, however, be uncertain what creating and assessing these multimodal texts mean in educational settings. Both students and the teacher thus have to negotiate what making and assessing such a task means.

Assessment is an integrated part of education which influences how teaching is organized and signals which knowledge is of importance (Erstad, 2008). Assessment can be done in several ways and serve different purposes. Broadfoot and Black (2004) stress the situatedness of assessment in education. Decisions about who and what is to be assessed as well as for what purpose, reflect the social setting in which the assessment takes place (ibid.). When processes as well products are assessed, attention needs to be paid to the setting in which the assessment occurs (Gipps, 2002, p. 74). With a sociocultural approach to learning and assessment the meaning of a task, and the assessment of it, is situated. During the process of performing and assessing a task, what it entails is discussed, clarified and negotiated.

Generally assessment criteria in curricula are what Sadler (1989) calls fuzzy criteria. Fuzzy criteria are abstract terms with no absolute or unambiguous meaning independent of their context. Therefore, the meaning of fuzzy criteria has to be established in the particular context where they are used, otherwise it is difficult to understand and utilize them. To concretize the meaning of assessment criteria the skills to be learned need to be described, and performances adhering to different grades need to be demonstrated as few skills can be acquired simply by being told about them (ibid.).

The relation between the use of digital technologies and assessment in education can be explored at different levels of the educational system. The case study presented here focuses on the negotiations of multimodal texts in the language classroom, in order to explore what assessing such a literacy object entails in an educational setting. The analysis of dialogues in particular classroom situations is regarded as important instances of negotiating the meaning of assessment in relation to the task of creating multimodal texts. The negotiations are part of a process of assessment and are meant to support the development of the students´ multimodal texts.

The multimodal texts can be regarded as an object at the boundary in the sense that creating such texts is not generally an established practice in language classrooms. Moreover, the multimodal texts are more commonly found in contexts outside the educational setting and they may therefore facilitate coherence between activities carried out in and outside of education. Analyzing how such literacy objects at the boundary are assessed may increase the understanding of how emerging and established practices of creating texts in language classrooms relate to each other. The following research questions will be addressed in this paper;

- What aspects of the multimodal text do the teacher and the students negotiate as important?
- When reflecting on the assessment of their multimodal text in the interviews, what aspects of their multimodal text do the students regard as important?
- How are contextual references from settings outside of education negotiated?

Activity and dialogue

This article takes a socio-cultural theoretical approach, drawing on dialogism and activity-theoretical thinking. Learning is considered to originate in social actions and is mediated through interaction and the use of various tools (e.g., Säljö, 2000).

In dialogism, as conceptualized by Linell (2009), responsivity and addressivity are central concepts as dialogism emphasizes that people are social beings who are thoroughly interdependent of each other (Linell, 2009, p. 69). When uttering something, speakers anticipate a potential response and this influences what speakers say as well as how utterances are phrased (Linell, 2009, p. 167). Every utterance is addressed to somebody and utterances are also selective responses to contextual conditions which include the utterances of others. Utterances can therefore be seen as part of on-going conversations, conversations which differ depending on the context in which they are situated. The message and how it is expressed in a multimodal text may hence depend upon whether it is seen as part of an on-going conversation with peers or with the teacher.

In educational settings there are established practices of how activities are performed and assessed which influence students´ and teachers´ actions as well as the activities carried out in classrooms. Certain rules and division of labor apply in a classroom and both students and teacher relate to these when engaging in activities. Linell (2009) points out the importance of what he calls double dialogicality. Double dialogicality refers to that participants in activities are in dialogue both with the actual situation they are in, as well as with situation-transcending practices in that setting (ibid.). Activities both respond to and address this double dialogicality.

In activity theory, or Cultural Historical Activity Theory (hereafter CHAT), as conceptualized by Engeström (e.g., 2009), the prime unit of analysis is "the object-oriented, collective and culturally mediated human activity, or activity system" (Engeström and Miettinen, 1999, p. 9). How the different components in activity systems affect and constitute each other is the focus of analysis in this paper.

Depicting activity systems as neat triangles may contribute to a sense that activity systems are stable and harmonious, but instead, Engeström (1993, p. 72) states that they are characterized by tensions and contradictions. When creating multimodal texts both the meditational means and the object of the activity acquire new qualities, which in turn leads to tensions and contradictions within the activity system. These tensions and contradictions are often not open conflicts, but may be noticed in interaction as some aspects of the activity attract greater attention while other aspects largely are ignored.

In what Engeström (2009, p. 56) calls the third generation of activity theory, the basic model of activity has been expanded to include at least two interacting activity systems. When several activity systems are involved, the object of the activity becomes potentially shared and can be seen as a boundary object. Star and Griesemer (1989) regard boundary objects as an analytical concept which refer to objects that inhabit several intersecting social worlds (ibid., p. 393). The boundary object is recognized since the structure of it is common enough and because of this they may facilitate to the developing of coherence between the related social worlds. In a review of the literature on boundary crossing and boundary objects, Akkerman and Bakker (2011, p. 141) conclude that descriptions of boundaries, and of people and objects at the boundary, show signs of ambiguity as in-between and belonging to both one world and another. This means that boundaries connect, as well as divide, the activity systems involved, so that people and objects at the boundary simultaneously act as bridges and represent a division .

The analysis of interactions in this article focuses on tensions and contradictions concerning the assessment of multimodal texts in classrooms. Moreover, tensions between intersecting activity systems and whether the multimodal text is related to as a boundary object, will be focused on in the analysis.

The Study

The study has been carried out during lessons in Swedish, in a class where the students have individual laptops. One-to-one solutions such as this, where the students are given their own personal laptop, are becoming relatively common in Sweden. The class consisted of 19 students, 4 girls and 15 boys, who are taking a compulsory course in Swedish. They are studying the social science program at an inner city school in southern Sweden.

The task the students were given was to create an argumentative text in the shape of a multimodal text, or digital story, where they use their own voices as well as images and music to put forward their arguments for or against a topic. The students were asked to create argumentative texts, as this is stated in the national curricula as one of the aims of the course in Swedish. To practice argumentation, verbally or in writing, is part of the national curriculum so the task of arguing for or against a topic is known to the students. The students were given a topic by the teacher and initially they worked in pairs where each pair had the same topic, but had to argue for opposite views. The topics were contestable subjects such as whether homosexuals should be allowed to adopt children or whether to legalize drugs.

The students have created multimodal texts once before. When evaluating the task the students stated that they would like to create multimodal texts again. However, when they were asked to create their second multimodal text they wanted to know how their multimodal texts would be assessed. Based on the questions raised by the students, a task was designed which related to the goals in the curricula and where the assessment and grading criteria were explicitly stated. As the upper-secondary school curriculum in Sweden at this particular time was changing, the task was designed to relate to both the old and the new curricula. That students should be able to pose arguments and draw conclusions as well as work with images and ICT was stated in both the new and the old Swedish language curriculum.

According to the criteria given to the students at the start of the project, the multimodal text would be assessed in relation to four different aspects;
- the argumentative disposition of the multimodal text
- the different ways of expressions used
- the students´ participation when discussing and analyzing texts
- the language used in the multimodal text.

Empirical material and analysis

The empirical material on which the analysis is based consists of short talks between the teacher and students, as well as interviews with the students. Fifteen assessment-talks between teacher and individual students have been audio recorded, and interviews with seven students where the assessment of their text is the main topic, has been video recorded. The recorded material is part of a larger set of empirical material which has been collected in an iterative cycle of Design Based Research (DBR). By designing, studying and refining innovations in realistic classroom environments, DBR aims to develop theoretical understanding as well as to influence practice (McKenney and Reeves, 2012). Researchers and practitioners collaborate in DBR by negotiating and developing the studies together. Through multiple iterations the intervention evolves (Anderson and Shattuck, 2012). In the iterative process the creation, as well as the assessment, of multimodal texts has been in focus during different cycles in the design process.

The aim of the interviews was to give supplementary information about how the students experienced the assessment of the multimodal texts. By reflecting on the assessment in the interviews the students further expand on what was negotiated in the assessment-talks. In the interviews, the students are also given the opportunity to reflect on how they reasoned when creating their multimodal text. Moreover, the interviews were conducted in order for the students to voice what may, in situated interaction, not be explicitly stated. Shared understandings are often silent as students and teacher have developed a common knowledge and the need to be verbally explicit then declines (Mercer, Littelton and Wegerif, 2004). The interviews were done individually, and can, in turn, be seen as dialogues or negotiations of meaning between the students and the researcher. As such, they are considered to be complimentary to the recordings of the assessment-talks between teacher and student.

In the analysis of the interactions the interpersonal processes as well as how the students utilize the resources available to them are taken into account (Mercer, Littleton and Wegerif, 2004; Jordan and Henderson, 1995). Neither the setting, nor the mediational means can be separated from activities and the analyses therefore concern the *"content, function and the ways shared understanding is developed in social context, over time"* (Mercer, Littleton and Wegerif, 2004, p. 203).

Findings

In the following sections, excerpts from the assessment-talks as well as the interviews with individual students will be presented. The annotations used in the excerpts are adapted from Jefferson (1984). For details about the transcript notation see Appendix. The chosen excerpts serve as examples of what is being negotiated in relation to the assessment of the multimodal text and of the students´ reflections on the process of creating and assessing multimodal texts. The excerpts hence seek to illuminate what is made relevant and salient, in relation to assessment and ICT in an educational setting as established in negotiations.

The excerpts presented are taken from the assessment-talks and interviews of two students. As the assessment of their multimodal texts differed from what the students had anticipated, the students elucidate how their notion of the assessment of a multimodal text differs from the teacher´s. The two students also reflect on their own process and product as well as on each other´s product, and refer to each other to exemplify differences in their multimodal texts and in the assessment of them. The students have different topics as Harry argues for eating meat while Ihsam argues for the use of surveillance cameras in public places.

Assessment-talks; negotiations between teacher and students

Harry attempts to make an amusing film but in the assessment-talk, the teacher remarks on Harry´s argumentation not being solid enough and points out that he brings up matters which do not concern his topic.

Excerpt 1
T   and then you had humans in prison that has nothing to do with your subject
H   um but it was a bit like ((T laughs))
T   you have made a funny movie
H   yes
T   but you should learn to argue
H   um
T   *kill your darlings* that means you that you have to remove things which do not belong to your topic things that are funny like you the hamburger motorbike you had a picture of that is funny but it has nothing to do with your subject.

The assessment-talk focuses on what Harry says in his multimodal text. His oral argumentation is considered to be weak and unfocused. The teacher makes it clear that it is the argumentation that is in focus in the task. Both what Harry says and the images he uses stray from the main topic and as his use of images is considered to enhances the weak argumentation the images are seen as one of the reasons for his flawed argumentation.

In the assessment-talk between Ihsam and the teacher, Ihsam is surprised by the positive evaluation of his multimodal text. The teacher focuses on Ihsam´s verbal argumentation and says that he got high grades for his clear argumentation. Ihsam, on the other hand, appears to think that his argumentation was simple.

Excerpt 2
T   I think that you have very very good and wise arguments
I   it really didn't feel like that when I worked with it
T   no I don't understand
I   it really didn't (1) I thought it was well ok and then when I talked about the school there it felt ok that maybe the argument is too simple.

The teacher here refers to the verbal argumentation in Ihsams multimodal texts and that the argumentation has received high grades. At a later stage in the assessment-talk the teacher briefly refers to other forms of expressions than the verbal argumentation.

Excerpt 3
T   the transitions between your images are not very exciting but they are like this but that is still good
I   yes:::
T   slow
I   they went like that all of them ((refers to the movement of the transitions))
T   yes yes
I   you mean that they should move in another direction or
T   no but you could have varied them so that some came from the other direction
I   ok you mean like that
T   yes you know you should but anyway good choice of transitions, images and music let's say

Initially the teacher claims that the transitions are "not very exciting" but after clarifying to Ihsam what she means by that she concludes that his choice of transitions as well as images and music are good. Other forms of expressions then the verbal argumentation are mentioned twice in the assessment-talk. At first it is mentioned in this sentence and then it is also mentioned at the end of the talk when the teacher put grades on the four different aspects the multimodal text is assessed on. The use of different expressions receives the grade past with distinctions.

Students´ reflecting on the assessment

In the interviews with the students they are asked about the assessment of their multimodal text in order to enable the students to reflect on the process and product of the activity and how they experienced the assessment of their multimodal text. Ihsam claims that he did not aim at any particular grade and was surprised by the quite high grades which his multimodal text was given. Harry, on the other hand, aimed for high grades but was told to remake his multimodal text since the argumentation was too weak.

In the interview Harry is asked whether he agrees with the critique of his multimodal text and also to explain what he would have needed to know to do better.

Excerpt 4
A um do you understand what T means like can you agree with her or do you
H yes I mean I had (2) had I known a bit earlier then I wouldn´t have spent so much time either I mean
A no what is it you wanted to know
H I mean that it was only like that the argument was what she wanted to get like not that it should be a nice film or something like that
A um um ok
H I kind of got that like it should look nice as well

Harry articulates that he spent a lot of time making the multimodal text "look nice". Had he known that it was "only" the arguments that counted, he would have done differently. Harry thereby emphasizes the importance of the visual aspects of his multimodal text and makes it clear that he spent time and effort on these aspects, but this did not make a positive difference in the assessment of his multimodal text. Looking at the criteria which were given for making the multimodal texts it was not "only" the arguments which were going to be assessed. From what Harry says, however, his impression is that it was mainly the spoken arguments that were taken into account in the assessment.

In excerpt 5 Ihsam talks about Harry and how much effort Harry put into making his multimodal text. Ihsam finds it hard to believe that his multimodal text got high grades, but Harry´s did not.

Excerpt 5
I Harry oh this is going to get the highest grade and that with the meat and I just shit this is really good and look at mine and what the hell yeah it is only simple and then it was the complete opposite I mean (.) he sat there with blood, sweat and tears and just like failed or he felt like that anyway when he got his
A but wh what do you think is the difference what is it that he or that you have done and what is what does it depend on
I the simple is that I have done (.) three arguments only ((shrugs his shoulders)) I did three arguments and added some counterargument to one of the arguments

When asked what differs between the two multimodal texts, Ihsam says that his multimodal text is simple and contains three arguments. Though Ihsam is pleased with the high grades his text received, he finds his own multimodal text simple in comparison with Harry´s. The difference in the anticipated assessment and the actual assessment given of their multimodal texts indicate that the students consider several forms of expression as bearers of meaning but the multimodal texts have been assessed on the premises that it is what they say that conveys the meaning and that their speech carries the argumentative structure of their multimodal text.

Harry refers to Ihsam´s text during the interview and takes it as a point of reference when explaining why his own text is different. He refers to Ihsam´s multimodal text in excerpt 6 as "reading from a book with facts", whereas he tried to do his multimodal text with "a bit of feeling".

Excerpt 6
H because Ihsam for example take him he made his with only arguments
A um
H I mean like it wasn´t how should I put it it was just like reading from a book with facts like
A um
H and there was nothing that was a bit but I tried to do a bit more (.) with a bit more expression
A um um

H   with a bit more feeling
A   um
H   but eh it (1) well it went wrong

From what Harry and Ihsam say about their own, and each other's texts, they find the assessment of both the texts difficult to understand as it mainly focuses on the spoken argumentation whereas visual aspects, which are important to the students, are largely overlooked.

Conclusion

The main topic in the assessment-talks between teacher and students is what the students say in their multimodal text and how they argue verbally for or against a subject. The use of other ways of expressing meaning is only briefly mentioned. It is hence the spoken word which is considered to be primary when expressing meaning as well as the bearer of the argumentation in the multimodal texts. Though the students appear to regard other ways of expressing meaning than written and spoken language as bearer of the argumentation as well as primary in expressing making, it is the institutional practice, as voiced by the teacher, which appears to have the preferential right of interpretation.

In the interviews with the students they reflected on the process and product of the activity of creating a multimodal text. The students find it difficult to comprehend the assessment of their use of images and sound as well as what they needed to do to improve their work, as they do not appear to have any previous assessment of these ways of expressing meaning to relate to. As the meaning of the criteria related to the assessment of images and sound are not negotiated, the students and the teacher do not appear to share a common understanding of how to interpret them (Godhe, 2013). When the students and the teacher do not share a roughly similar concept of quality to the task it becomes difficult for the student to judge the quality of the texts they are producing (Sadler, 1989).

To incorporate features which are familiar to the students from out-of-school-contexts in a school task can be regarded as crossing boundaries so that the multimodal text becomes a boundary object where ingredients from different contexts are combined (Engeström, 2009). This appears to invite the students to address their text to different audiences (Linell, 2009). Students who relate to the assignment as a school-task and focus on the spoken language in their multimodal text and the argumentative structure of their language mainly address the teacher and the school setting. Students who focus on the appearance of the multimodal texts by emphasizing their use of images and sound, mainly address their peers. The difference in addressivity and responsivity affects the assessment of the multimodal texts as those which are addressed to the school context generally are given higher grades. Since the students combine different ways of expressing meaning as well as contextual references from different settings in their multimodal texts, the texts become boundary objects which potentially connect different activity systems (Akkerman and Bakker, 2011).. Although the students use different kinds of expressions as bearer of meaning, these expressions are largely overlooked in the assessment of the multimodal texts, as the teacher primarily relate to the spoken word as the main bearer of meaning.

When the assessment of the multimodal texts largely overlooks images and sound as bearers of meaning, important aspects of the multimodal texts may be lost. Consequentially, this may cause the multimodal texts to represent the difference between practices in different settings, rather than connecting them (ibid.). Moreover, creating multimodal texts in an educational setting becomes an ambiguous activity since students are assigned to do a task incorporating ways of expression which are not usually part of the task of writing a text in language education, but in the assessment of the outcome of the activity these ways of expression are largely ignored. This ambiguity may lead to a reinforcement of the written and spoken language as valued ways of expressing meaning in education, rather than different ways of expression being evaluated and incorporated in language education. At a time when the use of technology is becoming increasingly common in classrooms it is important to consider how assessment practices relate to new activities and outcomes, so that significant aspects of them are not overlooked.

References

Akkerman, S. F., & Arthur, B. (2011). Boundary Crossing and Boundary Objects. *Review of Educational Reserach*, 81(2), 132-169.

Anderson, T., & Shattuck, J. (2012). Design-Based Research: A Decade of Progress in Education Research? *Education Researcher*, 41(16), 16-25.

Barton, D. & Hamilton, M. (1998). *Local Literacies.* London: Routledge.

Broadfoot, P., & Black, P. (2004). Redefining assessment? The first ten years of assessment in education. *Assessment in Education: Principles, Policy & Practice*, 11(1), 7-26.

Cope, B., Kalantzis, M., McCarthey, S., Vojak, C., & Kline, S. (2011). Technology-Mediated Writing Assessments: Principles and Processes. *Computers & Composition*, 28(2), 79-96.

Engeström, Y. (1993). Developmental studies of work as a testbench of activity theory: The case of primary care medical practice. In S. Chaiklin, & J. Lave (Eds.), *Understanding practice: perspectives on activity and context* (pp. 64-103). Cambridge: Cambridge Univ. Press.

Engeström, Y. (2009). Expansive learning: toward an activity-theoretical reconceptualization. In K. Illeris (Ed.), *Contemporary theories of learning: learning theorists in their own words* (pp. 53-73). New York: Routledge.

Engeström, Y., & Miettinen, R. (1999). Introduction. In Y. Engeström, R. Miettinen, & R. Ounamaki (Eds.), *Perspectives on activitiy theory* (pp. 1-16). Helsinki, Finland: Orienta-Konsultit Oy.

Erstad, O. (2008). Changing assessment practices and the role of ICT. In J. Voogt & G. Knezek (Eds.), *International Handbook of Information Technology in Primary and Secondary Education* (pp. 181-194). New York: Springer.

Gipps, C. (2002). Sociocultural perpsectives on assessment. In G. Wells, & G. Claxton (Eds.), *Learning for life in the 21st century* (pp. 73-83). Oxford: Blackwell Publishers.

Godhe, A-L (2013). Negotiating assessment criteria for multimodal texts. *International Journal of Assessment and Evaluation*, 19(3), 31-43.

Hung, H-T., Chiu, Y-C. J., & Yeh, H-C. (2013). Multimodal assessment of and for learning: A theory-driven design rubric. *British Journal of Educational Technology*, 44(3), 400-409.

Jenkins, H., Clinton, K., Purushotma, R., Robison, A. J., & Weigel, M. (2006). *Confronting the Challenges of Participatory Culture: Media Education for the 21st Century.* Chicago: The MacArthur Foundation.

Jewitt, C., & Kress, G. (2004). *Multimodal literacy.* New York: Peter Lang publishing Inc.

Lankshear, C., & Knobel, M. (2008). *New Literacies: Everyday Practices and Classroom Learning.* Maidenhead: Open University Press.

Linell, P. (2009). *Rethinking language, mind, and world dialogically : interactional and contextual theories of human sense-making.* Charlotte, NC: Information Age Publ.

Livingstone, S., Bober M., & Helsper, E. (2005). Active participanation or just more information? *Information, Communication & Society*, 8(3), 287-314.

McKenney, S., & Reeves, T.C. (2012). *Conducting Educational Design Research..* New York, NY: Routledge.

Mercer, N., Littleton, K., & Wegerif, R. (2004). Methods for studying the Processes of Interaction and Collaborative Activity in Computer-based Educational Activities. *Technology, Pedagogy and Education*, 12(2), 195-212.

The New London Group (1996). A pedagogy of multiliteracies: designing social futures. *Harvard Educational Review*, 66(1), 60-92.

Sadler, D.R. (1989). Formative assessment and the design of instructional systems. *Instructional science*, 18, 119-144.

Star, S. L., & Griesemer, J. R. (1989). Institutional Ecology, 'Translations' and Boundary Objects: Amateurs and Professionals in Berkeley's Museum of Vertebrate Zoology, 1907-39. *Social Studies of Science, 19*(3), 387-420.

Säljö, R. (2000). *Lärande i praktiken: ett sociokulturellt perspektiv.* [Learning in practice: A socioculturell perspective. Stockholm, Sweden: Prisma.

Appendix: Transcription Notations

The annotation conventions are adapted from Jefferson, G. (1984). Transcription Notation, In J. Atkinson and J. Heritage (Eds.), *Structures of Social Interaction,* New York: Cambridge University Press.

(# of seconds)	A number in parentheses indicates the time, in seconds, of a pause in speech.
(.)	A brief pause, less than one second.
:::	Indicates prolongation of a sound.
((text))	Annotation of non-verbal activity.
Italic text	words said in English instead of Swedish
xx xxx xx	Speech which is unclear or in doubt in the transcript.

From Creation to Curation:

Evolution of an Authentic 'Assessment *for* Learning' Task

Peter R Albion
University of Southern Queensland, Australia
Peter.Albion@usq.edu.au

Abstract: Authenticity is an important characteristic of learning experiences and contributes to transfer of learning into practice but maintaining authenticity as practice changes is challenging. This paper describes action research undertaken to guide the evolution of an authentic assessment task in a teacher preparation course responding to changes in the program and the wider educational environment. As teaching resources have become more readily available online, the task has evolved from one of creating teaching resources to curating and sharing collections of resources that may be adapted or adopted. Lessons learned through reflection during the evolutionary process and prospective developments are discussed in light of the effectiveness of the evolution of the task in responding to the changing circumstances.

Background

Despite 30 years of effort, schooling lags society in adapting to information and communication technology (ICT) (Ertmer & Ottenbreit-Leftwich 2013). Belland (2009) used *habitus* to explain the challenges in moving teacher graduates toward integrating ICT in classroom practice; teacher preparation programs must overwrite understandings of teaching developed during 12 years of learning in conventional classrooms. Ertmer, Ottenbreit-Leftwich, Sadik, Sendurur, and Sendurur (2012) argued that teacher professional development for ICT should be authentic, using the same ICT and pedagogical approaches that teachers are able to use in their classrooms.

The implication is that widespread change in teachers' ICT practices will be facilitated by first implementing changes within programs for teacher preparation and ongoing development. That is, teacher education at all stages should authentically represent the contexts within which teachers will be expected to perform. Authenticity in teachers' learning should facilitate transfer of learning to professional practice. The challenge, in a time of rapid change, will be to ensure that the learning experiences are authentic and meet requirements of teacher education.

This paper describes the evolution of a task that represents a substantial proportion of the assessment for a final year course in an initial teacher preparation program. The task is also a significant learning activity that develops relevant knowledge and professional dispositions. In its recent iteration the task engages students in *curation* as they gather and present online resources using processes analogous to curation of exhibitions in art galleries or museums. It is assessment *for* learning as much as, or more than, assessment *of* learning. The evolution of the task will be considered in the context of the bachelor degree program within which the course is placed.

The activity described may be best characterized as action research undertaken for progressive improvement in pedagogy (Somekh 2006). It involved a series of cycles in which the author's experiences provided the basis for reflection and subsequent action to improve a teacher preparation course.

The changing educational environment

Biological evolution occurs in response to environmental changes. As conditions change the relative advantages of specific characteristics shift and organisms with more favorable combinations of characteristics are more likely to survive and reproduce. Similarly, educational evolution occurs in response to changes in societal and institutional conditions. In this instance some of the key changes that affected evolution of the course assessment included the increasing abundance of information, increasing focus on learning networks as a site of professional learning, emergence of curation as a professional activity, changes to curriculum and its implementation by education systems, and desire of students for more flexible learning opportunities.

Abundance of information

Historically information was scarce and changed slowly. Initially it was stored in human memory and transmitted orally. The invention of writing changed that, but reproduction of handwritten documents was slow and expensive, so copies were rare and information was still conveyed orally by those with access to written copies. Printing made it possible to produce more copies cheaply but it was still necessary to physically distribute them. Traditional approaches to education developed in this context as a *pedagogy of scarcity* (Weller 2011). When access to information was limited, transmissive teaching by lectures and similar methods made sense.

Four technological waves have changed the ecology of information (Albion 2011), which is now expanding and changing very rapidly. Publishing was expensive and restricted to specialists, but in the 1980s desktop publishing enabled almost anybody to print professional looking materials. In the 1990s the World Wide Web made a single electronic copy of a document available globally. In the 2000s Web 2.0 made it easy for anybody to instantly publish material to the world. Now mobile Internet access allows smartphones to access and publish information from almost anywhere.

The *pedagogy of scarcity* was based on transmitting scarce information from teacher to learners and is less relevant in an age when information is abundant and easily accessible to all. What we need now is a *pedagogy of abundance* (Weller, 2011). Unlike material property, the value of information is often increased by sharing and linking with information available elsewhere.

Based on a traditional understanding of information it was natural to think of education and learning as being about transfer of information from teacher to learner. A constructivist view of knowledge encouraged us to think of learning as building knowledge by extending on the known (Bereiter 2002). Connectivism (Siemens 2005) suggested that knowledge may exist in the network as much as, or more than, in an individual and that learning is about making connections. The challenge for educators is to be lifelong professional learners using the power of the network to support user-generated learning (Swanson 2013).

Personal/Professional Learning Networks

Whether or not they realize it, people have learning networks. We all learn from others in family, school, or community and they form part of a personal learning network that develops without much conscious effort. Warlick (2012) compares developing a personal learning network to cultivating a garden. Teachers, including those in preparation, need to give serious thought to how to extend and shape a learning network that meets their needs for ongoing professional learning. Their personal learning network will evolve to become a personal/professional learning network (PLN) with interlinking segments related to different areas of interest and blurred boundaries between professional and personal connections. In a world of abundant and rapidly changing information developing an effective PLN is an important strategy for maintaining professional currency. For teachers, a strong PLN is a way to maintain professional links with distant colleagues and engage in lifelong learning.

A network is typically looser than a group or community. It may include people who are known personally as well as others with whom there is no personal contact but who are followed as sources of information without necessarily engaging in direct exchanges. It may begin with people known in the real world and be extended through social networking services like Facebook, Twitter, or Google+ to include people with whom there is no other connection.

Curation

One approach to dealing with the abundance of information on the Internet is *content curation*, a process through which somebody gathers and presents material similarly to how a curator brings together an exhibition in a museum or art gallery. Jarche (2012) linked curation to the processes of personal knowledge management that are essential for professionals working with an abundance of information.

Jarche (2012) and Kanter (2011) described curation as having three phases - Seek, Sense, Share. In the Seek phase topics are defined, sources are organized and scanned, and high quality material is captured. In the Sense phase a useful artifact is produced by adding annotations to contextualize the selected material and make sense of it in relation to other material. In the Share phase the artifacts are made available to the PLN and comments are offered on artifacts similarly shared by others. Weisgerber (2012) described eight steps rather than three in the curation process – find, select, editorialize, arrange, create, share, engage, track – but her process is essentially similar, especially when viewed alongside the more detailed processes described by Jarche (2012) and Kanter (2011) within each of their phases. Curation as a response to abundance of information is still an emerging practice but the essential features appear to be that it:
> presents high quality content selected for its relevance to a specific topic (seek),
> includes description and comment that adds value to the content (sense), and
> is published so that it is available to, and engages, interested colleagues (share).

As the practice of digital curation has become more common, the processes and tools have evolved. At its most basic, curation could be undertaken using a web search engine and web publishing software to develop and publish a website displaying the curated items. Curators have appropriated tools such as social bookmarking sites, Delicious (delicious.com) and diigo (diigo.com), and media sharing sites, Flickr (flickr.com) and YouTube (youtube.com), to their purposes, adding Twitter (twitter.com) and other channels for dissemination. New tools such as Pinterest (pinterest.com) have been taken up as they have emerged and tools such as Scoop.it (scoop.it) have been developed specifically to support curation.

Implementing new curriculum initiatives

Education systems are changing in response to societal change. In Australia there has been a progression from broad agreement among state and federal governments about goals for education (MCEETYA 1989) toward a national Australian curriculum (ACARA 2011). In Queensland, the State Education Department has responded to the Australian curriculum by developing the Curriculum into the Classroom (C2C) materials (Education Queensland 2013) which are described as a "digital resource that can be adapted to meet different school contexts" but have been adopted rather than adapted in some schools as the definitive interpretation of the curriculum.

The C2C materials are just one, admittedly influential, source of plans available for adaptation, or adoption, by teachers in their classrooms. The Web offers a profusion of sites from which lesson plans and teaching resources can be downloaded by teachers to support their planning. There are marketplaces like Teachers Pay Teachers (teacherspayteachers.com) and others from which resources can be downloaded and adopted or adapted. While some teachers may choose to create their own plans and resources based on curriculum requirements it is increasingly likely that most will prefer to begin with existing materials and adapt them to meet their own needs.

Flexible learning

Most undergraduate students at Australian universities have significant commitments to employment. In 2006, almost 5% worked full-time, 15% worked more than 20 hours per week, and 70% worked an average of 15 hours per week (James, Bexley, Devlin, & Marginson 2007). They include a proportion of mature age students likely to have family commitments. In 2006, 45% of teacher education students were 25 years or older and 10% were at least 40 years old (DEST 2006) and those proportions continue. The availability of students to attend classes is affected by work and family commitments and many choose to study by distance or online in order to achieve the flexibility to meet their other commitments.

Universities use Learning Management Systems to facilitate online access to study materials and learning activities. From 2001 to 2010 multimodal enrolments (mixed on and off campus) in Australia rose from 4% to 8% (DEEWR 2011). At USQ the proportion of web-based enrolments increased by more than 400% from 2006 to 2010 (USQ 2012) and by 2012, up to 70% of students in the 4-year Bachelor of Education studied at least some subjects online. Students enrolled on campus also access materials and activities online. These demographic changes inevitably affect the design of courses.

Evolution of the Assessment Task

A previous paper described the evolution of the course, *EDP4130 Technology Curriculum and Pedagogy*, with respect to how its design might be revised with a more explicit focus on development of pre-service teachers' TPACK (Albion 2012). *Technology* in the course title refers to the subject specified in Queensland (QSA 2013) and Australian (ACARA 2013) curriculum documents and corresponds to *design and technology* or similar in other jurisdictions. It is more similar to what is widely understood as STEM (Science, Technology, Engineering, and Mathematics) education than to Information Technology, although information and digital technologies do feature in the curriculum documents. This paper focuses on the evolution of the major assessment piece in the course and the contribution that it might make to pre-service teachers' learning specific to the course and technologies education, and to more general development of professional dispositions.

Year 1

Prior to introduction of *EDP4130* in 2011, a technology education course had been offered from 2002 until 2005. Like *EDP4130*, that course was offered in the final year of a 4-year teacher preparation program. The major assessment piece engaged the entire annual cohort (typically 150 students), working in tutorial classes, in collaboratively developing technology curriculum resources and making them available to all cohort members. The approach was based on the relate-create-donate pattern advocated by Shneiderman (1998) and each student completing the course had the potential to acquire a collection of curriculum materials for use in their future classrooms. The task was designed to provide students with a technology challenge through application of the technology design cycle (design-make-appraise or investigation-ideation-production-evaluation in the then national and state curriculum documents). The task also included a requirement to reflect and report on their learning as it related to the technology curriculum. Students appreciated the practicality of the assessment task and the teaching resources that they acquired through it. In some cases that was confirmed by contact from former students a year or more after graduation requesting details of the site where the resources could be accessed.

When *EDP4130* was first offered in 2011 the major assessable task was retained without significant change. A significant point of difference between *EDP4130* and the previous course was the mode of offer. The earlier course had been offered each year to about 120 students on the main campus and a further 30 students on a smaller campus about 400 km distant, with both groups taught by face-to-face lecture and tutorial. By 2011, consistent with the move toward flexible learning described above, all undergraduate courses were offered fully online as well as in face-to-face mode on three campuses. The online class in 2011 numbered about 25 students and was treated as equivalent to a face-to-face tutorial class for the major assessment task. Each tutorial class (or equivalent) was charged with developing a number of sets of curriculum support materials to support 6 to 8 hours of technology curriculum learning over a period of 3 to 4 weeks. The number of sets required from each class varied according to the size of the class, with a set required for every five students. Classes were jointly responsible for negotiating the process of development and typically formed smaller groups and made each responsible for developing a set of materials. As was observed in the previous course, students appreciated the focus on activities that had direct relevance to their professional futures. Management of the development process was generally simple in face-to-face classes that met at least weekly but was more challenging for the online class where communication was mostly by email and asynchronous discussion forums with the option for synchronous links using Wimba or Skype.

Year 2

Review of the 2011 offer noted the challenges that all students had encountered with managing the large group activity and the particular challenges for those studying online. For the 2012 offer the assessment task was modified so that students were required to develop a plan and associated resources for teaching the technology curriculum but had a choice to work individually or in small groups rather than in a class group with collective responsibility. Consistent with the relate-create-donate model (Shneiderman 1998), the materials developed were still made available to all members of the cohort, thereby maintaining the authenticity of developing an artifact of value for a real audience. In order to preserve the benefits attached to working with the larger group, students were required to develop a personal reference network with which to discuss their materials development and to participate in a studio-style environment (Brown 2006) so that their work in progress was open for comment by peers. This Virtual Learning Design Studio (VLDS) was mediated through the ePortfolio environment (mahara.org) provided by the university so that students might develop familiarity with the ePortfolio tools that they would be required to use in the following semester.

Most students engaged effectively with the task, although a small proportion delayed engagement with the VLDS until close to the end of semester, thereby minimizing any benefit from comments of their peers. Working individually addressed the issues experienced by online students in the previous offer while retaining the benefits of developing and sharing resources. By the time the course was offered in 2012, the C2C initiative (Education Queensland 2013) was being implemented in schools. C2C was confined to English, Mathematics, Science and History, and did not directly affect teaching of technology except insofar as one of its characteristics appeared to be to focus teaching on single learning areas and discourage curriculum integration. However, the emergence of C2C and the increasing availability of other teaching materials rendered the assessment task less relevant because of the move toward adapting teaching materials rather than developing them from scratch. Hence some further rethinking of the task design was required.

Year 3

Revision of *EDP4130* for the 2013 offer was informed by the environmental changes described above. Rather than requiring students to develop plans and teaching materials from scratch, the design recognized the ready availability of plans and resources on the Web and required students to curate digital resources that would support learning in some part of the curriculum. The course design was thereby moved toward a *pedagogy of abundance* (Weller 2011). The requirement to engage with a personal reference network introduced in the 2012 offer was recast around the important role that a PLN plays in curation as both source of items to be curated and destination for sharing. The description of the assessment task began by declaring that the focus for the project was to "**curate a publicly accessible collection of online resources relevant to the classroom implementation of technology education in the Australian context.**" That was followed by details of requirements and assessment criteria.

Because some students in the 2012 offer had reduced the value of the VLDS by delaying their engagement with it, the curation task was developed with two assessable phases. The intention was to ensure that students made a start early in the semester and received feedback to ensure that they were on track. The first phase submission was due two weeks into semester, carried 15% of the semester marks, and required identification of a theme for curation, steps toward development of a PLN, selection of tool(s), and presentation of a sample curated item. Table 1 lists the assessment criteria.

Criterion	Description
Theme	Identify and justify a theme for its professional relevance to technology education
PLN mechanics	Explain the choice of 2 or more online services as sources of information for curation
PLN membership	Explain the choice of 3 to 6 experts as sources of information
Curation tool(s)	Explain the selection of a curation system
Curation sample(s)	Provide a sample of a curated item with an explanation of the curation process

Table 1: Criteria for first phase of curation assessment

The final submission was due at end of semester, carried 18% of the semester marks, and addressed criteria related to the content of the collection and its dissemination to a wider audience. Table 2 lists the assessment criteria.

Criterion	Description
Publication	Curated collection published on a professionally presented public site
Content of collection	A number of properly attributed items linked to the collection theme
Value added	Evidence of selection, editorial comment, contextualisation and critique
Curation process	Explanation of the curation process, role of PLN, etc.
Audience engagement	Evidence of efforts to promote the collection and of responses and further dissemination
Professional learning	What was learned and what is the continuing value of curation for professional growth?

Table 2: Criteria for final phase of curation assessment

At the beginning of semester students were provided with task descriptions and marking guides for both phases. The LMS also offered an 18 minute recorded presentation about curation (repeated in class for those attending on campus) and notes addressing the same content. The materials included suggestions about suitable tools. Tools freely available on the Internet (diigo, Delicious, Twitter, Wordpress, Facebook, Scoop.it, Storify, Pinterest, etc.) were suggested but no specific tools were required and students were informed that they could meet course requirements using tools of their own choice, including those provided through the university.

Students were encouraged to sign up to Twitter and use it for dissemination . To provide access to the tweet stream for those with reservations about social media, a Twitter widget displaying tweets with a hashtag, #edp4130, was embedded in the LMS and those using Twitter were asked to include the hashtag in relevant tweets. Similarly the RSS tool in the LMS was used to display items posted to a diigo group.

Student Response to the Curation Task

Student submissions for the first phase confirmed the value of including it as a check on directions. Despite the clear course focus on the *Australian Curriculum: Technologies* document (ACARA 2013) several students declared themes, and provided examples, directed toward ICT integration rather than technologies curriculum. Feedback advised those students that ICT integration was important but not the specific subject for the curation task and, in most cases, that clarification assisted them to better direct their work for the second phase. The idea of a PLN and processes for developing it had been discussed in class but some students identified their PLN with a specific page on a website rather than the network of contacts linked to that page. Again they were provided with feedback to refocus their efforts. The most popular curation tool was Scoop.it, which had featured in examples provided to the class, but others selected by students included Pinterest, Facebook, pages in their ePortolio (mahara.org) and websites developed using Weebly (weebly.com), Wix (wix.com) or other tools. Issues included doubtful relevance of curated items, and comments that did not link curated items to curriculum or classroom application. Some students using blogs and simple websites did not use features such as tagging and categories to organize access to their collections. Feedback provided guidance to assist students with better meeting the task requirements in their submissions at the end of semester.

In the submissions at the end of semester it was evident that most students had benefited from feedback on the first phase and had made appropriate adjustments. Most of their sites were well presented but some students failed to include sufficient information about themselves to enable a user of their site to confirm their credibility as a source. That would not reduce the basic utility of the curated items but gave no basis for confidence in comments they offered. The comments by student curators on their selected items varied from a perfunctory 'Great resource' or similar to identification of specific sections of curriculum documents and suggestions for use in teaching.

All but a very few students met, or slightly exceeded, the target of one curated item per week, but most of the tools used for curation included indications of the dates on which items were curated and it was clear from that evidence that almost without exception students had engaged with the activity in the first weeks and again in a burst late in semester. There was little evidence of a sustained pattern of curating across the semester. Dissemination to their PLNs was similarly concentrated in two periods of peak activity with little sustained effort across the semester. There was some evidence of linkages formed among the students with items curated by one being picked up by others and some students had clearly developed extended professional links with practicing teachers or other professionals via Twitter and other channels as a result of engagement in the curation and PLN activity.

Where students wrote about their learning through the task, most offered positive comments about its value for developing a collection of teaching resources curated by themselves and colleagues. Some of that might be attributed to writing what they thought would please a marker but much of it appeared to be genuine appreciation of the value of the task, and especially of a developing PLN, for their future as professional educators. A check conducted on a selection of curation sites three months after the end of the assessment task found no activity beyond the required period, suggesting that they were not continuing the activity or at least not in the same spaces.

Conclusion

The curation task was intended to provide students ongoing access to collections of ideas and resources to support classroom learning linked to the *Australian Curriculum: Technologies* and assist them in developing an active professional learning network with a life beyond the course. They should have enhanced their professional Web presence and developed enduring professional links within their own cohort and beyond.

As noted above, the quality of the curated collections varied – both in the selection and curation of items with comments and in the actual presentation on the websites. This probably resulted, at least in part, from lack of exposure to suitable models of curation. Although the desired qualities were explained in course materials and in classes, some students evidently had not internalized the appropriate standards for their own work. One possible approach to improvement would be to engage students in reviewing a selection of curation sites and discussing the merits of their content and presentation. Such a learning activity early in the semester should help to build consensus about the qualities that make some curated collections more valuable than others. Students could then apply that knowledge in developing their own collections.

Engagement with a PLN is most effective if it is consistent. The pattern of peaks in activity observed around assessment dates indicated that students were not consistently engaged and unlikely to develop an habitual pattern of interaction with their PLN. One possible solution would be to require that the curation activity demonstrate consistent engagement over the semester. Because students' other commitments vary and a steady stream of curatable items on any topic cannot be guaranteed, there would need to be some flexibility but it would still be possible to require demonstration of activity across the semester as part of the assessment.

These changes based on experience will prompt evolution of the assessment task toward a form that is more fit for the prevailing environment. As the environment continues to change it is unlikely that it will ever be a perfect fit but continuing reflection on the environment and experience will ensure that it remains authentic.

References

ACARA. (2011). *The Australian Curriculum*. Canberra: Commonwealth of Australia (Australian Curriculum, Assessment and Reporting Authority) Retrieved from http://www.acara.edu.au/curriculum/curriculum_design_and_development.html.

ACARA. (2013). *Technologies*. Canberra: Commonwealth of Australia (Australian Curriculum, Assessment and Reporting Authority) Retrieved from http://www.acara.edu.au/curriculum/learning_areas/technologies.html.

Albion, P. R. (2011). Connected learning: What do our widening social networks mean for the future of learning? In A. Dashwood & J.-B. Son (Eds.), *Language, Culture and Social Connectedness* (pp. 89-100). Cambridge: Cambridge Scholars Publishing.

Albion, P. R. (2012). Designing for Explicit TPACK Development: Evolution of a Preservice Design and Technology Course. In P. Resta & R. Rose (Eds.), *Proceedings of Society for Information Technology & Teacher Education International Conference 2012* (pp. 2680-2685). Chesapeake, VA: Association for the Advancement of Computing in Education (AACE).

Belland, B. R. (2009). Using the theory of habitus to move beyond the study of barriers to technology integration. *Computers & Education, 52*(2), 353-364. doi: 10.1016/j.compedu.2008.09.004

Bereiter, C. (2002). *Education and mind in the knowledge age*. Mahwah: L. Erlbaum Associates.

Brown, J. S. (2006). New Learning Environments for the 21st Century: Exploring the edge. *Change, 38*(5), 18-24.

DEEWR (2010). *Students: Selected Higher Education Statistics*. Retrieved from http://www.deewr.gov.au/HigherEducation/Publications/HEStatistics/Publications/Pages/2009FullYear.aspx

DEEWR (2011). *uCube - Higher Education Statistics*. Retrieved from http://www.highereducationstatistics.deewr.gov.au/

DEST (2006). *Survey of Final Year Teacher Education Students*. Retrieved from http://www.dest.gov.au/sectors/school_education/publications_resources/profiles/documents/FinalYrTeachStudentsSurveyReport_pdf.htm.

Education Queensland. (2013). *Curriculum into the Classroom (C2C)*. Brisbane: The State of Queensland (Department of Education, Training and Employment) Retrieved from http://education.qld.gov.au/c2c/.

Ertmer, P. A., & Ottenbreit-Leftwich, A. (2013). Removing Obstacles to the Pedagogical Changes Required by Jonassen's Vision of Authentic Technology-Enabled Learning. *Computers & Education, 64*, 175-182. doi: 10.1016/j.compedu.2012.10.008

Ertmer, P. A., Ottenbreit-Leftwich, A. T., Sadik, O., Sendurur, E., & Sendurur, P. (2012). Teacher beliefs and technology integration practices: A critical relationship. *Computers & Education, 59*(2), 423-435. doi: 10.1016/j.compedu.2012.02.001

James, R., Bexley, E., Devlin, M., & Marginson, S. (2007). Australian University Student Finances 2006: Final Report of a National Survey of Students in Public Universities. Retrieved from http://www.universitiesaustralia.edu.au/documents/publications/policy/survey/AUSF-Final-Report-2006.pdf

Jarche, H. (2012). *PKM as pre-curation*. Retrieved from http://www.jarche.com/2012/07/pkm-as-pre-curation/

Kanter, B. (2011). *Content curation primer*. Retrieved from http://www.bethkanter.org/content-curation-101/

MCEETYA. (1989). The Hobart Declaration on Common and Agreed National Goals for Schooling in Australia, from http://www.mceecdya.edu.au/mceecdya/hobart_declaration,11577.html

QSA. (2013). *Years 1-9 Technology*. Brisbane: The State of Queensland (The Office of the Queensland Studies Authority) Retrieved from http://www.qsa.qld.edu.au/7299.html.

Shneiderman, B. (1998). Relate-Create-Donate: a teaching/learning philosophy for the cyber-generation. *Computers & Education, 31*(1), 25-39. doi: 10.1016/S0360-1315(98)00014-1

Siemens, G. (2005). Connectivism: a learning theory for the digital age. *International Journal of Instructional Technology & Distance Learning, 2*(1).

Somekh, B. (2006). *Action Research: a Methodology for Change and Development*. Maidenhead, UK: Open University Press.

Swanson, K. (2013). Professional Learning in the Digital Age: The Educator's Guide to User-Generated Learning. Larchmont, NY: Eye On Education.

USQ. (2012). *University of Southern Queensland 2011 Annual Report*. Toowoomba: University of Southern Queensland.

Warlick, D. (2012). Cultivating Your Personal Learning Network: A Gardener's Approach to Learning (2nd ed.): The Landmark Project.

Weisgerber, C. (2012). *Teaching Students to Become Curators of Ideas: The Curation Project*. Retrieved from http://academic.stedwards.edu/socialmedia/blog/2012/04/16/teaching-students-to-become-curators-of-ideas-the-curation-project-3/

Weller, M. (2011). A Pedagogy of Abundance. *Spanish Journal of Pedagogy*, (249), 223-236.

Video Self Modeling via iPods:
The Road to Independent Task Completion

Julie Bucalos
Jefferson Public Schools, USA
juliebucalos@gmail.com

Debra Bauder
University of Lousiville, USA
debra.bauder@louisville.edu

Anne Bucalos
Bellarmine University, USA
abucalos@bellarmine.edu

Abstract: General and special education teachers can promote skill development, especially for children with autism in the general education classroom by using video self-modeling techniques. One skill area that is important in the general education classroom is independent task completion. Independent task completion is a challenge for many students with an autism spectrum disorder (ASD). This skill is especially important to develop independence with academic tasks in a socially acceptable and motivating way. There is an easy and efficient means of creating video self-modeling scenarios by using an iPod Touch ™. The iPod Touch™ promotes individualized instruction in an easily accessible format that can be generalized to a variety of environments, including the student's home.

Introduction

Wesley, a 12-year-old fifth grader with an autism spectrum disorder (ASD), is educated for most of the day in a general education classroom with collaboration support from Ms. Laurent, a special education teacher. In all subject areas, Wesley is responsible for completing written seatwork tasks, which, as testing data suggest, are in his range of capability for completing individualized independent work. Wesley is quiet, but compliant at school. He gets along well with his peers, but rarely initiates conversations or volunteers answers in class. He also rarely completes tasks independently. His mother, a teacher at a different school in the same district, had requested that teachers send home his unfinished schoolwork, so every day his teacher checks his desk and sends his papers home. She reports, "Wesley stuffs a lot of his work in his desk because he knows he can take it home and his mom will help him." She says that when she tries to help him with his work he demonstrates "anxiety" by twitching his face and jerking his body.

This is not an unfamiliar scenario for both general and special education teachers who struggle to find ways to successfully facilitate independence in children with autism spectrum disorders. His teacher found herself prompting Wesley continuously during collaboration and resource time. She said "He just sits there and waits for me to come over to help him." If he did not get assistance relatively quickly he would stuff the paper in his desk knowing he could take it home. Continuous prompting is one of the behaviors that teachers recognize as counterproductive for fostering independence in the classroom. His teacher recognized that Wesley was not alone among his 5th grade peers receiving special education services. She identified two additional students, John and Luke, who also demonstrated poor classroom independence and independent task completion behaviors. How could she decrease her prompting while increasing the students' independent behaviors in ways that would fit into typical classroom procedures and strategies? His teacher decided to incorporate the students' interest in technology and created individualized video self-modeling interventions for each student using an Apple iPod Touch™.

With the relative ease of technology, participants act as their own models in videos. This method is described as video self-modeling (VSM) and has been shown to be effective across a wide range of behavior, ages, and abilities (Bellini & Akullian, 2007; Bellini, Peters, Benner & Hopf, 2007; Buggey, 2005; Buggey & Ogle, 2010; Delano, 2007; Gelbar, Anderson, McCarthy, & Buggey, 2012; Hitchcock, Dowrick, & Prater, 2003; Prater, Carter, Hitchcock, & Dowrick, 2012). Additionally, video self-modeling has been an effective strategy in studies across multiple disciplines, such as psychology, and speech pathology, and in improving academic achievement in general. It is thought that by watching edited self-modeling videos, individuals acquire mastery of targeted behaviors (Bellini, Akullian, & Hopf, 2007). Numerous studies report that VSM interventions are effectively generalized across situations, persons, and environments (Bellini & Akullian, 2007; Bellini, Akullian et al., 2007; Buggey, 2005; Charlop-Christy et al., 2000; Corbett, 2003; Delano, 2007; Maione & Mirenda, 2006; McCoy & Hermansen, 2007; Nikopoulos & Keenan, 2003; Prater et al., 2012).

The greatest advantage to using an Apple iPod Touch™ for a video self-modeling intervention (VSM) is the social acceptability of a device that is intrinsically motivating to most children – those with and without disabilities. This intervention promotes independence for students functioning in the least restrictive environment, which is one of the major challenges particularly for students with an ASD. Many individuals with an ASD acquire and demonstrate a wide range of skills, yet research is expanding to identify evidence-based practices that will support the independence of such individuals over time (Hume, Loftin, & Lanz, 2009). For individuals with an ASD, difficulty with independent functioning may impact lifelong outcomes and narrow opportunities for inclusion into society through higher education or vocation. Research suggests that individuals with various disabilities who rely on close supervision, prompting, or contingencies by adults may experience a recurrence of off-task behaviors or a decline in engagement and a lack of productivity across settings when these factors are removed (Bock, Bakken, & Kempel-Michalak, 2009; Dunlap & Johnson, 1985). For elementary aged students with an ASD, (who may be heavily conditioned to rely on adult prompting), completion of simple written tasks may be the first step toward autonomy. Yet, it is challenging to find ways to use initial prompting and then extinguish it over time that do not draw undesired attention to a specific child's needs. The use of an iPod™ not only encourages independence, but in a way that is socially acceptable within one's peer group.

Steps to Successful Implementation

Methodology

This study examined chained steps toward independent task completion using a multiple probe across participants design (Gast, 2010; Kennedy, 2005; Horner & Baer, 1978). According to Gast and Ledford (2012), a multiple probe across participants design requires that the researcher collect probe data across three or more participants. This design can be conceptualized as a series of stacked A-B designs in which the length of the baseline (probe) condition is measured repeatedly and systematically across the tiers. The multiple probe design is a practical design which is well suited for practicing teachers or clinicians to conduct research in their school or clinical environment because there is no withdrawal of intervention requirements and the design is relatively easy to conceptualize and implement (Gast & Ledford, 2010).

Developing a Self Model Video

After determining baseline, a video self modeling (VSM) was created as an intervention for each student. The steps process for creating a VSM include process for creating a VSM includes the following 10 steps: (1) Observe the student to determine the target behavior; (2) Write a script for the VSM (Be sure your the VSM is not more than 1 minute, 30 seconds); (3) Train student to determine they can access the video using an iPod Touch™; (4) Plan a 20 minute uninterrupted video-taping session when other students are not in the classroom; (5) Videotape the student in his environment; (6) Prompt student through the completion of the task; (7) Edit the video using video-editing software such as MovieMaker or iMovie; (8) Edit out all verbal and physical prompting so the completed intervention shows the student completing the task independently; (9) Narrate over the video if necessary; (10) Export the edited video to the iPod Touch™. The teacher spent between 30-40 minutes to create each individualized VSM.

After the video was created, the teacher assessed each student's ability to access a sample video on the iPod Touch™, and recorded each student's proficiency using the device on a chart. All of the students easily accessed the sample video and manipulated the device successfully. If they were not able to independently access the VSM on the iPod Touch ™, Ms. Laurent had planned a series of instruction to train each student to access the intervention. Ms. Laurent ensured that each VSM intervention was no more than two minutes in duration (Buggey, 2007; Dowrick & Raeburn, 1977), concise, and specific to the task. To begin, she observed each student individually. First, she chose John and worked with him alone in the classroom while the other students were in a special area. She videotaped John performing the steps necessary to complete a written task - a "Nouns" worksheet. She verbally and at times, physically, prompted him through the steps to complete the task during the videotaping. The videotaping process lasted about 10 minutes. Next, Ms. Laurent edited the raw footage using a MacBook and iMovie software, removing all prompting and narrating over the completed video. The video was 1:38 minutes in length. Once the VSM was completed, she implemented the intervention in John's English/Language Arts (ELA) classroom for the next five days.

Plan Implementation

After collaboration meetings with the classroom and student teacher, a plan was developed to implement the VSM with the students. Upon receiving a written assignment in his ELA classroom, the student teacher handed the student an iPod™ and instructed him to "Please watch your video." The "video" was the VSM the teacher created that showed the student as he completed each step necessary to finish the independent academic task while the teacher's voice narrated the steps the student performed. The teacher stood within close proximity to the student in case assistance was needed in accessing the video or in the event of mechanical error. The student also had 60 seconds to begin before the teacher was signaled to prompt. However, throughout the study, adult assistance was not needed for both accessing the VSM and prompting to begin the written task. Upon being handed the iPod™, the student put his earbuds in his ears and watched his video in its entirety. Upon finishing the video, the student completed the steps necessary to finish the written task. As of day one, the student made significant gains in his independence as a result of the VSM. He demonstrated quick rates of initiation of the task as well as time-on-task behavior. He also completed the entire assignment within the required time. The trend continued throughout the remainder of the five-day intervention period. Each session lasted approximately 10 minutes and was during the regular "morning work" time in the general education classroom. The student had a total of 10 minutes to watch the VSM and independently complete the steps necessary to finish at least 80% of the academic task. Once criterion of 100% had been met for the first student during the intervention phase for at least three out of five days, the researcher ended the intervention. Next, the teacher completed the steps described above and created and implemented an individualized VSM for two other students. Each student made steady progress and demonstrated more independence in task completion in the classroom. Reinforcers, such as adult attention and games on the iPod™ were planned, but not used, because students did not demonstrate a need to be reinforced to complete the written work.

Generalization Across Content Areas

Following the implementation of the VSM, the teacher continued to observe each student in their ELA class as well as their Math class (with a different teacher in a different classroom) to determine if the effects of the VSM would persist over time and generalize to another environment and subject area. All three students were given the same mathematics tasks for two days in the afternoon during the maintenance phases. The generalization task had one overall direction, then three sets of sub-directions, which was similar to the ELA task. She found that for all three students the effects of the VSM were lasting. Students completed the steps to finish the math tasks independently and without the need for adult prompting to begin and persist. The results are consistent with the research and suggest that VSM may be a very effective and efficient intervention to increase task completion of written work for students with an ASD. As a result of implementing the VSM intervention, all students immediately increased their time on task and independent task completion, and decreased their level of prompt dependence and off-task behavior as displayed in Figure 1.

The graph in Figure 1 provides the data collected regarding the implementation of the VSM strategy. The first probe (also known as baseline) is a condition in which the teacher requested the student to complete his work. For each student a 20% or lower completion rate was observed and graphed. The next condition shows the data collected when using VSM with each student. After the student reached a criterion of 100% over three data points, a probe condition gathered the student completing his task without VSM. Probe data continued to be collected for each student after mastery and also in the generalization and maintenance conditions. During the generalization (gen.) condition, student data was collected completing tasks in other classrooms and with other teachers. The maintenance (M.) condition demonstrated that the student continued to complete tasks over time, which was after 30 days.

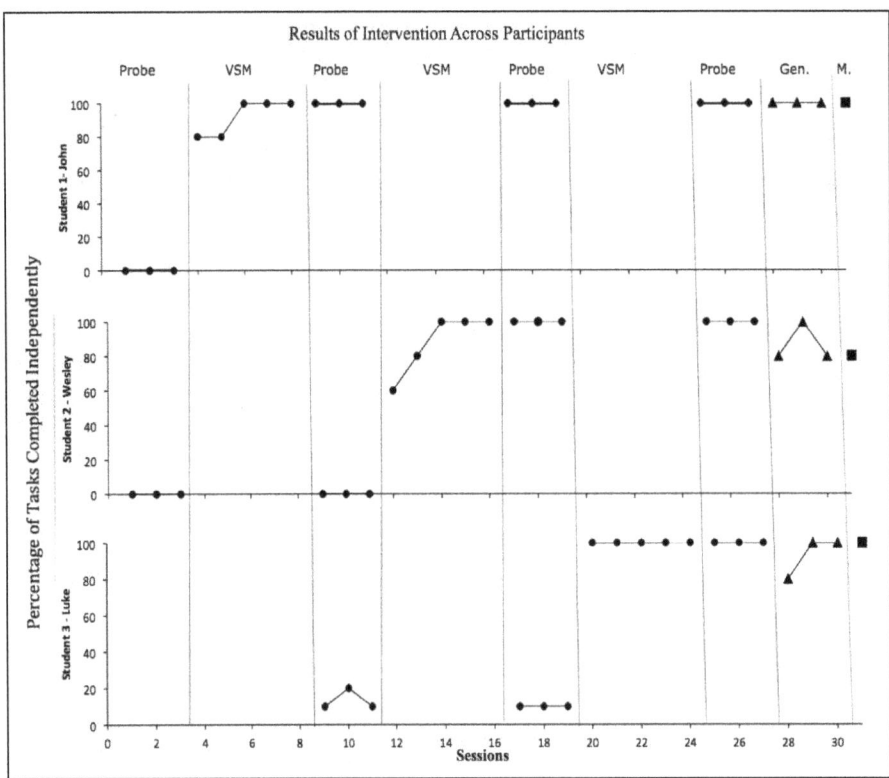

Figure 1: Results of VSM Intervention Across Participants

Benefits to Using VSM with an iPod™

VSM is an efficient intervention as demonstrated by the relative ease of creation and implementation in an inclusive classroom. In the example, the teacher created each individualized VSM in less than 1 hour, including the videotaping and editing. Training of students occurred efficiently as all students had previous experience manipulating an iPod™. Implementation of the VSM intervention was also non-invasive to instructional time for the teacher and other students. Yet, the results revealed that each student increased his time on task, decreased the amount of time it took to complete written assignments, and demonstrated significant gains in his ability to complete the necessary tasks of an academic assignment.

As students transition through grade levels, the amount of written work increases, while in many cases, the level of support decreases. Students who have relied on adult prompting in the primary grades are often left unprepared to meet the increased academic challenges. Therefore, by using video self modeling strategies, students with disabilities are more confident in their ability to complete tasks.

Finally, generalization of acquired behavior across settings and disciplines may be one of the most important skills a student can demonstrate following the implementation of an intervention. IDEA (2004) mandates that special education teachers should administer specially designed instruction as well as accommodations to ensure that achievement gaps are narrowed. The ultimate goal of specialized instruction is generalization of acquired skills across disciplines and settings. Since there is not a universally applied curriculum for children with ASDs, studies suggest that teachers report feeling ill-equipped and untrained to support the specialized needs of their students (Ravet, 2011).

VSM is a relatively easy intervention for teachers to create and implement. The technology has become more accessible to schools and classroom teachers. All three students who received the VSM intervention were heavily prompt dependent, including Wesley, who was conditioned to bring all unfinished work home, making his school day even longer. Despite this, all three students attended to the VSM and demonstrated high rates of acquisition and independence in task completion. The classroom teachers both observed fewer tics and twitching from Wesley while viewing the VSM and afterward.

Challenges in Inclusive Settings

Consistent with the implications related to the practice of teaching, some special education teachers may subconsciously reduce opportunities for independence because they have more frequent interactions with students who have special needs than with typically developing students in inclusive settings and, therefore, a more intimate, familial relationship. This may be true especially for teachers and students who spend multiple years together. These results are consistent with the research of Cameron, Cook, & Tankersley (2012) which examined the frequency and patterns of one-to-one interactions of general education, special education, and paraprofessionals with students who were typically developing, mildly disabled, and severely disabled in inclusive elementary and middle school settings. The teacher's observations also supported the research which suggests that special education teachers interact significantly more with children with disabilities as compared to general education teachers, and paraprofessionals interacted significantly more with students with severe disabilities than with mildly or non-disabled students. This suggests that the more severe the disability, the less independent the student is encouraged to be in an inclusive classroom. The findings also suggest that special education teachers, who teach small groups of children, may rely heavily on prompting which may stifle students' independence.

Ease of Use by General Education Teachers

VSM could serve as a viable solution to general education teachers without special education training to work more effectively with their students with an ASD. Video self modeling may be successful in the classroom because it is individualized to the needs of the student, yet requires very little training or effort to implement on the part of the general education teacher (Buggey, 2009). The VSM movie took approximately 25 minutes to create but implementation was nearly effortless and actually eliminated the time teachers spent prompting and re-teaching individual students. In addition, all students' task completion time improved as well as their on-task behavior, resulting in feelings of increased independence and success as expressed by students and teachers. The use of the iPod Touch™ enhanced the motivational aspects of the intervention by using a device that was familiar, unobtrusive, and socially acceptable to peers, with and without disabilities.

Advantages to VSM using an iPod Touch™

There are 6 key advantages to using an iPod Touch™ when using the VSM strategy. First, most students are familiar with iPod™ devices and can manipulate them with little assistance. Second, iPod™ devices are socially acceptable across environments. Third, iPod™ devices are unobtrusive (the VSM can be a private intervention). Fourth, iPod™ devices are affordable relative to other technological devices. Fifth, creating a VSM and uploading it to an iPod™ device does not require elaborate training or a significant investment of time. Lastly, students who can access a VSM on an iPod™ may require less adult assistance to complete independent tasks.

Conclusions

Video self modeling appears to have been an effective intervention for all of the student participants. The results are consistent with the research that acquisition of skills are almost immediate, skills are maintained over time, and skills are generalized to other academic disciplines. The results also support that VSM may provide a way to support the specialized needs of students with an ASD by positively affecting task completion and giving students access to general education curriculum. Perhaps the most significant asset to implementing VSM is using the iPod Touch™

This type of device is easy to use, portable across any number of environments, including at home, and is socially accepted by peers in the general education classroom.

References

Bellini, S., & Akullian, J. (2007). A meta-analysis of video modeling and video self modeling interventions for children and adolescents with autism spectrum disorders. *Exceptional Children, 73,* 264-287.

Bellini, S., Akullian, J., & Hopf, A. (2007). Increasing social engagement in young children with autism spectrum disorders using video self modeling. *School Psychology Review, 36,* 80-90.

Bellini, S., Peters, J. K., Benner, L., & Hopf, A. (2007). A meta-analysis of school-based social skills interventions for children with autism spectrum disorders. *Remedial and Special Education, 28,* 153-162.

Bock, S. J., Bakken, J. P., & Kempel-Michalak, N. (2009). Behavioral interventions for children and youth with autism spectrum disorders. *In a handbook for teachers:Teaching students with autism in the general education classroom* (pp. 109-141).Waco, Texas: Prufrock Press, Inc.

Buggey, T. (2005). Video self modeling applications with students with autism spectrum disorder in a small private school setting. *Focus on Autism and Other Developmental Disabilities, 20,* 52-64.

Buggey, T. (2007). A picture is worth…Video self-modeling applications at school and home. *Journal of Positive Behavior Interventions, 9,* 151-158.

Buggey, T. (2009). *Seeing is believing: Video self-modeling for people with autism and other developmental disabilities.* Bethesda, MD: Woodbine House.

Buggey, T. & Ogle, L. (2012). Video self-modeling. *Psychology in the Schools, 49,* 52-70.

Cameron, D., Cook, B. G., & Tankersley, M. (2012). An analysis of the different patterns of 1:1 interactions between educational professionals and their students with varying abilities in inclusive classrooms. *International Journal Of Inclusive Education, 16(12),* 1335-1354.

Charlop-Christy, M. H., Le, L., & Freeman, K. A. (2000). A comparison of video modeling with in vivo modeling for teaching children with autism. *Journal of Autism & Developmental Disorders, 30,* 537-552.

Corbett, B. A. (2003). Video modeling: A window into the world of autism. *The Behavior Analyst Today, 4,(3),* np.

Delano, M. E. (2007). Video modeling interventions for individuals with autism. *Remedial and Special Education, 28,* 33-42.

Dowrick, P. W., & Raeburn, J. (1977). Video editing and medication to produce a therapeutic self-model. *Journal of Consulting and Clinical Psychology, 45,*129, 1156–1158.

Dunlap, G., & Johnson, J. (1985). Increasing the independent responding of autistic children with unpredictable supervision. *Journal of Applied Behavior Analysis, 18,* 227–236.

Gelbar, N. W., Anderson, C., McCarthy, S., & Buggey, T. (2012). Video self-modeling as an intervention strategy for individuals with autism spectrum disorders. *Psychology in the Schools, 49,* 15-22.

Hitchcock, C. H., Dowrick, P. W., & Prater, M. A. (2003). Video self-modeling intervention in school-based settings: A review. *Remedial and Special Education, 24,* 36-45.

Hume, K., Loftin, R., & Lanz, J. (2009). Increasing independence in autism spectrum disorders: a review of three focused interventions. *Journal of Autism and Developmental Disorders, 39,* 1329-1338.

Maione, L., & Mirenda, P. (2006). Effects of video modeling and video feedback on peer-directed social language of a child with autism. *Journal of Positive Behavior Interventions, 8,* 106-118.

McCoy, K., & Hermansen, E. (2007). Video modeling for individuals with autism: a review of model types and effects. *Education and Treatment of Children, 30,* 183-213.

Nikopoulos, C. K. & Keenan, M. (2003). Promoting social initiation in children with autism using video modeling. *Behavioral Interventions, 18,* 87-108.

Prater, C. A., Carter, N., Hitchcock, C., & Dowrick, P. (2012). Video self-modeling to improve academic performance: A literature review. *Psychology in the Schools, 49,* 71-81.

Ravet, J. (2011). Inclusive/exclusive? Contradictory perspectives on autism and inclusion: the case for an integrative position. *International Journal Of Inclusive Education, 15,* 667-682.

Using Digital Resources to Support Personalized Learning Experiences in K-12 Classrooms: The Evolution of Mobile Devices as Innovations in Schools

Savilla Banister
Bowling Green State University, USA
sbanist@bgsu.edu

Rachel Vannatta Reinhart
Bowling Green State University, USA
rvanna@bgsu.edu

Abstract: The challenges facing the United States in educating its youth have been widely documented. The dropout rate in the past decades has been staggering, hovering around the 20% mark, with students of color and in lower socio-economic circumstances posting an even higher rate (Barton, 2005). Perhaps more troubling are the indicators that students who are staying in school until high school graduation are largely disengaged and disenfranchised with their experiences (Balfanz, Herzog, & MacIver, 2007; Henry, Knight, & Thornberry, 2012). However, educators are now beginning to embrace the promise of ubiquitous digital technologies in the classroom. This study examines the practice of adopting mobile devices in K-12 environments in a geographic region of the Midwestern United States. The findings suggest that active learning environments, addressing personalized needs and providing evidence of student competencies, may be accomplished effectively by integrating mobile technologies more prominently in K-12 classrooms.

Introduction

The challenges facing the United States in educating its youth have been widely documented. The dropout rate in the past decades has been staggering, hovering around the 20% mark, with students of color and in lower socio-economic circumstances posting an even higher rate (Barton, 2005). Perhaps more troubling are the indicators that students who are staying in school until high school graduation are largely disengaged and disenfranchised with their experiences (Balfanz, Herzog, L & MacIver, 2007; Henry, Knight & Thornberry 2012). Finally, emphasis on standardized tests that may or may not be relevant in determining how successful or productive students will be in our information-age world, have created an ambiance of confusion and stress for both teachers and students. (Au, 2011; Hanushek & Rivkin, 2010; Sahlberg, 2008). Yet for all of the investment of time and money in public education in an effort to promote productivity and democracy throughout the U.S., the results appear to be dismal.

But there are signs that major changes are coming to our educational institutions; changes that will drastically alter the traditional models that have long held across the years and have, for the most part, been resistant to promising models of reform. These changes are largely fueled by the reality of the digital world we now live in. Since the advent of the World Wide Web (circa 1995), the digital generation and exchange of information has become the norm. In the past decade, the interconnectivity and collaborative possibilities in the use, reuse, and co-construction of digital texts, images, audio, video, and databases (loosely identified as "Web 2.0" functionalities) has forced teachers to abandon their long-held positions as the ultimate possessors and distributors of knowledge (Barnett, 2012; Drexler, 2010; Ertmer & Ottenbreit-Leftwich, 2010). Students come to school knowing that the "information is in the air" (Williams, Karousou, & Mackness, 2011) and that they have the ability to connect with experts around the world in multiple venues, in order to learn about all sorts of content, academic or practical.

Beyond the amount of resources available for learner consumption, in the support of educational growth, our digital tools now afford us the communicative and data-management power to truly provide individualized learning experiences for students. In addition, state and national policies are directing districts and schools in how the ever rising expectations can met. The United States Department of Education (US DoE) is supporting the Digital Promise initiative, using their League of Innovative Schools as a conduit to encourage implementation of powerful technologies to support meaningful learning. The US DoE's Office of Educational Technology is promoting strategies including one-to-one mobile devices for students, personalized learning networks, a national registry of learning resources, data management learning dashboards and competency-based education models to provide direction for dramatic changes in our nation's schools (Hwang, Kuo, Yin, & Chuang, 2010; Miller & Lake, 2012; Wang & Liao, 2011). In the state of Ohio, educational legislation in recent years has pushed schools to implement a variety of initiatives: the Common Core, online state assessments, end-of-course exams, teacher evaluation systems, and district report cards (Lieszkovszky, 2012). These statewide initiatives have placed enormous pressure on districts to have the resources to implement online state assessments and increase student achievement growth especially among marginalized groups.

This study sought to examine how schools are embracing the educational possibilities of the digital age. More specifically, the researchers studied regional K-12 Ohio schools and were guided by the following research questions:

1. What types of initiatives, related to the Digital Promise of DoE's Office of Educational Technology, are schools in this region exploring or deploying?
2. What are the identified priorities of these schools, specifically related to student learning outcomes?

Methodology

In order to address these research questions, the researchers employed a mixed methods explanatory design in conjunction with the Center of Excellence for 21st Century Educator Preparation of a state university. The School Initiative Survey was distributed online in early Fall 2013. The survey consisted of 16 questions. The first three items garnered background information. Then 11 questions asked the respondent to indicate their use of 10 technologies and initiatives (BYOD--Bring Your Own Device, one-to-one laptops, one-to-one tablets, one-to-one handhelds, digital textbooks (in lieu of paper texts), flipped classroom models, blended or online course options, online assessment tools, a focus on individualized or differentiated instruction, and the alignment of their work with the Partnership for 21st Century Skills. Three options were provided for these items: (1) Not familiar, (2) Exploring—talking about implementing, and (3) Deploying—actually doing. The final two items were open-ended and asked:

- What other initiatives are you investigating or implementing to support student learning?
- What are your highest priorities, connected to student learning, for your school/district at this time?

Surveys were not anonymous, but were confidential, as far as keeping individual responses from being distributed. Principals supplied their school names, addresses and an email contact, so that researchers could follow up on specific responses, and data was aggregated and shared back to the districts for comparison and conversation. This type of protocol was utilized to support a more open and collegial model of working towards meaningful change, grounded in the philosophy of the Open Source and Open Education mindsets.

The survey was sent to principals of all schools (n=657) within a 50-mile radius of the Center with an email requesting completion of the online survey, or an option to complete the survey over the phone. Administrators were informed that they could forward the survey completion task on to another teacher/administrator of their choice, and that they would receive a follow up phone call in upcoming weeks, in order to acquire their responses, in the event that the online survey was not completed. As a perk for completing the 5-minute survey, principals were offered a complimentary registration to a full-day technology symposium being hosted at the university in the spring. Fifty-six administrators accepted this offer and attended the event later in the year. The target population represents a variety of school settings ranging from rural, small town, suburban to urban. Out of 657 school principals invited, 110 completed the survey. This response rate of 16.7% represented a reasonable sampling of the schools in the region with 4 charter schools and 13 private schools with the remaining as public schools. Among the participating schools, most were located in districts with a Small Town (36.5%) typology followed by Urban (28%), Rural (18.7%), and Suburban (16.8%).

Because the survey included items that were both quantitative and qualitative in the response choices, a mixed methods explanatory approach was used in that the quantitative data was first analyzed, with qualitative results being used to explain the quantitative results. This paper present descriptive statistics regarding the initiatives being explored or deployed followed by a synopsis of themes that emerged from the open-ended items.

Results

Results (see Table 1) indicate that the surveyed schools are focusing on the initiatives of: 1) Individualized and Differentiated Instruction (M=2.64) and 2) the use of Online Assessment Tools (M=2.48). At least 90% of the respondents indicated that they were either exploring or deploying these initiatives. One-to-one student devices was also a top initiative, with 78% of schools exploring or deploying one-to-one laptop programs.

Table 1: Summary of initiatives being explored or deployed.

Initiative	f			n	M	SD
	1 Not Familiar	2 Exploring	3 Deploying			
BYOD (Bring Your Own Device)	20	40	30	90	2.11	0.74
One-to-One Mobile Devices for Students:	13	52	26	91	2.14	0.64
Laptops	6	30	41	77	2.45	0.64
Tablets (iPads, etc.)	10	35	41	86	2.38	0.68
Handhelds (iPods, cell phones, etc.)	12	29	27	68	2.22	0.73
Digital Textbooks (online academic resources)	18	52	20	90	2.02	0.65
Flipped Classrooms	32	40	16	88	1.82	0.72
Online or Blended Classes	24	42	26	92	2.02	0.74
Online Assessment Tools	9	36	58	103	2.48	0.65
Individualized/Differentiated Instruction	3	30	68	99	2.64	0.54
P21 (Partnership for 21st Century Skills) Alignment	32	38	17	87	1.83	0.73

The qualitative results of the open-ended response items provided more descriptive details as to the actions and priorities of the school districts. Sixty-four participants responded to the first open-ended question, which asked about other initiatives being implemented. Many participants (n=26) elaborated on their technology initiatives, further discussing their one-to-one programs. However, 16 of these 26 spoke of technology in relation to other initiatives, such that the technology was a means to fulfilling other goals. Three other themes emerged from the data: 1) state-wide initiatives; 2) curriculum changes; and 3) meeting the needs of all students. The theme of statewide initiatives was the focus for 13 respondents and included the topics of Ohio Teacher Evaluation System, Race to the Top, Formative Instructional Practices, and the Third Grade Reading Guarantee. Many mentioned the PARCC (Herman & Linn, 2013) assessments specifically and the challenge of administering these assessments online in upcoming years. Curricular initiatives were also identified by many respondents (n=10), as many discussed Common Core, the new Ohio Academic content standards, STEM, project-based learning, and curriculum mapping. Finally, equally important was the emphasis on meeting the needs of all learners. Many school leaders (n=10) identified initiatives that addressed interventions, enrichment, credit-recovery, ESL support, individualized instruction. The desire to have students and teachers perform well, as gauged by these state standards, assessments, and value-added parameters was paramount among approximately 20% of the responses submitted in this area. The following quote is representative of the comments received:

Our focus has been directed at improving scores in the state mandated assessments. (OAA< OGT). We are also preparing for new statewide, end-of-course exams that will be implemented in the next few years. The development of new learning standards, formative assessments, and preparation for online assessments (PARCC) is also a priority. The implementation of Ohio's New Learning Standards (Common Core State Standards, Ohio Revised Standards), technology integration included in curriculum maps, measuring student growth, and evaluation are all connected in this plan.

Finally, when asked about their school's highest priority related to student learning, 95 educational leaders responded, with 33 indicated technology as a top priority, followed by student achievement. Other priorities echoed the initiatives identified in the previous question.

Discussion and Implications

While research is lacking that identifies the initiatives that schools are implementing, the literature regarding educational initiatives focuses on state and national policies and guides. These results show that school leaders are exploring or implementing a variety of initiatives that are parallel to state legislation and policy. Along with their commitment to the standards and legislated assessments, principals espoused a strong allegiance to innovation, personalized learning experiences for students and 21st century skills. They spoke of "giving our staff the tools for learning that allow them to teach our students the way the students are learning with their personal devices at home while all the while maintaining the high standard of excellence that we demand from both staff and students." The commitment to connect the curriculum to student success beyond the classroom was evident in the explanations associated with the one-to-one deployments, which were mentioned in detail, providing the names of the devices (Chromebooks, iPads, laptops, BYOD, cell phones, etc.). One school leader stated, "Our priority is that students will learn the curriculum necessary to be successful in life. We are preparing students for the future. We want to make sure our students are receiving the best education possible with the best tools that are available."

In other words, school principals connected one-to-one deployment initiatives to providing more personalized learning environments for students and ultimately increasing student success. One commented that, "We want to see more individualized strategies, one-on-one teaching time...we want to spend more time making learning relational, but also use higher level thinking skills." Another said, "We want to raise the rigor of our instruction in order to prepare our students better for life after high school. We are implementing a more challenging curriculum, and we need to do more with lesson planning and assessing learning objectives." Finally, a principal described their broader vision, explaining,

> Regarding student learning, our focus is on creating/maintaining student centered classrooms that foster and promote creativity, communication, and collaboration. Instructional goals should always include relevance; students should utilize 21st century learning skills to solve real world problems. Learning best takes place during the application of knowledge to accomplish real work.

These statements provide context for the infusion of the digital technologies in these schools. A context that connects curriculum and standards to meaningful, personalized learning. Of course, not all comments were as lofty and promising, as one principal noted, "...but we also need to work on getting more use of technology by our teachers in their instruction. We have gone to BYOD, but our students have indicated they see no value in bringing such devices to school because they can't use them in the classroom." This observation ties in to multiple comments related to professional development for teachers, and these will be unpacked and addressed in another article, as they are currently beyond the scope of this piece.

Results have implications for teacher preservice and inservice training. With 78% of participating schools exploring or deploying one-to-one technology initiatives, teachers need training on instructional methods that capitalize on a one-to-one learning environment while meeting the needs of all learners. While most teacher preparation programs include technology integration courses and experiences, preservice teachers are likely receiving inadequate preparation to teach within a one-to-one classroom. Teacher education courses need to address the instructional ramifications of a one-to-one environment as well as blended and online environments (Yoon & Chang, 2012).

Conclusions

While it is apparent that school leaders are working to accommodate the legislative demands of the national Common Core curriculum, online PARCC achievement testing and value-added criteria for teachers, they are doing so with an eye towards preparing students for a future outside these parameters and restraints. Implementing one-to-one mobile device initiatives, while providing an infrastructure for online testing (PARCC) and access to other state and national assessment systems, creates opportunities for teachers and students to individualize, customize and differentiate instruction for students. Teachers continue to need professional development, not only to learn more about how to integrate the digital tools and resources being provided in their schools, but to "retool" as educators that facilitate personalized learning environments for all of their students. The interconnected, communicative, responsive, data-rich world in which we live now makes this possible. It is up to these pioneers to lead the way.

References

Au, W. (2011). Teaching under the new Taylorism: High-stakes testing and the standardization of the 21st century curriculum. *Journal of Curriculum Studies, 43*(1), 25-45.

Balfanz, R., Herzog, L., & MacIver, D. J. (2007). Preventing student disengagement and keeping students on the graduation path in urban middle-grades shools: Early identification and effective interventions. *Educational Psychologist, 42*(4), 223-235.

Barnett, R. (2012). Learning for an unknown future. *Higher Education Researh and Development, 31*(1), 65-77.

Barton, P. E. (2005). One-third of a nation: Rising dropout rates and declining opportnities (pp. 1-47): Policy Information Center.

Drexler, W. (2010). The networked student model for construction of personal learning environments: Balancing teacher control and student autonomy. *Australasian Journal of Educational Technology, 26*(3), 369-385.

Ertmer, P. A., & Ottenbreit-Leftwich, A. T. (2010). Teacher technology change: How knowledge, confidence, beliefs, and cluture intersect. *Journal of Research on Technology in Education, 42*(3), 255-284.

Hanushek, E. A., & Rivkin, S. G. (2010). Generalizations about using value-added measures of teacher quality. *American Economic Review, 100*(May), 267-271.

Henry, K. L., Knight, K. E., & Thornberry, T. P. (2012). School disengagement as a predictor of dropout, deinquency, and problem substance use during adolescence and early adulthood. *Journal of Youth and Adolescence, 41*(2), 156-166.

Herman, J., & Linn, R. (2013). On the road to assessing deeper learning: The status of Smarter Balanced and PARCC Assessment Consortia CRESST Report 823 (pp. 20). Los Angeles: CRESST.

Hwang, G.-J., Kuo, F.-R., Yin, P.-Y., & Chuang, K.-H. (2010). A heuristic algorithm for planning personalized learning paths for context-aware ubiquitous learning. *Computers and Education, 54*(2), 404-415.

Lieszkovszky, I. (2012). State Impact: What's coming up in Ohio education in 2013. stateimpact.npr.org/ohio/2012/12/24/whats-coming-up-in-ohio-education-in-2013

Miller, R., & Lake, R. (2012). Federal Barriers to Innovation (pp. 1-14). Seattle, Washington: Center for Reinventing Public Education.

Sahlberg, P. (2008). Rethinking accountability in a knowledge society. *Journal of Educational Change, 11*, 45-61.

Wang, Y.-h., & Liao, H.-C. (2011). Data mining for adaptive learning in a TESL-based e-Learning system. *Expert Systems with Applications, 38*(6), 6480-6485.

Williams, R., Karousou, R., & Mackness, J. (2011). Emergent learning and learning ecologies in Web 2.0. *International Review of Research in Open and Distance Learning, 12*(3), 1-11.

Yoon, H.J. & Chang, H.M. (2012). Instructors' modeling of technology integration in preservice teacher preparation program with one to one laptop initiative. In P. Resta (Ed.), Proceedings of Society for Information Technology & Teacher Education International Conference 2012 (pp. 4910-4916). Chesapeake, VA: AACE.

The Impact of a Digital Storytelling Assignment on Non-English-Major-Students' Motivation for Learning English in a Japanese University

Naoko Kasami
J. F. Oberlin University, Japan
naoko.kasami@gmail.com

Abstract: The purpose of this study was to investigate how a digital storytelling assignment affected non-English-major-students' motivation for learning English. Sixty five university students from a Faculty of Information and Communications participated in a course entitled 'Information English'. The study goal of the course was to acquire skills and knowledge to present ideas and messages effectively with the use of ICT and English. As a final assignment of the course, students were encouraged to create digital stories to introduce Japanese culture to people abroad. In this research, the impact of the digital storytelling assignment was analyzed based on Keller's ARCS model. The findings showed that the digital storytelling assignment might be a potential way to enhance non-English-major-students' motivation for learning English. Also, the digital storytelling assignment contributed to increased motivation to learn compared with essay assignments in a traditional style.

Introduction

The purpose of this study was to investigate how a digital storytelling assignment affected non-English-major-students' motivation for learning English. Sixty five university students from a Faculty of Information and Communications participated in a course entitled 'Information English' for 15 weeks. The study goal of the course was to acquire skills and knowledge to present ideas and messages effectively with the use of Information and Communications Technology (ICT) and English. As a midterm assignment of the course, students were required to write a short essay in English using Microsoft Word. Then, as a final assignment of the course, they were encouraged to create digital stories to introduce Japanese culture to people abroad. In this research, the effectiveness of the digital storytelling assignment was analyzed in terms of motivation for learning based on Keller's ARCS model. Also, this research focuses on the impact of a digital storytelling assignment by comparing with an essay assignment. In Japan, the Ministry of Education, Culture, Sports, Science and Technology (MEXT) promotes the establishment of an environment corresponding to globalization and has released the English Education Reform Plan. In spite of high expectations, many university students do not have enough confidence in their communication abilities. It is commonly observed that non-English-major-students have relatively low confidence, motivation and autonomy in learning English. This research introduces how the digital storytelling assignment can be integrated into ICT and English education for university students, and reports the outcomes of the impact of the assignment on the students' motivation for learning.

Literature Review

Digital stories provide opportunities for students to engage in authentic projects that allow students to perform self-construction of meaning (Jonassen, 1999). According to the Center for Digital Storytelling (2010), the major components of a digital story have been rationalized in "The Seven Elements of Digital Storytelling": (a) Point of view, (b) A dramatic question, (c) Emotional content, (d) The gift of your voice, (e) The power of soundtrack, (f) Economy and (g) Pacing.

According to Robin (2006), "There are many different definitions of "Digital Storytelling," but in general, they all revolve around the idea of combining the art of telling stories with a variety of digital multimedia, such as images, audio, and video. Just about all digital stories bring together some mixture of digital graphics, text, recorded audio narration, video and music to present information on a specific topic. As is the case in traditional storytelling, digital stories revolve around a chosen theme, and often contain a particular viewpoint. The stories are typically just a few minutes long and have a variety of uses, including the telling of personal tales, the recounting of historical events, or as a means to inform or instruct on a particular topic."

Numerous researchers have discussed the process of digital storytelling and how to introduce digital storytelling technology into classes (Frazel, 2010; Jakes, 2005; Lambert, 2007; Susono et al., 2010). There are also studies which examine the effectiveness of digital storytelling in terms of students' motivation for learning. Digital storytelling increases students' motivation and engagement. Yu and Robin (2010) stated that 72% of students agreed that digital storytelling made the course more motivational and engaging in university forensic science education in the online learning environment. Plankis and Hwang (2010) reported that digital storytelling projects enhanced students' creativity and enthusiasm in high school science classrooms in the USA, and more students enjoyed creating a digital story with Microsoft Photostory compared to the standard laboratory written report with Microsoft Word. According to the study, 68.6% of the student comments focused on the digital storytelling process being more enjoyable because it was fun or entertaining, visually or aurally oriented, and allowed for creativity and freedom of choice. Xu et al. (2011) indicated that digital storytelling might encourage people who did not like writing or who had no confidence in writing. Sadik (2008) reported that students were encouraged to work through the process of producing their own digital stories.

In this research, Keller's ARCS model is used as the conceptual framework because this model is comprehensive and useful for the courseware design (Keller & Suzuki, 1988). Keller (1983, 2010)'s motivational design model called the ARCS (Attention, Relevance, Confidence and Satisfaction) model was used as the guiding framework for the evaluation of the enhancement of motivation for learning based on the following four categories.
    1) Attention: Capturing the interest of learners; stimulating the curiosity to learn
    2) Relevance: Meeting the personal needs/goals of the learner to effect a positive attitude
    3) Confidence: Helping the learners believe/feel that they will succeed and control their success
    4) Satisfaction: Reinforcing accomplishment with rewards (internal and external)

These four categorical components of ARCS cover major factors influencing the motivation for learning, and comprise the following subcategories based on the major motivational variables (Keller, 1983; Keller, 2010).
    1) Attention: Perceptual arousal, Inquiry arousal, Variability
    2) Relevance: Goal orientation, Motive matching, Familiarity
    3) Confidence: Learning requirements, Success opportunities, Personal control
    4) Satisfaction: Intrinsic reinforcement, Extrinsic rewards, Equity

The ARCS model provides typology for educators to know learner motivation and motivational strategies. Moreover, Keller (2010, p.7) developed ARCS-V: an expansion of the traditional ARCS model, considering volitional skills, otherwise known as self-regulatory behaviors.

Kogo and Suzuki (2000) created a Japanese version of a questionnaire for Japanese students to evaluate motivational characteristics of instruction using 12 sub-categorical items with a 9-point Likert scale based on Keller's ARCS model. Also, a web version of this questionnaire was developed and introduced in English (Suzuki et al., 2004).

Method

The steps in the digital storytelling assignment and data collection

During the 15-week course which ran from April to July 2013, the digital storytelling assignment was conducted from the week 10 onwards. The length of each class was 90 minutes per week. The procedure of the assignment was as follows.

In the week 10 class, students wrote a scenario in English with the use of a scenario sheet. It was necessary to take enough time to write the scenario before moving on to editing the digital story. It took more than two weeks to write and review the scenario sheet. Students who wanted their English writing checked by a teacher received individual feedback. Students who could not finish writing in the class were required to finish the writing as a homework assignment. All students had to submit the final version of their scenario sheet within three weeks as it constituted one of the important tasks of the course.

In the week 11 class, students watched the demonstration of how to create a digital story by the teacher. After that, each student was supposed to get hands-on practice to make a digital story with sample photos and image data. Other basic rules such as copyright rules were also taught.

In the week 12 and 13 classes, each student made his or her own digital story over the 2 week period. Each student was allowed to write by themselves or to create a digital story with classmates as a team. Some students who could not create their digital story were required to create it as a homework assignment.

In the week 14 class, after recapping what had been learned in the course, each digital story was uploaded in Windows Media Audio/Video file (wmv) format to Google Drive and shared with the classmates. All students had to submit the final version of their digital story by the beginning of the week 15 class as another important task of the course.

In the week 15 class, a final test of the course was conducted and each student was required to review and evaluate other students' digital stories and to give comments and scores on a peer review sheet.

In this digital storytelling project, each student was allowed to select whether to create a digital story individually or with classmates as a group (comprising 2 to 4 participants). The group participants were self-selected. As a result, 34 students (52.31%) chose an individual task and 31 students (47.69%) chose a group task.

For the data collection, in the first class, a pre-assessment questionnaire was conducted and in the last class, a post-assessment questionnaire was conducted. Every student was required to answer the questionnaire survey as they were compulsory. The surveys were administered with the use of Google Docs. Participants were required to log in to their Gmail account under the university domain.

The subject of research

This study focuses on the practices of the courses entitled 'Information English' for students at a Faculty of Information and Communications in 'A University' in Japan. The study comprised 65 students in three classes. The study goal of the course was to acquire skills and knowledge to present ideas and messages effectively with the use of ICT and English. The courses were conducted in a CALL (Computer-assisted language learning) room, and each student used one computer.

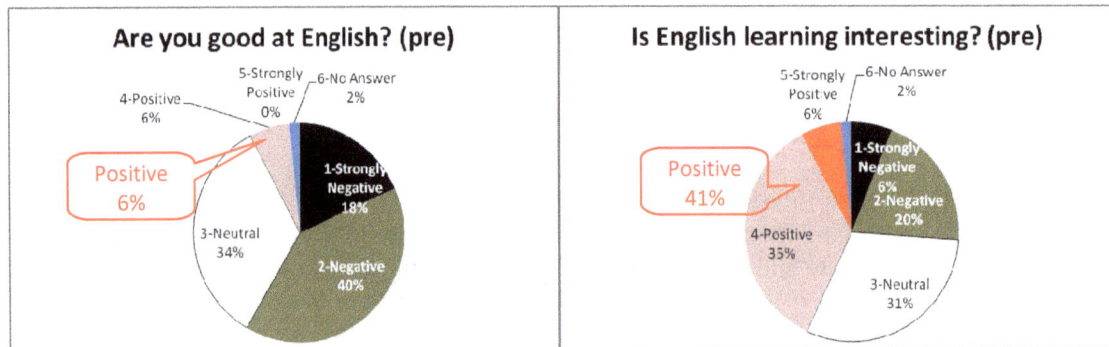

Figure 1: The students' self-evaluation for their own English and English learning

At the beginning of the course, it was revealed that 58% of the 65 students did not have confidence in their English ability. According to the pre-assessment questionnaires conducted in the spring term of 2013, only 6% of all students answered "Yes (Positive)" and nobody answered "Strongly Positive (Agree)" to the question "Are you good at English?", and more than 90% of all students answered "Negative (Disagree)", "Strongly Negative (Strongly Disagree)" or "Neutral (Neither)". Similarly, only 41% of students answered "English learning is interesting" at the beginning of the course. (35% of the students answered "Positive (Agree)" and 6% of the students answered "Strongly Positive (Strongly Agree)" to the question "Is English learning interesting?"

In this course, the mid-term assignment was to write a short essay. The general theme of the essay was to introduce his or her university life. There were some students who seemed uninterested in writing essays or who felt that it was difficult to write an essay in English. At the end of the course, every student was supposed to create a digital story with the use of ICT. The digital storytelling assignment allowed each student to exhibit his or her originality and to consider the audience.

There were three goals for this assignment and the goals were introduced with the keyword of "Happy": Heartfelt Acceptance and Presentation for Peace with You. The general theme of the assignment was "Tips for Your Happy Life in Japan" and "Tips for Better Understanding Japanese Culture". Each student was required to create a digital story which enables people in other countries to amicably understand Japanese culture. The following message from the teacher was written on the syllabus of this course. "This course was conducted with a notion of 'Your differences make you beautiful and happy' and please don't hesitate to make a mistake or to be different from other students" Figure 2 shows screen shots of students' digital stories.

Figure 2: Screen shots of the digital stories of the students

Windows Live Movie Maker and PowerPoint 2010 were used as the software for creating the digital stories as they had been installed on the Windows 7 computers used for instruction in the course within the university. Students were allowed to choose either software to create a digital story. The software enables users to import graphical and movie data, to edit it by integrating it with sound data, and to export the product into a movie file. Students can create their digital stories with characters, graphics, movie files, sound and narration in order to take into account their audience's concerns.

Analysis

This research aimed to investigate the impact on students' motivation for learning. The participants of this course were 65 students. The results and findings are presented based on questionnaires as follows. First, in order to know students' learning motivation and general reaction towards the final project, the students were asked to rate the final digital storytelling assignment. The question statements of the questionnaires were set as the following with reference to the ARCS model and its process questions (Keller, 2010). In addition to the sub-categorical 12 question items (A-1, A-2, A-3, R-1, R-2, R-3, C-1, C-2, C-3, S-1, S-2, S-3) referred to the research by Kogo and Suzuki (2000), the author added 5 question items shown in Italics (Attention, Relevance, Confidence, Satisfaction, and Volition) based on the ARCS-V: an expansion of the traditional ARCS model (Keller, 2010).

Questionnaire statement based on the ARCS model and the results

Attention: (1. The assignment was very boring. --- 5. Neutral ---9. The assignment was very interesting.)
    A-1: Perceptual Arousal (1. Felt sleepy --- 5. Neutral ---9. Didn't feel sleepy)
     Did the assignment capture your interest?
    A-2: Inquiry Arousal (1. Curiosity wasn't aroused --- 5. Neutral --- 9. Curiosity was aroused)
     Did the assignment stimulate an attitude of inquiry?
    A-3: Variability (1. Not stimulating --- 5. Neutral ---9. Variable and stimulating)
     Did the assignment maintain your attention?
Relevance: (1.The assignment was not relevant to me at all. --- 5. Neutral --- 9. The assignment was very relevant to me.)
    R-1: Goal-Orientation (1. No relevance to me --- 5. Neutral ---9. Relevant to me)
     Did the assignment best meet your needs?
    R-2: Motive Matching (1. Didn't want to acquire --- 5. Neutral --- 9. Wanted to acquire content)
     Did the assignment link to your learning styles and personal interests?

R-3: Familiarity (1. Learning process wasn't fun --- 5. Neutral ---- 9. Learning process was fun)
  Did the assignment tie to your experiences and did you enjoy the process?

Confidence: (1. I did not feel confident at all. --- 5. Neutral ----9. I felt very confident.)
  C-1: Learning Requirement (1. Objectives were vague --- 5. Neutral ----9. Objectives were clear)
  Did the assignment assist in building a positive expectation for success?
  C-2: Success Opportunities (1. Steady progress impossible --- 5. Neutral ----9. Steady progress was possible)
  Did the assignment support or enhance beliefs in your competence?
  C-3: Personal Control
    (1. Not creative in learning --- 5. Neutral ---9. Was creative in learning)
  Did you clearly know that the success was based upon your efforts and abilities in this assignment?

Satisfaction: (1. I am not very satisfied with the assignment very much. --- 5. Neutral --- 9. I am very satisfied with the assignment.)
  S-1: Natural Consequences
    (1. Not readily applicable --- 5. Neutral --- 9. Readily applicable)
  Did the assignment support your learning soon?
  S-2: Positive Consequences
    (1. Effort wasn't recognized --- 5. Neutral --- 9. Effort was recognized)
  Did the assignment provide rewarding consequences to your successes?
  S-3: Equity
    (1. Evaluation not consistent --- 5. Neutral --- 9. Evaluation was consistent)
  Did you have perceptions of fair treatment for your accomplishment?

Volition: (1. I didn't make continuous efforts to achieve the study goals at all. --- 5. Neutral --- 9. I made continuous efforts to repeatedly achieve the study goals.)

		Average	SD
Attention		**7.22**	**1.55**
A-1	Perceptual Arousal	7.32	1.64
A-2	Inquiry Arousal	6.85	1.63
A-3	Variability	7.17	1.43
Relevance		**7.35**	**1.48**
R-1	Familiarity	7.09	1.48
R-2	Goal Orientation	7.17	1.36
R-3	Motive Matching	7.11	1.56
Confidence		**6.54**	**1.47**
C-1	Learning Requirement	6.52	1.94
C-2	Success Opportunities	6.49	1.71
C-3	Personal Control	6.91	1.62
Satisfaction		**7.28**	**1.71**
S-1	Natural Consequences	6.17	1.73
S-2	Positive Consequences	7.06	1.43
S-3	Equity	6.92	1.42
Volition		**7.09**	**1.33**

Figure 3: The results of post-assessment questionnaires based on Keller's ARCS model

Questions regarding motivation for learning with the final project were asked using a 9-point Likert scale. The greater the numerical value, the stronger the motivating factor becomes. The average points of all question items were higher than 6.17, and there were no clear gaps between each category. It can be noted that the project was generally effective in enhancing students' motivation for learning to some extent [Figure 3].

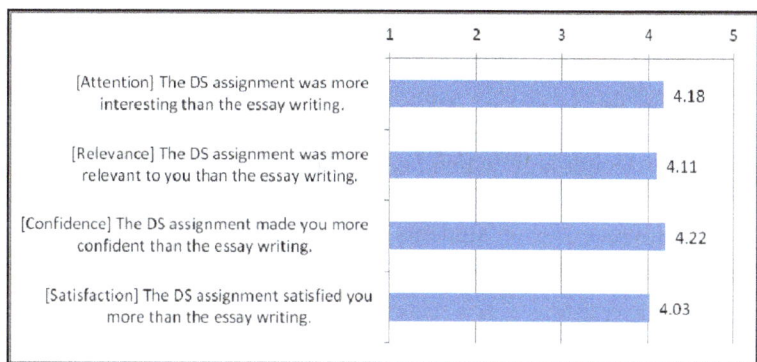

Figure 4: Comparison with the digital storytelling assignment and the essay writing assignment

Secondly, the learners were asked to compare the digital storytelling (DS) assignment with the essay writing assignment which was required to do as a mid-term assignment in a traditional writing style using Microsoft Word. The question statements were as follows. Q1: "Do you think that the digital storytelling was more interesting than the essay writing?", Q2: "Do you think that the digital storytelling was more relevant to you than the essay writing?", Q3: "Do you think that the digital storytelling made you more confident than the essay writing?", Q4: "Do you think that the digital storytelling satisfied you more than the essay writing?" The questionnaire was answered with a 5-point Likert scale (1-Stronngly Disagree, 2-Disagree, 3-Neutal, 4-Agree, 5-Strongly Agree). As a result, the average of each point was more than 4.03, which revealed that the students were motivated for learning through the digital storytelling assignment. The aspect of the confidence tended to be slightly lower than other aspects in the above graph, but when it came to the comparison with the traditional essay writing, the average point concerning confidence tended to be higher, and similar to the average points of the other aspects [Figure 4].

Thirdly, the open-ended question was given at the end of the course. Students were asked to "Please write down what you think was good about the digital storytelling assignment in this course." Comments were given by 38 students. The author categorized all comments into five aspects ((1) interesting, (2) collaborative learning, (3) English learning, (4) think deeply / discovery learning, and (5) utilizing ICT). The followings are examples of comments made. The whole questionnaires were asked and answered in Japanese, and then translated into English.

Positive comments
(1) Interesting (n=12)
- It was interesting to think and write English sentences for my digital story.
- It was interesting to watch classmates' digital stories because we enjoyed different ideas.
- It was interesting to watch digital stories at the end and there was a certain challenge to doing the assignment.

(2) Collaborative learning (n=9)
- As we exchanged ideas and discussed different ideas with classmates, we created a good digital story.
- It was good to discuss scenarios and to write English sentences with friends as I felt I had difficulty with my English writing.
- The classmates' digital stories inspired me.

(3) English learning (n=8)
- I learned English proactively not passively.
- It was good to have opportunities to manage my communication in an unfamiliar language. I found it interesting to challenge myself to communicate in English.
- I can learn English writing and speaking while making use of new functions which I used for the first time.

(4) Think deeply / discovery learning (n=6)

> - I thought deeply about how to write English sentences clearly while considering the audience.
> - Since the assignment requires me to present messages effectively, I thought deeply in order to devise ways of communicating effectively using both images and sound.
>
> **(5) Utilizing ICT (n=3)**
> - I have acquired new technology which I can utilize in my life.

From the above comments, it may be inferred that the assignment enhanced students' motivation for the final project. However, when students were asked to "Please write down what you think was bad about the digital storytelling assignment in this course.", there were several negative comments as follows.

> **Negative comments**
> - The length of time for the project was too short. (n=4)
> - I wanted to learn how to edit a movie file more with a technical manual. (n=2)
> - It was quite difficult to allocate roles appropriately between team members. (n=2)

Fourthly, at the end of the course, students were asked the same questions as those of the pre-assessment questionnaires. According to the post-assessment questionnaire, 16% of all students answered "Positive (Agree)" or "Strongly Positive (Strongly Agree)" to the question "Are you good at English?" Similarly, 53% of students answered that English learning was interesting at the end of the course [Figure 5]. Compared with the result of the pre-assessment questionnaire, it was not an outstanding growth; there was an improvement of the questionnaire result though it was only a slight improvement.

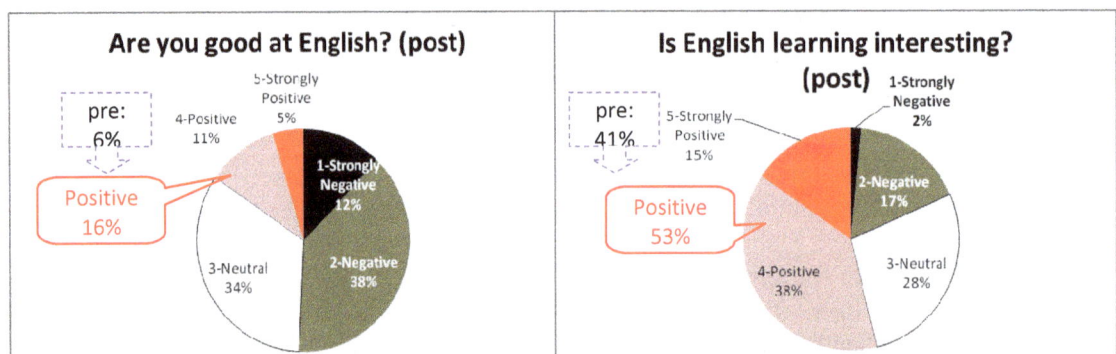

Figure 5: The students' self-evaluation for their own English and English learning at the end of the course

Findings

This study was designed to establish whether a digital storytelling assignment led to more positive attitudes and enhanced motivation for learning English by utilizing the advantages of ICT. The results show that the assignment encouraged the non-English major students' motivation for learning to some extent according to the following four points.

First, from the answers to the questionnaire based ARCS model, the aspect of 'Relevance' tended to mark slightly high in the aspects of ARCS, with the average point for all sub-category questions concerning 'Relevance' scoring higher than 7.09 (on a 9-point scale). It might be natural that students felt there was relevance because ICT was their specialty. On the contrary, the aspect of 'Confidence' seemed to be comparatively lower than the other three aspects. Second, when it came to the comparison with the essay assignment, it was revealed that the students were motivated for learning with the digital storytelling assignment. Third, the comments by students showed that some students felt the digital storytelling assignment was interesting and good for collaborative learning. In addition, the digital storytelling assignment made some students become proactive English learners, and it was likely that the assignment was good for English writing and speaking learning, through naturally being exposed to real communication. Fourth, based on the comparison of pre and post-assessment questionnaires regarding students' self-evaluation for their own English and learning, the percentage of students who answered positively to the questions of "Are you good at English?" and "Is English learning interesting?" were slightly increased. This might show that the digital storytelling assignment was effective not only for ICT but also for English learning to some extent.

Conclusions

The purpose of this study was to investigate the effects of the digital storytelling assignment in terms of motivation for learning.
The findings of this research are stated below:
1. The digital storytelling assignment is a potential way to enhance non-English-major-students' motivation for learning English to some extent.
2. The digital storytelling assignment contributed to increased motivation to learn compared with the essay assignment.

The above findings support the literatures which suggest that digital storytelling increases students' motivation for learning.

The limitations of this study should be pointed out. The major limitation was that this research does not analyze the effectiveness of achieving the learning outcomes, and it will be important to consider the method and measures for examining learning effectiveness. Also, statistically significant results were not observed for improved motivation for learning English. Therefore, further studies are needed to consider the method of evaluation of students' improvement on learning effectiveness. Also, the result of improvement should be indicated statistically. Moreover, the volition aspect of ARCS-V was only partially analyzed, though it should have been examined more clearly because this aspect might be a very important aspect to research into the motivation for learning English of non-English major students. Furthermore, this research has not indicated the comparison of individual and group tasks which might be a key factor for effecting student motivation for learning.

Moreover, there are some areas of improvement to be addressed in the course design for the higher satisfaction of students in the final project. This includes additional time being spent on the assignment and providing simple technical handouts to help them create their digital stories and advice for appropriate allocation of roles between group members.

References

Center for Digital Storytelling. (2010). Retrieved October 18, 2013, from http://www.storycenter.org
Frazel, M. (2010). *Digital storytelling guide for educators*. Washington DC: International Society for Technology in Education.
Jakes, D.S. (2005). *Capturing stories, capturing lives: An introduction to digital storytelling*. Retrieved January 16, 2011, from http://www.jakesonline.org/dstory_ice.pdf
Jonassen, D., Peck, K.& Wilson, B. (1999). *Learning with technology: A constructivist perspective*. NJ: Prentice Hall.

Keller, J. M. (1984).The use of the ARCS model of motivation in teacher training. In Trott, K. S. A. J. (ed.), *Aspect of educational technology volume XVII: Staff development and career updating.* London: Kogan Page.

Keller, J. M. (2010). *Motivational design for learning and performance: The ARCS model approach.* NY: Springer.

Keller, J. M., & Suzuki, K. (1988). Use of the ARCS motivation model in courseware design (Chapter 16). In Jonassen D. H. (Ed.), *Instructional designs for microcomputer courseware.* NJ: Lawrence Erlbaum Associates.

Kogo, C. & Suzuki, K. (2000). An analysis of the structure of course evaluation items based on ARCS motivation model (2). *International Conference on Computers in Education/International Conference on Computer-Assisted Instruction 2000,* Asia-Pacific Chapter of ACCE, Taipei, 1577-1578.

Lambert, J. (2007). *Digital storytelling cookbook.* Digital Diner Press. Retrieved October 18, 2013, from http://www.storycenter.org/cookbook.pdf

Plankis, B. & Hwang, S. (2010). Tapping student creativity and enthusiasm with digital storytelling in the K-12 science classroom: Guiding success stories and avoiding Hollywood. *Society for Information Technology & Teacher Education International Conference, 2010,* Association for the Advancement of Computing in Education, Chesapeake, VA. 2347-2354.

Robin, B. (2006). *The educational uses of digital storytelling. Society for Information Technology & Teacher Education International Conference, 2006,* Association for the Advancement of Computing in Education, Chesapeake, VA. 709-716.

Sadik, A. (2008). Digital storytelling: A meaningful technology-integrated approach for engaged student learning. *Educational Technology Research and Development,* 56(4), 487-506.

Susono, H., Kagami, A., Ikawa, T. & Shimomura, T. (2010). Online videos that teach digital storytelling to Japanese students and teachers. *Educational Multimedia, Hypermedia and Telecommunications, 2010,* Association for the Advancement of Computing in Education, Chesapeake, VA. 3929-3931.

Suzuki, K., Nishibuchi, A., Yamamoto, M. & Keller, J.M. (2004). Development and evaluation of Website to check instructional design based on the ARCS Motivation Model. *Journal of the Japanese Society for Information and Systems in Education,* 2(1), 63-69.

Xu, Y., Park, H., & Baek, Y. (2011). A New Approach Toward Digital Storytelling: An Activity Focused on Writing Self efficacy in a Virtual Learning Environment. *Educational Technology & Society,* 14 (4), 181–191.

Yu, C. & Robin, B. (2010). An action research: When digital storytelling meets forensic science education in an online learning environment. *Society for Information Technology & Teacher Education International Conference, 2010,* Association for the Advancement of Computing in Education, Chesapeake, VA. 1234-1239.

Psychosocial and Cognitive Dimensions of the 'Self' within Pre-service Teachers' Reflective Blogs

Shaunna Smith
sfs36@txstate.edu

Rubén Garza
Texas State University, USA
ruben.garza2001@gmail.com

Abstract: This study provides support for the importance of addressing Deng & Yuen's (2011) three blogging behaviors (write, read, and comment) as well as the psychosocial and cognitive dimensions that participants explore as they authentically represent the 'self'. Participants included 23 pre-service teachers from different content areas enrolled in an undergraduate field-based education course at a large southwestern university. Within the context of pre-service teacher education and field-based experiences, these findings indicate that the use of reflective blogs can support the development of a community of practice that can transcend space by extending beyond the walls of the classroom and possibly transcend time by extending beyond graduation.

Introduction

Reflective practice is key to pre-service teachers' development of teacher identity and self-efficacy (Farrell, 2004). As Boody (2008) explains within a framework on teacher reflection, reflective practice entails "(a) retrospection, (b) problem solving, (c) critical reflection, or (d) reflection in action" (p. 298). This means that teachers must reflectively examine the personal lens that informs their notions about teaching and learning. Research on the use of technology to facilitate reflection highlights the affordances of networked communication systems, such as blogs, in their ability to create interactive communities of practice both within bounded private systems of classroom groups and boundless public communities (Blau, Mor, & Neuthal, 2012; Luehmann, 2008). In order for reflection to be deemed authentic, Sakr (2012) points out the need to explore the relationships between the subjectivities of text, 'self', and technology suggesting that using technology to engage in reflective writing should focus on honesty (accurate self-representation) rather than the superficialities of an edited "public self" (p. 121).

Therefore, the researchers explored the participants' blog communications to uncover the presentation of 'self' within the psychosocial dimensions (self-expression, social connection, and social interaction) and cognitive dimensions (self-reflection, reflection triggered by reading, and reflective dialogue) amongst a group of secondary pre-service teachers.

A Framework for Facilitating Reflection through Blogging

This case study is guided by Deng and Yuen's (2011) framework for the educational affordances of blogs. The framework highlights the affordances of networked blogging technology within pre-service teacher experiences and courses to facilitate both cognitive and social/psychosocial development. Based on a constructivist model that emphasizes the impact of social interactions on individual learning (Jonassen, Davidson, Collins, Campbell, & Haag, 1995), the framework was originally composed of two major blogging behaviors: 1) individual *writing* generates self-expression which spawns self-reflection, and 2) community-based *commenting* generates social interaction which inspires reflective dialogue.

Through empirical research of multiple groups, Deng and Yuen updated their framework to emphasize that there is an additional blogging behavior in which the act of *reading* posts and comments generates a social connection that creates individual reflection (see Figure 1).

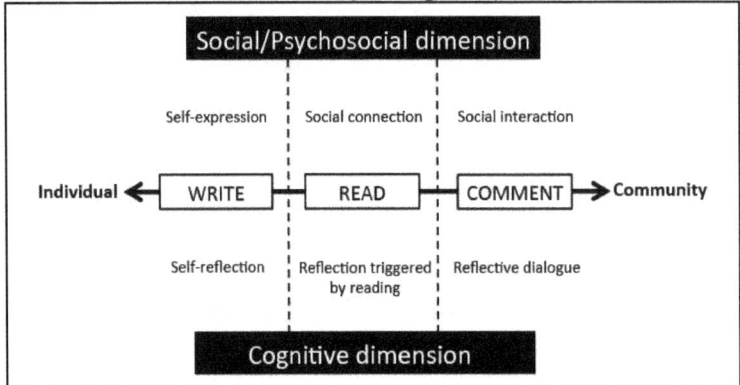

Figure 1. Deng and Yuen's "new framework for the educational affordances of blogs" (2011, p. 450).

Based upon this framework, pre-service teachers can engage in three blogging behaviors, 1) write, 2) read, and/or 3) comment that result in a reflective experience that resides along a continuum that ranges from an individual level to a community level.

Blogging for Enhanced Learning

Although not new, Blogs consist of a socially reflective networked capability that allows users to communicate using multimodal texts. Blogs can promote the co-construction of knowledge (Du & Wagner, 2007; Oravec, 2003), create opportunity for peers to provide emotional and informational support to one another across time and space; (Deng & Yuen, 2011; Hall & Davison, 2007), and promote a reflective environment (Hourigan & Murray, 2010). Blogging technology allows students to personalize their own communication space while simultaneously providing the teacher with a digital trail of all interaction.

Despite the aforementioned benefits, some empirical evidence also suggests that blogging cannot consistently promote individual reflective thinking (Xie, Ke, & Sharma, 2008). However, other researchers agree that the ability to use blogs to generate authentic reflective conversation through peer comments and feedback is directly related to the level of facilitation from the teacher (Hall & Davison, 2007; Kerawalla, Minocha, Kirkup & Conole, 2009; Miller & Williams, 2013). In addition, the community of practice will not be developed if students do not actively participate in the conversation. Advocating for the need to examine the presentation of 'self', Sakr (2012) notes that,

> analyzing multiple texts created by an individual in diverse modalities and media (textual life histories) will enable meaningful comparisons. It is through such comparisons that we will develop a genuine sense of the psychological and cultural changes that occur as a result of new technologies in education, and knowledge of the incremental mechanisms that underlie such changes. (p. 122)

While the related literature calls for studying ways in which blogging can promote teachers' critical thinking about their own practice, this study examined the role that networked blogging technology played in the psychosocial and cognitive dimensions of the 'self' within pre-service teachers' reflective blogs.

Methodology

As part of another study that examined preservice teachers' pedagogical growth through reflective practice, this mixed methods study quantitized the qualitative data in order to identify the depth of the qualitative patterns of behaviors amongst the participants (Sandelowski, Voils, & Knafl, 2009). By assembling instances and frequencies of each behavior, the researchers were able to visualize the impact of the networked blogging technology functions and technical capabilities. Martin (2004) supports the use of quantitizing narrative data in cases such as this because "counting is a process of individuating. We must be able to actively delineate and agree where one (something) ends and another begins (p. 925)." As a means of individuating the patterns of behavior, this case study was guided by the following question: In what ways did the functionality of the blogging technology contribute to the development of a community of practice within a pre-service teacher course?

Participants

Participants included 23 secondary pre-service teachers, 18 females (1 African American, 1 Latina, and 15 White) and 5 males (3 Latinos and 2 White) from different content areas enrolled in an undergraduate field-based education course at a large southwestern university. The participants attended class at the high school site on Tuesdays and Thursdays, 8 AM – 3:30 PM, and received instruction half the time and collaborated with a cooperating teacher the other half. Purposeful and convenience sampling (Gall, Borg, & Gall, 1996) were used to identify the participants.

Data Collection and Procedures

Data for this study, approved by the university's IRB, were gathered for 13 weeks. The participants created their blog during the first week of school with guided practice and received instructions for posting their weekly reflections during the semester. Blogs were shared only with the field-based professor and classmates enrolled in the course. Hall and Davison (2007) acknowledged that blogs are most effective for reflection if the teacher facilitates the blogging process by providing proper communication guidelines as well as continuously modeling reflective comments to support student reflection and to challenge their thinking. Therefore, participants were asked to answer reflective prompts provided by the professor, which included a scaffolded approach to support reflective writing about their course learning and field-based experiences. Additionally, the participants were asked to post a comment on at least one different classmate's blog each week, in which they provided constructive acknowledgement of specific items written within the post and added a personal reflection about a similar concept.

Data Analysis

This case study used qualitative data reduction strategies in order to identify themes through individual categorization and interpretation of the data (Marshall & Rossman, 1995). The first phase of data analysis was completed independently by the two researchers, which involved the use of open codes to inductively develop categorical themes that organized participants' frequently used words and responses (Strauss & Corbin, 1998). The second phase of data analysis involved the researchers' joint analysis and comparison of the initial codes, which resulted in the collaborative organization of the blog posts and comments within Deng and Yuen's (2011) three categorical blogging behaviors: 1) write, 2) read, and 3) comment. The data was then quantitized (Sandelowski, Voils, & Knafl, 2009), to determine frequencies of each behavior and plotted as data points to determine patterns between instances that aligned within the psychosocial domain and instances that aligned within the cognitive domain. Alignment within the psychosocial domain consisted of instances that emphasized social components and did not directly link to a discussion of course content. Alignment within the cognitive domain consisted of instances that emphasized reflective components with a direct link to a discussion of course content.

Findings

The very nature of blogs implies a social element in which users express ideas online and shared with the Internet-enabled world (Deng & Yuen, 2011). The added component of a commenting feature allows users to engage in dialogue as they share ideas and perspectives about various topics. Findings from this study shed light on how the use of this communicative networked technology facilitated out-of-class discussion of the 'self' to develop a stronger community of practice possessing both social components of the psychosocial dimensions and reflective learning components of the cognitive dimensions. Using these two dimensions as a guide, the participants' uses of the blogging technology functionality are juxtaposed within each categorical behavior, including a) writing: psychosocial self-expression vs. cognitive self-reflection, b) reading: psychosocial social connection vs. cognitive reflection triggered by reading, and c) commenting: psychosocial social interaction vs. cognitive reflective dialogue.

Representation of Authentic 'Self'

Sakr (2012) states the importance of networked technologies to produce self-representational texts because "the text acts as a form of expression that, while of course reflecting intersubjectivity, is not purely an attempt to engage with others" (p.122). In this sense, self-representational writing involves the participant producing reflective writing should focus on honesty (authentic self-representation) rather than the superficialities of an edited "public self." For example, the following is an instance that would characterize honest and authentic self-representation:

David, (pseudonym), February 22, 2013 at 9:28am:
What did you learn about yourself this week?
On Thursday, I presented my warm up activity. I was confident enough to only glaze at the material. Little did I know, I would forget the material and look foolish in front of the class. I learned that I need to review the material before class. I am frustrated by my own confidence because I feel/looked real stupid in front of the class! Lesson Learned :)

David's example characterizes honest and authentic self-representation because most people would not feel comfortable admitting to looking foolish in front of their students. The experience definitely had an impact on David and perhaps served as a way to comfort peers as they dealt with their own mistakes. Another example provides an instance that would characterize an edited "public self" because it focuses on superficialities instead of authentic language:

Jessica, (pseudonym), February 22, 2013 at 6:48pm:
What did you learn about yourself this week?
I paid attention in class and took notes, when needed. I came prepared for the class and brought my laptop and any printed notes I thought I would need.

Contrasting David's and Jessica's responses to the same prompt on the same week, one can easily see the difference between authentic self-presentation of what he learned from an embarrassing experience and Jessica's superficial presentation of public self that merely recounts her basic actions and preparation. Figure 2 illustrates the increase in authentic instances of self-presentation within reflective blog posts over the course of 13 weeks. Clearly, not all of the 23 students communicated authentic self-presentation; however, there was a steady increase.

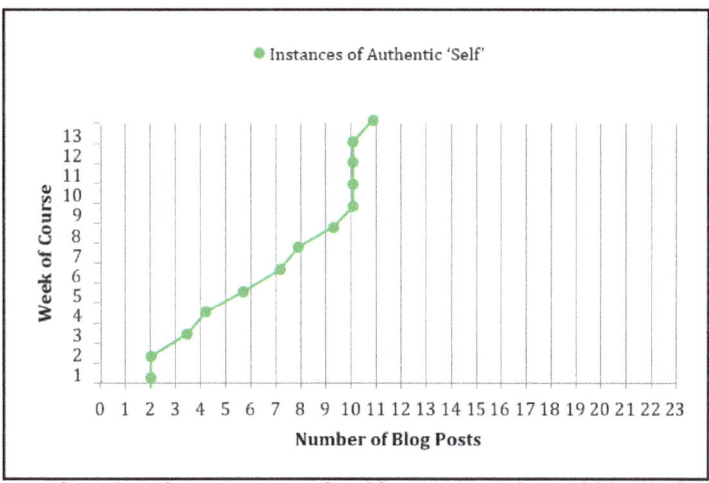

Figure 2. Increase of Authentic Instances of Self-representation within Reflective Blog Posts

Writing: Authentically Presenting the 'Self' through Psychosocial Self-expression vs. Cognitive Self-reflection

The writing behavior consists of participants' creating posts on their individual blogs. Posts that aligned with psychosocial self-expression primarily consisted of recounting the weekly events of their field-based experiences, whereas posts that aligned with cognitive self-reflection primarily consisted of making direct connections between events of their field-based experiences and reflecting on how those events will impact their future as a learner and a teacher.

The field-based professor's weekly reflective prompts required students to express their emotional state (psychosocial self-expression) and to reflect on their learning throughout the course and field-based experiences (cognitive self-reflection). Similar to the findings of Deng & Yuen (2011) the majority of the early posts recounted personal actions and events as opposed to reflectively discussing the implications for the future. Interestingly, the 'self' did not appear to be authentically presented until many weeks after the blogging experience had begun. Sakr (2012) noted that, "understood in this way, text-making is seen as a multi-faceted process involving various types of subjectivity: the self that is brought to the task, the self that is constructed as the text is made and the self that is read into the output by others (p. 120)." Figure 3 illustrates the growth in self-reflection over time by showing the increase in blog posts that contained cognitive self-reflection narrative components and instances that align with the notion of authentic self-presentation.

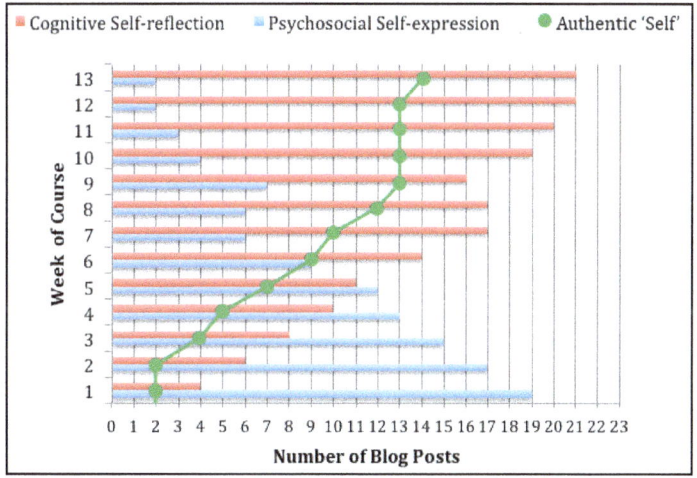

Figure 3. Pre-service Teachers' Growth In Self-Reflection Over Time

By week six, more participants began to post narratives that included personal reflections that linked their course material to actual experiences and postulated implications for their future practice. For example, in response to the prompt "What did you learn about yourself this week?" one participant articulated the following in a post:

Westin (pseudonym), February 12, 2013 at 3:33pm:
I learned that as a teacher I can't try to please these kids. As a person my fault is always trying to please people and get them to like me. This detracts from my personality and tends to have me be influenced by others rather than influencing them. As a teacher the last thing I can do is allow myself to try and "be cool" with my students.

This change in narrative construct suggests that participants began to feel comfortable enough with their peers to become seemingly vulnerable by sharing personalized reflections on their actual experiences. Dewey is often cited as the precursor of defining reflective thinking, which alludes to the vulnerability of negotiating with perplexity because "it involves (1) a state of doubt, hesitation, perplexity, mental difficulty, in which thinking originates, and (2) an act of searching, hunting, inquiring, to find material that will resolve the doubt, settle and dispose of the perplexity" (Dewey, 1933, p. 12). The participants' transition into generating more self-reflective posts also coincided with an increase in the number of posts that included honest representations of 'self'. This included discussing the meaning behind their actions, determining the implications of those actions on future experiences, all intertwined within raw narrative that was not encased in superficial language.

Reading: Psychosocial Social Connection vs. Cognitive Reflection Triggered by Reading

The reading behavior consists of participants' reading posts and comments from their peers' blogs. Though reading may be passive, it has a very powerful effect on participants because it "provides the missing link between posting and responding" (Deng & Yuen, 2011, p. 449). Categorization for the reading behavior reflected participants' explicitly communicating about their reading habits within their own posts and comments. Psychosocial social connections included posts that referred to social cues within peers' blogs to connect on a social level, whereas cognitive reflections were triggered by reading and consisted of specifically communicating how the reflection inspired or impacted the reader..

Many participants specifically indicated how they were impacted, either socially or cognitively, by a post or comment that they had read. The reading behavior of posts and comments was infinitely more difficult to track as compared to the other two behaviors; however, there were several instances in which participants used their narrative to express a psychosocial social connection or cognitively identified how their reflection was triggered by reading. Figure 4 illustrates how many individual narratives that mentioned reading behaviors align with the notion of authentic self-representation.

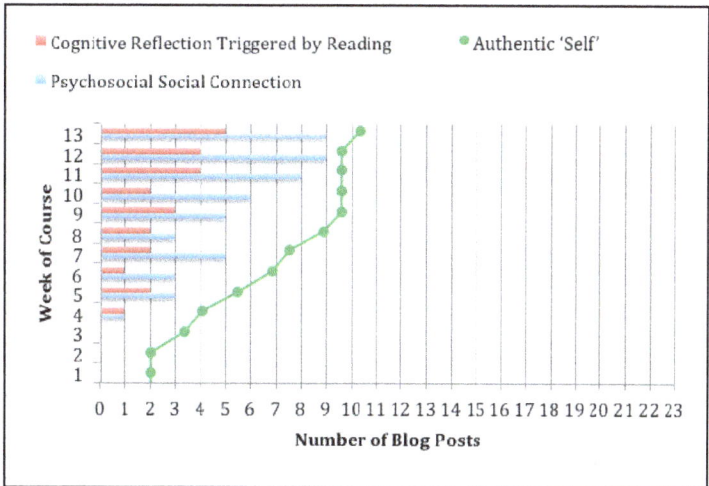
Figure 4. Pre-service Teachers' References to Reading Peers' Blogs Over Time

Through reading their peers' posts, students could compare with their own experiences and further contend with Dewey's notion of perplexity as they search for ways to make meaning, as reflected in this example of cognitive reflection triggered by reading within following communication exchange:

Margaret (pseudonym), February 28, 2013 at 6:11 PM:
When you mentioned that you had the opportunity to watch your CT teach the lesson and made you feel comfortable teaching for 3rd period, made me wish I had the opportunity to do that. With my CT, I do not get the opportunity to take notes, I am constantly active and working with the students on a lesson I do not know. But it got me thinking of finding ways I could observe and help at the same time.

Deborah (pseudonym), March 1, 2013 at 10:06 AM
I agree with Margaret! When you said you got to watch your lesson in action before you had to perform it yourself, I must admit I was jealous! That was a really great, practical and constructive idea because in order to teach the lesson effectively you have to see what the lesson looks like when it's taught effectively! I had not even considered this technique and thought my only option was to jump right in and see how I fared.

Though the number of reading behaviors are significantly lower than those recorded for the writing behavior, this communication exchange, acknowledges,that reading a peers' writing impacted many participants' reflections. This is noteworthy because it supports constructivist learning theories in that individual learning is impacted by the social setting around them. Within the context of developing a community of practice within a field-based experience course this finding is very important for "sustaining a sense of togetherness" and feeling like you are not alone in your journey (Deng & Yuen, 2011, p. 449).

Commenting: Psychosocial Social Interaction vs. Cognitive Reflective Dialogue

The commenting behavior consists of participants' exchanging communications by remarking on their peers' posts and comments. Comments that aligned with psychosocial social interaction primarily consisted of interactions that focused on enhancing social presence, whereas posts that aligned with cognitive reflective dialogue primarily consisted of engaging in reflective discourse of each other's perspectives as a learner and a teacher.

On the extreme of Deng & Yuen's (2011) framework lies the community end of the learning continuum. The comment functionality of the blogging technology allowed participants to purposefully engage with one another through psychosocial social interaction and cognitive reflective dialogue consisting of communicative exchanges. Similar to findings from studies by Hall and Davison (2007) and Deng and Yuen (2011), only a small percentage of first level comments embodied reflective dialogue attributes, indicating that comments were typically for social interaction purposes. Figure 5 illustrates the number of comments that contained narrative aligning with the psychosocial dimension and the cognitive dimension.

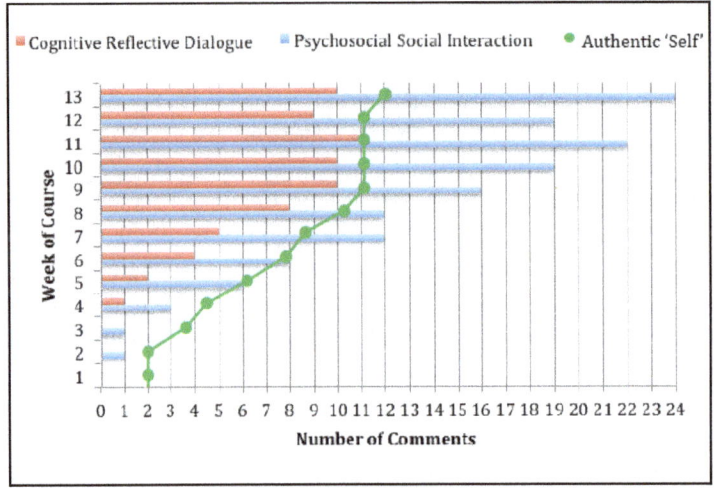

Figure 5. Pre-service Teachers' Comments Over Time

When juxtaposed with the instances of authentic 'self' the data shows interesting increases in the number of comments. First, in looking at week 9, after a significant number of participants began writing posts that authentically presented themselves, some participants commented on each other's blogs more than once (a total of 26 comments). This trend steadily increased over the following four weeks indicating that participants' vulnerable authenticity inspired richer dialogue, both for psychosocial social connections and cognitive reflective dialogue.

There were significantly more psychosocial comments than reflective dialogue comments, which is in part because of the very complex nature of reflective dialogue. As Hall and Davison (2007) noted, reflective dialogue within blogging environments is asymmetrical because the interaction of comments is driven by the verbal cues that make it easy or difficult to receive comments. An example of the use of open language within an exchange can be seen in this exchange by a participant who often posed questions to her peers throughout her posts:

> *Patsy (pseudonym), April 11, 2013 at 3:05 PM*
> That's good that you tried relating to your students and telling him about your own experiences. I feel like doing this makes people open up to each other more. And I can't believe this semester is almost over either!!! It went by SUPER fast!
>
> *Emma (pseudonym), April 12, 2013 at 3:42 PM*
> Thanks Passionate Patsy! :)

Emma's dedication to maintaining connections with her peers was evident both in her initial language throughout her posts and her consistent visits to her own blog to respond to peers' comments.

Discussion

Networked technologies have immense potential in educational settings because of their ability to be shared easily with teachers/professors and classmates. Blogs can be used to self-represent in an authentic and honest manner and also help peers going through similar experiences. Our findings are in concert with Deng & Yuen (2011) by showing the value of using blogs to encourage pre-service teachers to reflect on their authentic experiences, Within this socially-rich networked space, participants developed a collaborative community to support their transition from student to professional. Our findings also show a connection between authentic instances of 'self' (self-representation) and authentic reflection within participant blog narratives. One cannot truly reflect on his/her experiences and envision an impact on the future if one is not authentically representing the true 'self.'

Limitations

While the findings from our study add to the extant literature on pre-service teachers' representation of the 'self' through reflective dialogue, caution should be taken when generalizing the conclusions from this study due to the small sample size and the gathering of data from one secondary undergraduate field-based cohort during one semester. Pre-service teachers' field-based experiences at other universities and geographical areas may generate different perspectives than those reported here. Although all pre-service teachers blogged weekly responding to structured prompts, the attachment of a grade might have influenced participation. Perhaps a different set of structured prompts might have elicited different representations of the 'self.' Further research could examine the nature of reflective thinking without a grade attached to the task.

Conclusion

In line with findings from Deng and Yuen (2011) this study provides support for the importance of addressing the three blogging behaviors (write, read, and comment) as well as the psychosocial and cognitive dimensions that participants explored as they represented themselves emotionally and socially. Similarly, Miller and Williams (2013) found that pre-service teachers who reflected about assigned readings and field experiences through reflective blogging, built community, developed a professional online identity, took ownership of their learning, and promoted reciprocity of responses. And though blogs are not a 'flashy' new technology, their networked capability can allow peers to authentically express the 'self' and reflect through their writing, read each other's blogs to connect socially and activate deeper reflection, and engage in social interaction and reflective dialogue through commenting features. Teacher educators should consider how to encourage pre-service teachers to express authentic representations of 'self' as a way to reflect more deeply about their professional practice. Within the context of pre-service teacher preparation and field-based experiences, the use of reflective blogs can support the development of a community of practice that can transcend space by extending beyond the walls of the classroom and possibly transcend time by extending beyond graduation.

References

Blau, I., Mor, N., & Neuthal, T. (2012). Interacting for learning: Digital portfolios for a learning community in a university course. *Learning Media And Technology*, *38*(3), 241-255.

Boody, R. M. (2008). Teacher reflection as teacher change, and teacher change as moral response. *Education*, *128*(3), 498-506).

Creswell, J.W. (2003). *Research design: Qualitative, quantitative, and mixed methods approaches* (2nd ed.). Thousand Oaks, CA: Sage.

Deng, L., & Yuen, A. H. K. (2011). Towards a framework for educational affordances of blogs. *Computers & Education*, *56*(2), 441–451.

Dewey, J. (1933). *How we think*. Lexington, MA: D. C. Heath and Company.

Du, H. S., & Wagner, C. (2007). Learning With Weblogs: Enhancing Cognitive and Social Knowledge Construction. *IEEE Transactions on Professional Communication*, *50*(1), 1–16.

Farrell, T. S. C. (2004). *Reflective practice in action*. Thousand Oaks, CA: Corwin Press.

Gall, M. D., Borg, W. R., & Gall, J. P. (1996). *Educational research: An introduction*. White Plains, NY: Longman.

Hall, H., & Davison, B. (2007). Social software as support in hybrid learning environments: The value of the blog as a tool for reflective learning and peer support. *Library & Information Science Research*, *29*(2), 163–187.

Hourigan, T., & Murray, L. (2010). Using Blogs to Help Language Students to Develop Reflective Learning Strategies: Towards a Pedagogical Framework. *Australasian Journal of Educational Technology*, *26*(2), 209–225.

Jonassen, D., Davidson, M., Collins, M., Campbell, J., & Haag, B. B. (1995). Constructivism and computer-mediated communication in distance education. *American Journal of Distance Education*, *9*(2), 7-26.

Kerawalla, L., Minocha, S., Kirkup, G., & Conole, G. (2009). An empirically grounded framework to guide blogging in higher education. *Journal of Computer Assisted Learning*, *25*(1), 31–42.

Luehmann, A. L. (2008). Using blogging in support of teacher professional identity development: A case study. *The Journal of the learning Sciences*, *17*, (3), 287-337.

Marshall, C. & Rossman, G. B. (1995). *Designing qualitative research*. Thousand Oaks, CA: Sage Publications.

Martin, A. (2004). Can't any body count? Counting as an epistemic theme in the history of human chromosomes. *Social Studies of Science*, 34, pp. 923-948.

Miller, W., & Williams, R. M. (2013). Pre-service teachers and blogs: An invitation to extended reflection and conversation. *Art Education*, *66*(3), 47-52.

Sakr, M. (2012). "Wrighting" the self: New technologies and textual subjectivities. *Learning, Media and Technology*, *37*(1), 119-123.

Sandelowski, M., Voils, C. I., & Knafl, G. (2009). On quantitizing. *Journal Of Mixed Methods Research*, *3*(3), 208-222.

Strauss, A., & Corbin, J. (1998). *Basics of qualitative research* (2nd ed.). Thousand Oaks, CA: Sage.

Xie, Y., Ke, F., & Sharma, P. (2008). The effect of peer feedback for blogging on college students' reflective learning processes. *The Internet and Higher Education*, *11*(1), 18–25.

Patterns of Mathematics Teachers' Characteristics and Beliefs about Computer Use in Education: A Cluster Analytic Approach

Onder KOKLU	Elizabeth Jakubowski	Tayfun SERVI	Jiajing Huang
Adiyaman University	Florida State University	Adiyaman University	Florida State University
Turkey	USA	Turkey	USA
okoklu@fsu.edu	emjakubowski@fsu.edu	tservi@fsu.edu	jh11x@my.fsu.edu

Abstract: The purpose of this study was to investigate the complex relationship between Turkish mathematics teachers' gender, computer experience, teaching experience, and beliefs about integrating computers in teaching mathematics. The participants were 312 secondary mathematics teachers from different regions in Turkey. Data were collected through the application of a 20-item beliefs scale and included background questions. A confirmatory factor analysis was applied as a data reduction method in order to confirm different factors in the scale. Then a cluster analysis was used to determine homogeneous and well discriminated classes of teachers with five clusters identified. Gender differences, as well as teaching experience differences, and the resulting five clusters were investigated by MANOVA. It was found that male teachers are more likely to have better computer experience than female teachers and expressed more positive beliefs about integrating computers in teaching. Among the most experienced teachers females presented more positive beliefs about integrating computers in teaching than males. It was also found that more computer experience was associated with positive beliefs on using computers in teaching. Finally it was found that more experienced mathematics teachers showed negative beliefs about integrating computers in teaching.

Introduction

Technology, computer technology in particular, has rapidly progressed and expanded in education as well as in every field of science (Tas, 2011). Paralleling this progress, applications of computer technology in education have gradually increased in Turkey (Koray, 2011). According to Johnson (1999), although there have been hundreds of research studies conducted to understand effects of technology on education, there is still limited understanding on effects of computer technology on different types of learning. Kinnaman (1995) indicated that developments in technology have an important role in creating more effective and richer teaching and learning environments in schools. Paralleling these viewpoints and emphasizing the role of technology in education, O'Donnell (1996) highlighted that views on learning, such as those of transmission and receiving knowledge, should be changed in this new era. Furthermore, one of the important roles of teachers should not be providing knowledge but rather guiding students in order for them to obtain knowledge by themselves.

It is claimed that beliefs are the best indicators of the decisions that individuals make during the course of everyday life (Bandura, 1986). Therefore, there has been an increasing interest in defining belief systems. According to Pajares (1992), the concept of belief first needs to be defined and clearly conceptualized and then research studies should be conducted to identify connections between an individual's belief structures and actions in any setting. Since then numerous research studies have been conducted to define the term belief in the area of education including investigations of prospective and practicing teachers' beliefs about teaching, learning, and assessment in education (e.g., Levitt, 2001; Mueller & Wood, 2012; Oliver & Koballa, 1992; Pajares, 1992).

According to social learning theory, teaching, like any other behavior, is mediated by personal beliefs and contextual and external dynamics (Bandura, 1986). Organizational and educational theorists have similarly argued that individual and organizational belief systems influence the ability of organizations and its people to learn (Pajares, 1992; Ramsden, 1992). In other words, clearly establishing one's beliefs about teaching could directly influence teaching practices. For instance, beliefs of teachers about students would influence how they design instruction, teach, react to student actions, assess student understanding, and engage in professional development.

Oliver and Koballa (1992) developed eight different belief definitions based on data gathered from surveys and interviews of selected teachers. After coding the data, categories regarding teachers' definitions for "belief" were generated as follows:

- Consider belief as a functional representation of knowledge,
- View belief as antecedents of attitude, motivation, and behavior,
- Equate belief with knowledge,
- Explain belief as the acceptance or rejection of a proposition,
- Describe belief as a relationship between object and attribute that a person holds true,
- Reflect a definition of belief as a vision oriented by an epistemic system,
- Define belief as personal convictions that may or may not be based on observation or local reasoning, and
- States a dictionary definition of belief.

Considering all the responses from educators it can be seen that there is no consensus on a valid definition of beliefs. Although researchers in this arena agreed that knowledge should be distinguished from belief (Pajares, 1992; Nespor, 1987), most of the prospective and practicing teachers, in their definitions, associate belief with knowledge or see it as a reflection of knowledge. In an unquestionable manner, beliefs are personal truths that are not affected by dissuasion (Pajares, 1992). On the other hand, Ennis, Cothran and Loftus (1997) argued that knowledge is more factual or practical in nature.

Hannaford (1988) claimed a positive relationship existed between teachers' beliefs about integrating computer technology in education and their beliefs about how children learn and their beliefs about learning theories. For example, Tondeur, et al (2008) found a strong relationship between constructivist and traditionalist beliefs and using computers in teaching.

On the other hand, some research studies (e.g., Novek, 1999; Laffey, & Musser, 1998) indicated that teachers' beliefs about using computers in education was directly related to the value given to using computers in education by teachers. These studies found that some teachers believed that since computer technology had negative effects on relationships and interactions between student and teacher, using these technologies in education wss pointless.

A common agreement in the literature is that teachers' beliefs impact both their perceptions and judgments, and that these in turn affect their behavior, practices, and actions in classrooms. Therefore, the purpose of this study was to develop a valid and reliable instrument in order to examine teachers' beliefs and practices in the context of mathematics education and to seek potential mediating belief factors influencing instruction. Based on the purpose of the study, the specific research questions were:

- What is the factorial structure of mathematics teachers' beliefs about using computer technology in mathematics classrooms? Specifically, what is the factorial structure of the following variables: Cognitive Beliefs, Instructional Beliefs, Motivational Beliefs and Beliefs about Social Interaction?
- What is the influence of demographical and biographical data on mathematics teachers' Cognitive Beliefs, Instructional Beliefs, Motivational Beliefs and Beliefs about Social Interaction?
- What is the interrelationship between belief variables?

Method

Subjects

The target population was in-service (practicing) mathematics teachers who were actively teaching in grades six through eight in Turkish middle schools. In order to increase reliability of the study, an effort was made to include in-service (practicing) mathematics teachers from different cities located in 7 different regions in Turkey. The study included a total of 312 in-service (practicing) mathematics teachers with 103 (32.7%) having 0-10 years of teaching experience (YE), 127 (40.7%) with 10-20 years, and 83 (26.6%) with more than 20 years. The distribution of participants in terms of "gender (G)" was 138 females (44.2%) and 174 males (55.8%). Participants were asked about their experience with computers. The distribution for "self-evaluation of computer experience (SECE)" was 84 (26.9%) reported having a "poor" experience with computers, 128 (41%) having a "fair" experience, and 100 (32.1%) having a good experience with computers.

Research Instrument

The instrument "TBCAIM" (Teachers' Beliefs about Computer Assisted Instruction in Mathematics) developed by Koklu (2012) was used to evaluate in-service mathematics teachers' beliefs about using computer technology in mathematics classrooms. Specifically, there were four underlying components (factors): Cognitive Beliefs (CB), Instructional Beliefs (IB), Motivational Beliefs (MB) and Beliefs about Social Interaction (BSI). Figure 1 shows the operational definitions of each component and sample items on the belief scale (Koklu, 2012).

Components (Factors)	Operational Definitions	Sample Items
Cognitive	Giving emphasis to value of computer assisted instruction in terms of cognitive development of students.	I believe that students learn abstract concepts better by computer assisted instruction in mathematics classrooms.
Instructional	Giving emphasis to value of computer assisted instruction in terms of instructional benefits.	I believe that computer assisted instruction make more mathematics content teachable through the use of student explorations.
Motivational	Giving emphasis to value of computer assisted instruction in terms of increasing motivation.	I believe that computer assisted instruction increases the level of student involvement.
Social Interaction	Giving emphasis to value of computer assisted instruction in terms of increasing social interaction.	I believe that computer assisted instruction constrains classroom discussions.

Figure 1. Operational definitions of factors of belief scale and sample items from TBCAIM

With 20 items on the instrument, mathematics teachers were asked to read each statement starting with the phrase "I believe that" and then indicate their level of agreement with each statement. Scale items were rated as "strongly agree", "agree", "undecided", "disagree" and "strongly disagree". Positive statements were rated from 5 to 1 starting with "strongly agree" choice, while negative statements were rated from 1 to 5 starting with "strongly agree" choice.

Data Analysis

Factor Analysis

As previously indicated, the TBCAIM inventory was comprised of four belief scales (Koklu, 2012). It was hypothesized that the TBCAIM had a four-factor structure, including the factors of "cognitive beliefs", "instructional beliefs", "motivational beliefs", and "beliefs about social interaction". Confirmatory factor analysis (CFA) techniques were performed for the purpose of confirming the hypothesized four-factor structure of the beliefs scale of the TBCAIM. Latent variables cannot be measured directly but rather must be represented by one or more observed variables. Therefore, a total of 20 continuous factor indicators, which were individual items in the TBCAIM instrument, referred to the observed factor indicators in the model.

Confirmatory factor analysis was conducted to confirm hypothesized factors in the scale. Kaiser-Meyer-Olkin Measure of Sampling (KMO) and Bartlett's Test of Sphericity tests were applied in order to ensure whether the sample size was acceptable or not and whether the data had multivariate normal distribution or not. As seen in Table 1, the KMO value (0.807) shows the sample size was acceptable; and Bartlett's Test of Sphericity was significant ($p < 0.05$), so the data had multivariate normal distribution. In light of the factor analysis, it was observed that items have been distributed under four factors which had eigenvalues greater than 1.00. Principle Component Analysis was used as an extraction method. The four factors that were extracted were identical to the four factors of the original TBCAIM study (Koklu, 2012). In the second phase of the confirmatory factor analysis, reliability of each subscale or each factor was computed with results provided in Table 2. Reliability analysis yielded satisfactory Cronbach's alpha values for each subscale.

Table 1. KMO and Bartlett's Test of Sphericity

Kaiser-Meyer-Olkin Measure of Sampling Adequacy		0.8074
Baerlett's Test of Sphercity	Approximately Chi-Square	2,235.359
	df	190
	Significance	0.000

Table 2. Reliability analysis of all subscales

	Cronbach's Alpha	Cronbach's Alpha Based on Standardized Items	N of Items
CB (Cognitive Beliefs)	0.745	0.749	5
IB (Instructional Beliefs)	0.755	0.760	6
MB (Motivational Beliefs)	0.812	0.816	6
BSI (Beliefs on Social Interaction)	0.682	0.686	3

Cluster Analysis

Cluster analysis was used to determine homogeneous and clearly discriminated classes of teachers. The results of the cluster analysis were used to confirm the results of the factor analysis and to enhance the depth of the analysis by developing more interpretable classes of the participants (mathematics teachers). The cluster analysis method used was the K-means method.

Following a careful examination of the clusters, it was hypothesized there would be a 5-cluster partition. Initial five clusters were formed by using a hierarchical cluster analysis (Ward criterion). Table 3 shows the distribution of teachers based on gender and years teaching experience within each cluster.

Table 3. Distribution of cases by gender and years of experience (YE) across clusters

	Cluster Number				
	1	2	3	4	5
% of Cases	23.4	22.5	19.2	20.5	14.4
% of Male in Cluster	77.0	36.6	46.2	47.7	73.9
% of Female in Cluster	23.0	63.4	53.8	52.3	26.1
% of 0-10 YE in Cluster	67.6	7.0	17.9	15.4	58.7
% of 10-20 YE in Cluster	25.7	32.4	62.5	53.8	32.6
% of 20+ YE in Cluster	6.7	60.6	19.6	30.8	8.7

In order to investigate differences between the five clusters, a multiple Analysis of Variance (MANOVA) was used with the five clusters variable used as the independent variable and five variables used in developing the clusters (SECE, CB, IB, MB, and BSI) as the dependent variables. The multivariate test resulted in statistically significant differences between the five clusters.

The statistical significance between the mean values of the five clusters was tested by using Tukey's pair-wise comparison test. From the five univariate tests that followed (one for each of the dependent variables), statistically significant differences were found between the mean values of the five clusters and each of the five dependent variables ($p < .001$). Table 4 provides the mean value for each cluster across each dependent variables. Self-evaluation of computer experience was based on a 3-point scale (poor, fair, or good) while the remaining four dependent variables were on a 5-point scale.

Table 4. Mean values for dependent variables

Factor Means	Cluster Number				
	1	2	3	4	5
SECE	2.77	1.48	2.02	1.85	2.41
CB	4.61	1.53	2.35	2.19	3.12
IB	4.72	1.67	2.92	2.21	3.95
MB	4.89	2.23	3.78	3.17	4.74
BSI	2.13	1.32	1.56	1.60	2.09

Both descriptive and graphical summaries of the clusters comparing self-evaluation of computer experience with belief factors (Figure 2) and mean values of dependent variables for each cluster (Figure 3) are given below.

Cluster	SECE	CB	IB	MB	BSI
1	Good	Strongly Positive	Strongly Positive	Strongly Positive	Negative
2	Poor	Strongly Negative	Strongly Negative	Negative	Strongly Negative
3	Fair	Negative	Neutral	Positive	Strongly Negative
4	Fair	Negative	Negative	Neutral	Strongly Negative
5	Good	Neutral	Positive	Strongly Positive	Negative

Figure 2. Cluster analysis summary including self-evaluation of computer experience

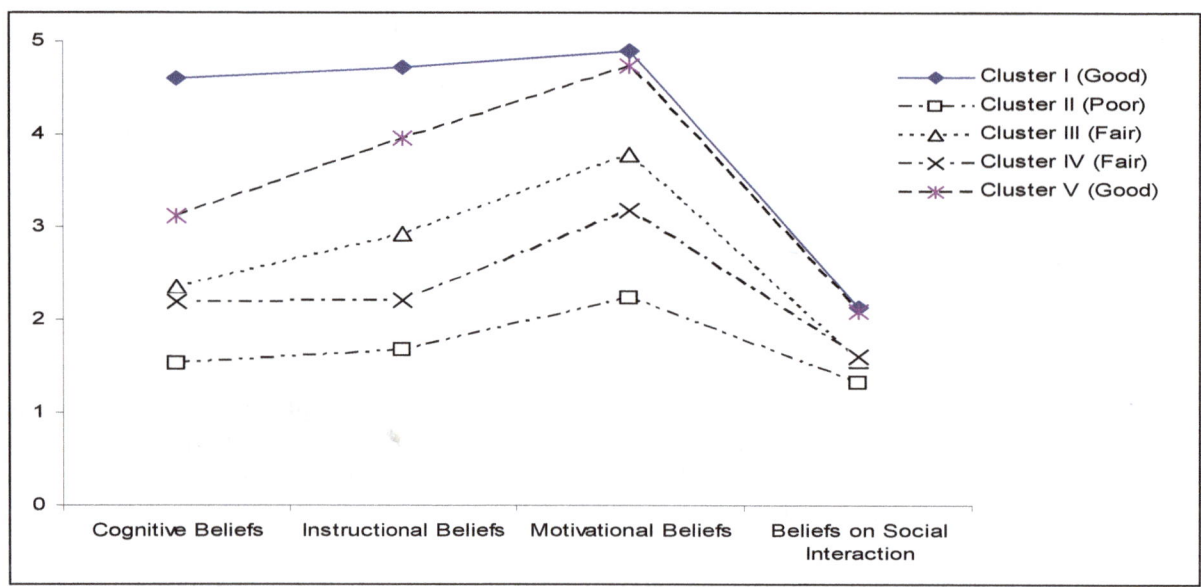

Figure 3. Graphically representation of mean values for each cluster across the four belief factors

Findings

From the tables and figures above the following are findings related to differences in "Gender" and "Years of Experience" for each of the resulting five clusters and their relation to "Self Evaluation of Computer Experience".

1. Cluster 1, with 23.4% of participants, consisted of mathematics teachers with good computer experience, strongly positive cognitive, instructional and motivational beliefs and negative beliefs on social interaction about using computers in mathematics classes. Cluster 1 type teachers were statistically significantly more likely to be males (77.0%) than females (23.0%). Cluster 1 type teachers were also statistically significantly more likely to have 0-10 years of experience (67.6%).
2. Cluster 2, with 22.5% of participants, consisted of mathematics teachers with poor computer experience, strongly negative cognitive and instructional beliefs, negative motivational beliefs and strongly negative beliefs on social interaction about using computers in mathematics classes. Cluster 2 type teachers were statistically significantly more likely to be females (63.4%) than males (36.6%). Cluster 2 type teachers were also statistically significantly more likely to have 20 and over years of experience (60.6%).
3. Cluster 3, with 19.2% of participants, consisted of mathematics teachers with fair computer experience, negative cognitive beliefs, neutral instructional beliefs, positive motivational beliefs and strongly negative beliefs on social interaction about using computers in mathematics classes. Cluster 3 type teachers were statistically significantly more likely to be females (53.8%) than males (46.2%). Cluster 3 type teachers were also statistically significantly more likely to have 10-20 and years of experience (62.5%).
4. Cluster 4, with 20.5% of participants, consisted of mathematics teachers with fair computer experience, negative cognitive and instructional beliefs, neutral motivational beliefs and strongly negative beliefs on social interaction about using computers in

mathematics classes. Cluster 4 type teachers were statistically significantly more likely to be females (52.3%) than males (47.7%). Cluster 4 type teachers were also statistically significantly more likely to have 10-20 and years of experience (53.8%).

5. Cluster 5, with 14.4% of participants, consisted of mathematics teachers with good computer experience, neutral cognitive beliefs, positive instructional beliefs, strongly positive motivational beliefs and negative beliefs on social interaction about using computers in mathematics classes. Cluster 5 type teachers were statistically significantly more likely to be males (73.9%) than females (26.1%). Cluster 5 type teachers were also statistically significantly more likely to have 0-10 years of experience (58.7%).

Discussion and Conclusions

The results from statistical analyses indicated teachers with good computer experience held positive beliefs on using computers in mathematics classes. It could be argued that excellence in computer experience yields more positive beliefs in using computers in mathematics classes.

Additionally, the analysis of data also revealed that less experienced teachers held more positive beliefs about using computer in mathematics classes than more experienced teachers. Likewise, some research studies (e.g., Aduwa-Ogiegbaen, 2009; Albirini, A., 2006; Mueller & Wood, 2012; Mueller, Wood, Willoughby, Ross & Specht, 2008; Yang & Huang, 2008) found a strong relationship between teachers' experience with computers and their beliefs about using computer technology in education. Since undergraduate programs in Colleges or Schools of Education in Turkey started to offer more courses related to educational technology and computer assisted instructions, it could be argued that less experienced teachers have had more opportunities with computer usage for educational purposes. Akpinar (2003) reported that courses related to educational technology and computer assisted instructions were initiated in 1999 by the effort of Turkish Higher Education Council (THEC). He also stated that many practicing teachers do not have sufficient training on how to use and integrate educational technology in their classroom instruction. Ertmer (2005) reported that according to US Department of Education survey data 85% of US teachers indicated that they feel well-prepared to use technology for educational purposes in their classrooms. On the other hand, one of the most important findings in this research was that less than 50% of the practicing teachers in Turkey expressed that they have had good experience with using computers. Therefore, extent of computer experience for educational purposes could be an intervening variable here yielding less experienced teachers holding more positive beliefs about using computer in mathematics classes than more experienced teachers. This result also shows that educational authorities should engage experienced teachers in more in-service trainings and workshops on effective use of computer technology in classrooms.

One of the most important findings of this research was that only 24% of the practicing mathematics teachers held positive beliefs regarding the integration of computers in terms of how that integration will lead to improved student understanding of mathematics concepts. Findings of the study revealed that this group consists of teachers with good computer experience and more likely to have less experience in teaching compared to the other groups. On the other hand, more than 60% of the practicing teachers held positive beliefs that integrating computers will improve students' motivation. In other words, although most of the teachers did not believe in the usefulness of computer technology in students' conceptual understanding of concepts, they mostly believe that computers are good motivators in educational settings. According to Blease and Cohen (1990), teachers who see themselves incapable and not well-prepared to use technology are reluctant to learn and use new technologies. In addition, they also indicated that some teachers may refuse to use new technologies in classrooms because they think that some students are more competent than them. Thus, this way of thinking may affect teacher beliefs on using computers in mathematics classes.

Moreover, results of the present study indicated male teachers were more likely to have had better computer experiences than female teachers. Therefore, male teachers with good computer experience held more positive beliefs about using computers in mathematics classes than female teachers. On the other hand, among the most experienced teachers the results showed that females held more positive beliefs about integrating computers in teaching than males.

Finally, the analysis of data clearly indicated that generally participants in all clusters held negative beliefs regarding the impact on social interaction. In other words, teachers generally thought that using computers in mathematics classes reduced or constrained classroom discussions and social interactions between students. Some research studies (e.g., Novek, 1999; Laffey & Musser, 1998) have indicated that teachers' beliefs about using computers in education were directly related to the value given to using computers in education by teachers. These researchers stated that some teachers believed that since computer technology has negative effects on relationships and interactions between student and teacher, using these technologies in education was pointless.

Implications

The findings of this present study are consistent with findings with earlier studies about beliefs and use of technology (e.g., Tondeur, Hermans, van Braak, & Valcke, 2008). As with previous studies, the consistency between stated beliefs and beliefs-in-action is an area to examine. While an educator might strongly agree with a belief regarding the use of computer technology how the use is actually implemented in the classroom could present a different picture (Haney, Lumpe, Czerniak, & Egan, 2002). Through qualitative research the practices of middle grades Turkish mathematics teachers should be observed to study the ways in which teachers are or are not using computer technology. Through observations and subsequent interviews inconsistencies between stated beliefs and teaching practices could be examined to better identify constraints preventing the belief from being actualized.

Case studies representative of the various clusters would provide information for teacher educators and those involved with professional development. Understanding why and how a teacher does (or does not) integrate computer technology in mathematics lessons could inform the process of teacher change. Positive experiences with computer technology opens the mind to considering and understanding how to use technology to facilitate meaningful learning whereby students are able to construct deep and connected mathematical knowledge and apply this to real situations.

As professional development is being designed for middle school mathematics teachers in Turkey, consideration should be given to providing meaningful opportunities for practicing teachers to explore integrating computer technology into teaching and learning experiences. Through purposeful activities teachers would be challenged to confront their beliefs and examine these in light of their engagement in experiences involving computer technology. Through these experiences teachers have opportunities to discuss how technology might be used to engage students in productive learning activities, to share best practices related to using technology to facilitate student learning, and to personally practice in safe environments and gain additional experience with the technology. These opportunities are consistent with the recommendations indicated by Etmer & Ottenbreit-Leftwich (2010) in order to facilitate teacher change regarding use of technology.

Finally, the positive results on three of the scales for teachers with less than 10 years would suggest that as teacher preparation programs continue to include a focus on technology integration into the curriculum for mathematics teachers more will enter the profession feeling comfortable with the use of computers in teaching. However, these programs should examine the opportunities preservice teachers have to consider best practices in using technology to engage students in communities of learning whereby a change in beliefs in the positive aspects of social interaction might be evident.

References

Aduwa-Ogiegbaen, S. (2009). Nigerian in-service teachers' self-assessment in core technology competence and their professional development needs in ICT. *Journal of Computing in Teacher Education, 26*(1), 17-28.

Akpinar, Y. (2003). Öğretmenlerin yeni bilgi teknolojileri kullanımında yükseköğretimin etkisi: İstanbul okulları örneği (The effect of higher education on teachers' use of new information technologies: A sample of Istanbul schools). *The Turkish Online Journal of Educational Technology – TOJET, 2*(11). ISSN: 1303-6521.

Albirini, A. (2006). Teachers' attitudes toward information and communication technologies: The case of Syrian EFL teachers. *Computers and Education, 47*, 373-398.

Bandura, A. (1986). *Social foundation of thought and action: A social cognitive theory.* Englewood Cliffs, Prentice-Hall, New Jersey, USA.

Blease, D. & Cohen, L. (1990). *Coping with computers: An ethnographic study in primary classes.* Paul Chapman Educational Publishing.

Ennis, C.D., Cothran, D.J., & Loftus, S.J. (1992). The influence of teachers' educational beliefs on their knowledge organization. *Journal of Research and Development in Education, 30*, 73–86.

Ertmer, P. A. (2005). Teacher pedagogical beliefs: The final frontier in our quest for technology integration? *Educational Technology Research and Development, 53*(4), 25–39.

Ertmer, P., & Ottenbreit-Leftwich, A. (2010). Teacher technology change: How knowledge, confidence, beliefs, and culture intersect. *Journal of Research on Technology in Education, 42*(3), 255-284.

Haney, J. J., Lumpe, A. T., Czerniak, C. M., & Egan, V. (2002). From beliefs to actions: The beliefs and actions of teachers implementing change. *Journal of Science Teacher Education, 13*, 171-187.

Hannaford, M.E. (1998). Teacher attitudes toward computer use in the classroom. Paper presented at the *Annual Meeting of the Pacific Northwest Research and Evaluation Conference of the Washington Educational Research Association.* Seattle, USA.

Johnson D. (1996). Evaluating the impact of technology: the less simple answer. From now on. *The Educational Technology Journal.* Retrieved from http://www.fno.org/jan96/reply.html.

Kinnaman, D.E. (1995). Cannibalism. Convergence and the mother of all networks. *Technology Learning, 16*, 86.

Koklu O. (2012). Developing a belief scale related to computer assisted instruction. *Energy Education Science and Technology Part B: Social and Educational Studies, 4*(3), 1741-1752.

Koray, O. (2011). The effectiveness of problem-based learning supported with computer simulations on academic performance about buoyancy. *Energy Education Science Technology Part B,3*, 293–304.

Laffey, J., & Musser, D. (1998). Attitudes of preservice teachers about using technology in teaching. *Journal of Technology Teacher Education, 6*, 223–241.

Levitt, K. (2001). An analysis of elementary teachers' beliefs regarding the teaching and learning of science. *Science Education, 86*, 1–22.

Mueller, J., & Wood, E. (2012). Patterns of beliefs, attitudes, and characteristics of teachers that influence computer integration. *Education Research International, 2012*, 1-13. doi:10.1155/2012/697357

Mueller, J., Wood, E., Willoughby, T., Ross C., & Specht, J. (2008). Identifying discriminating variables between teachers who fully integrate computers and teachers with limited integration. *Computers & Education, 51*, (40), 1523–1537.

Nespor, J. (1987). The role of beliefs in the practice of teaching. *Journal of Curriculum Studies, 19*, 317–328.

Novek, E.M. (1999). Do professors dream of electronic students? Faculty anxiety and the new information technologies. Paper presented at the *Eastern Communication Association Annual Meeting.* Charleston, WV, USA, (ED 429 582).

O'Donnell, J. (1996). The Digital Challenge. *Wilson Quarterly, 20*, 42–55.

Oliver, J.S., & Koballa, T. (1992). Science educators' use of the concept of belief. Paper presented at the meeting of the *National Association of Research in Science Teaching,* Boston, MA.

Pajares, M.F. (1992). Teacher beliefs and educational research: Cleaning up a messy construct. *Review of Educational Research, 62*, 307–332.

Ramsden, P. (1992). *Learning to teach in higher education.* Routledge, London.

Tas, E. (2011). A new web designed material approach on learning and assessment in science education. *Energy Education Science Technology Part B. 3*, 567–578.

Tondeur, J., Hermans, R., van Braak, J., & Valcke, M. (2008). Exploring the link between teachers' educational belief profiles and different types of computer use in the classroom. *Computers in Human Behavior, 24*(6), 2541–2553.

Yang, S. C. & Huang, Y. F. (2008). A study of high school English teachers' behavior, concerns and beliefs in integrating information technology into English instruction. *Computers in Human Behavior, 24*(3), 1085–1103.

Developing an Open Online Course for Teachers and Student Teachers

Louise Mifsud
louise.Mifsud@hioa.no

Tonje Hilde Giæver
tonje.h.giaever@hioa.no

Vibeke Bjarnø
Vibeke.Bjarno@hioa.no

Eli Gjølstad
Eli.Gjolstad@hioa.no

Irene Beyer -Log
irene-beyer.log@hioa.no

Faculty of Education,
Oslo and Akershus University, Norway

Abstract: In this paper, we describe and analyze the process of developing an open and flexible online course for teachers and student teachers. The aim of this course is to increase as well as formalize teachers' and student teachers' digital competence. This course is developed as both an open online learning resource as well as an accredited higher education course of 30 credits, and it will be delivered as an open online course. We apply activity theory (Engeström 1996, 1999; Jahreie 2010) as a theoretical framework to analyze the development of the course, and we take into consideration organizational and pedagogical activity systems. We address the question of how the different systems present influence the development of the goals—the course description and the course.

Introduction

Creating new courses in teacher education is crucial for teacher education to keep in tune with the needs of society and of national curricula. Furthermore, the creation of new courses for teacher education competes with existing courses and course compositions, giving rise to the need for the new course to legitimize itself. Therefore, it is important to understand the processes of developing new courses and course descriptions. To bypass some of these issues, one solution is to deliver courses for teachers as open online and flexible courses and resources. Delivering a course as an open and online one circumvents concerns with competing courses and content.

In this paper, we describe and analyze the process of developing an open and flexible online learning resource and course in digital competence for teaching and learning (Digital Skills for Teachers, 2013). This course is developed as both an open online learning resource as well as an accredited higher education course of 30 credits. The aim of this course is to formalize as well as increase teachers' and student teachers' digital competence. We address the question of how organizational and pedagogical issues influence the development of an open online course in digital competence for teachers and student teachers. In developing a course at the higher education level, certain tensions may arise between different interest groups with different goals. We argue that it is crucial to be aware of these tensions as these can be risk factors in goal attainment. Therefore, as a theoretical framework to analyze the development of the course, we have applied activity theory (Engeström 1996, 1999; Jahreie 2010) by taking into consideration organizational and pedagogical activity systems. Activity theory has its roots in the legacy of Vygotsky and Leontiev (Wertsch 1981), and it incorporates notions of intentionality, history, and mediation, among others. An activity theoretical approach allows for focusing on tensions and contradictions as well as mutually supportive possibilities. In this paper, we focus on tensions and contradictions, which, from an activity theoretical perspective, are the root of transformation.

We will first describe our activity theoretical approach to course development. Then we describe our methodological approach and discuss two of the activity systems present and analyze how these two systems influenced the development of the course.

An Activity Theoretical Approach to Understanding the Process of Course Development in Teacher Education

From an activity theoretical approach, activities are considered embedded in activity systems, as described in the activity triangle (see Figure 1). The activity triangle reveals the "social and material resources that are salient in activity" (Jahreie 2010, p. 47), and one activity can consist of two or more interacting activity systems. Each of the elements (tools, rules, division of labor) in the activity system, and consequently the activity system as a whole, undergoes continuous change and can be understood only through a combination of historical analysis and analyses of the situated actions. Benson, Lawler and Whitworth (2008) argue that in activity theory, contexts are conceived of as activity systems in which "human, technological and organizational elements are interrelated and largely inseparable" (p. 456), allowing for a focus on different levels of an organization. As such, applying an activity theoretical perspective to the development of a course at the higher education level turns the focus on the interrelations, internal contradictions, possibilities, challenges, tensions, and concerns that are present.

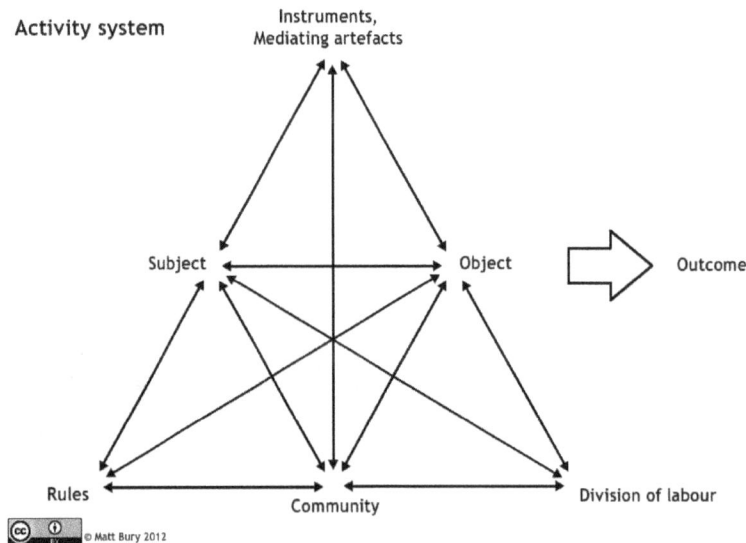

Figure 1: Model of activity system (Engeström 1987).
Image source: http://commons.wikimedia.org/wiki/File:Activity_system.png

In the case that we present in this paper, we found that the pedagogical, technological, and organizational systems are interrelated. In this paper, we focus on the pedagogical and organizational systems to highlight the underlying tensions and contradictions that exert force in the process of creating new courses in teacher education. An activity system can be seen in relation to other activity systems, which also consist of a community of different views, divisions of labor, and histories. In applying an activity theoretical approach, contradictions and tensions are viewed as fundamental to transformation.

In studying collaboration, tensions, and negotiations between activity systems, the notion of "boundary crossing" is often used (Jahreie 2010). Boundary crossings can be referred to as the "process of collective concept formation" (Engeström, Engeström & Kärkkäinen 1995, p.321). In the context of this study, boundary crossings occur when administrative staff (organizational system) and pedagogical faculty (pedagogical system) cross the systems to form a collective understanding of the aims of the course. The two systems are rooted in different histories, intentions, and cultures. However, they have a common aim: the outcome, in this case a course description and a course that gives teachers and student teachers digital competence. These two systems are also mutually dependent, and have to co-exist. We examine these two separately for analytical purposes.

Method

We analyze the process of creating a course description and a course. Data comprises of e-mail communication between administration staff and educational faculty members, comments on drafts of the course description by the administration staff, and records of discussions and meetings in the form of minutes between faculty and administration and between faculty and in-service teachers, comprising of notes from a period of two years. E-mail correspondence about the course was filed separately. Data was analyzed to look for patterns in two activity systems—the organizational and the pedagogical. In analyzing the data, we found patterns of tensions, contradictions, and challenges in the organizational and pedagogical systems. To present our findings, we will first present the process and then add our analysis to the process.

The Process

In initiating the process of creating a course in digital competence for teaching and learning (see Figure 2), we started by assessing the students' need to increase their digital literacy, where we found that the students' information and communication technology (ICT) knowledge was not homogenous. In addition, we saw that some students and teachers needed to improve their knowledge, while others needed to formalize their knowledge. Digital literacy is one of five basic skills in the Norwegian curriculum (2006) for compulsory and upper secondary schooling (compulsory schooling in Norway is from age 6–16). The five basic skills are reading, writing, numeracy, oral, and digital skills (*Framework for Basic Skills*, 2012). Digital skills have to be integrated in the different subjects taught in school. Consequently, this means that teachers and student teachers need to know how to use ICT to support teaching, teaching through ICT, as well as imparting digital literacy to their pupils. Digital literacy entails more than "tool literacy" or skills. It also includes what Tyner (1998) describes as "literacies of representation" (p. 92), which incorporates a deeper understanding beyond skills. The National Curriculum (2006) as well as the Framework for Basic Skills (2012) emphasize this. Therefore, the need to increase students' and teachers' competence in digital literacy can be described as being rooted in the notion of "what counts as knowledge" (Ludvigsen, 2011)—digital literacy is given place in the school curriculum, which consequently means that teachers need to know how to impart digital literacy to their students.

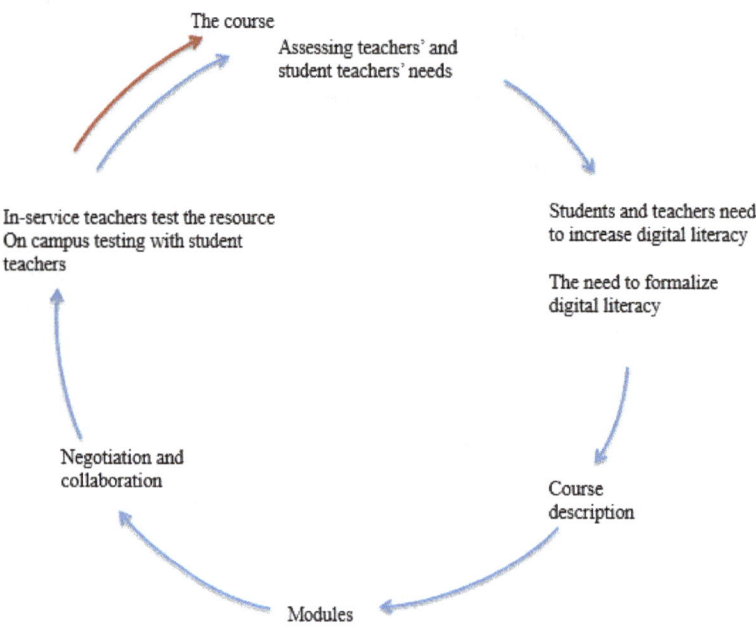

Figure 2: The process of creating a course

As we see in Figure 2, there was also the need to formalize digital literacy in the form of an accredited course. The historical background is necessary to understand the need for creating a new course. Information Technology (IT) has been offered as a subject at the Faculty of Education and International Studies at Oslo and Akershus University College since 1997, starting with an introductory course for student teachers. Courses at this time were separate from the rest of the subjects studied for the teaching degree. Students and faculty members did not see the need for taking the IT course. The issue was how to make ICT relevant to the students' studies as well as their future practice as teachers. In 2001 I(C)T was not offered as a separate course but integrated with the other subjects through ICT-related course requirements for both assignments and exams (Bjarnø 2008, Johannesen 2004). However, in 2010, a new teacher education degree was introduced. The previous degree covered grades 1 through 10. The new degree has two tracks: a primary and middle school track and a middle school and secondary school track. One of the main aims of the new degree is more subject specialization. One consequence is that students do not all take the same subjects, fewer subjects are compulsory, and there are few multidisciplinary projects. Students following the secondary school track take fewer subjects, but over a longer period of time and with more credits in the same subject. This consequently means that students do not all have the same platform, and ICT is now fragmented. This led to the need to formalize digital competence at the teacher education level. Therefore, the aims of developing a course in digital literacy were twofold—to increase teachers' digital competence and to formalize teachers' and student teachers' digital competence. In retrospect, we see two activity systems that both conflict and support each other and that both contributing toward the outcome—the course description and the course—the organizational system and the pedagogical system.

As a result of the design process, an online and flexible course in digital literacy was designed, containing six modules. The first module has a theoretical focus comprising learning theories applied to ICT, classroom management, cyber ethics, online safety, and assessment. The other five modules are a combination of practical skills and reflections on the use of digital tools in the classroom, where student reflection include an application of theory (module 1) and practice. The five practical modules take up topics such as digital texts and presentations, audio and video, Web 2.0 technologies, digital learning resources, and their assessment. Course requirements are in the form of articles, lesson plans, reports, and instructional videos, and the final assessment for students choosing to formalize their competence is an oral exam where the students have the option of sitting for the exam online.

We will now analyze each of the systems individually before turning to a discussion of how the different systems present influenced the development of the goal—the course and the course description.

Organizational System

We have defined the organizational system as comprising the administration, leaders, and management the Committee for Academic Affairs within the community of Teacher Education as well as the Curriculum for Teacher Education. These had an agenda ruled by the laws for higher education as well as the curriculum for teacher education, ensuring that laws and rules are followed. Several agents in this organizational system influenced the creation of the course, from merging institutes, changes in leadership, and ownership relations to the project and teaching loads to the new teacher-education curriculum (see Figure 3).

Tensions and Challenges

In teacher education, the didactic aspects are as important academic subjects. In addition, creating new courses for teacher education competes with existing courses and course compositions, where the need for the new course to legitimize itself also arises. Tensions arose when the community, in this case the faculty members at the Faculty of Education, did not see the need for increasing student teachers' digital literacy. Kennedy (1990) describes two extremes when it comes to choosing aims in vocational and professional education: to choose new topics and subjects that fulfill society's changing expectations of innovation and to give students the tools to become self-sufficient in attaining new knowledge. Faculty members tend to work in isolated groups focusing on their own subjects, which means that there is little time for collaboration and for the integration of ICT in course requirements. Furthermore, collaboration with the faculty members also depends on their attitudes toward the use of ICT in their subject. Departments at the university are divided according to subjects, and collaboration requires boundary crossing. At present, ICT is, to a certain extent, integrated within the teaching degree, through course requirements. However, the integration is not always incorporated in subjects' course descriptions and is sometimes based on individual collaboration among faculty members rather than collaboration at the organizational level (Engen & Øgrim 2009). Therefore, there is a need to formalize digital literacy competence.

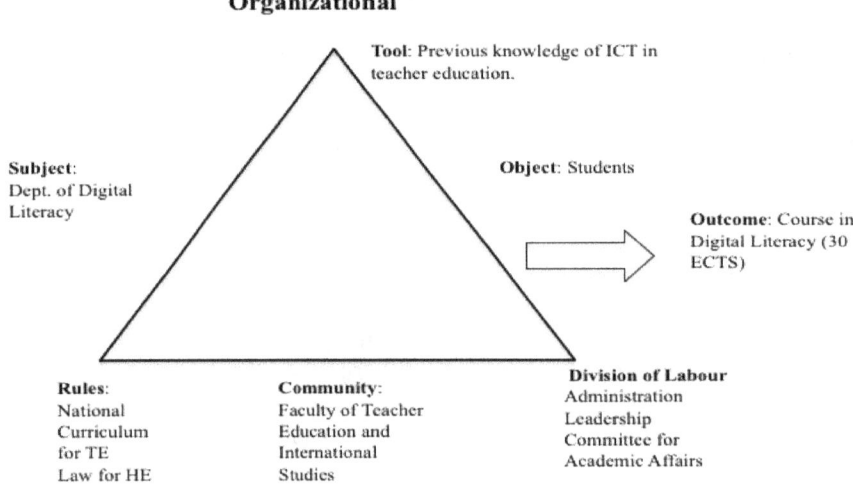

Figure 3: The Organizational System

In creating a new course, timing is essential to its acceptance. In the case of the course described in this paper, the timing could have been better for three reasons. First, the process of establishing the course started at the same time as a new teacher education course was introduced. We did not have a good overview of how the other subjects planned on integrating ICT. The national curriculum for teacher education was developed in parallel. Second, the guidelines from the Ministry of Education specified a different construction of teacher education. Owing to changes in the new curriculum, new subject compositions emerged and fewer subjects were compulsory. For example, students have to take a minimum of 60 credits in subjects such as English, Norwegian, and Mathematics to be qualified as teachers in the secondary school. This gives less room for subjects such as digital literacy, which is not classified directly as a "school subject" but a "school-related subject." "School subjects" are timetabled subjects in schools, such as Norwegian, English, Mathematics, and Social Science. ICT/digital literacy is not a timetabled subject in school, and it is not directly taught in class; instead, it is one of the five basic skills that have to be covered in all subjects at all levels. Third, two universities merged into one institution at the time that the process with the course description started. This resulted in faculty members being relocated and given new posts as well as a new leadership. The focus at the organizational level was on building a new organization.

Another issue that appeared was that the rules and regulations that govern courses offered at university did not always match. As faculty members, our aims did not always match the administration's rules, and they were a source of conflict and negotiation. The course design is online, open, and flexible. As a resource, we aimed to design the course so that users could use it both as a resource to enhance their classroom teaching, as well as an accredited course, formalizing their knowledge by sitting for the relevant exams. Exam guidelines and formats had to follow the organizational regulations as well as being adaptable to being taken online. In analyzing email correspondence between faculty and administrative members we see these are characterized by utterances such as "unfortunately there are major problems with what you suggest" and "my suggestions involve relatively major changes in the course descriptions" (our translation). These excerpts refer to flexibility in the course, such as taking modules in a non-chronological order, which was not acceptable from an administrative viewpoint, and the exam format, portfolio, and two exams were not acceptable. These tensions and challenges were experienced as obstacles in the process of designing the course, and tensions between the pedagogical and organizational system. In analyzing the data, we see that the organizational system conflicted with several of the aims, such as flexibility. We discuss the didactical and pedagogical aims further in the next section.

Pedagogical System

In creating a teacher education course, the didactics and pedagogy that come to the fore are important conceptual ideas that must be included. In creating the course, one of the aims was to make the course relevant for several groups. The course should be relevant to student teachers and in-service teachers as well as be in keeping with the directives of the National Curriculum for Compulsory Schooling (2006). The course has to meet the needs of teachers teaching through the first to the tenth grades, and the practical assignments had to be applicable through these grades as well. In-service teachers therefore tested the modules as distance learners whereas the students tested the modules on campus. Therefore, in this paper, we have defined the pedagogical system as comprising digital literacy specialists from the university. Furthermore, to meet the needs of the diverse groups that the course was aimed at, in-service teachers as well as student teachers tested the course modules during the development phase, being thus also encompassed in the pedagogical system.

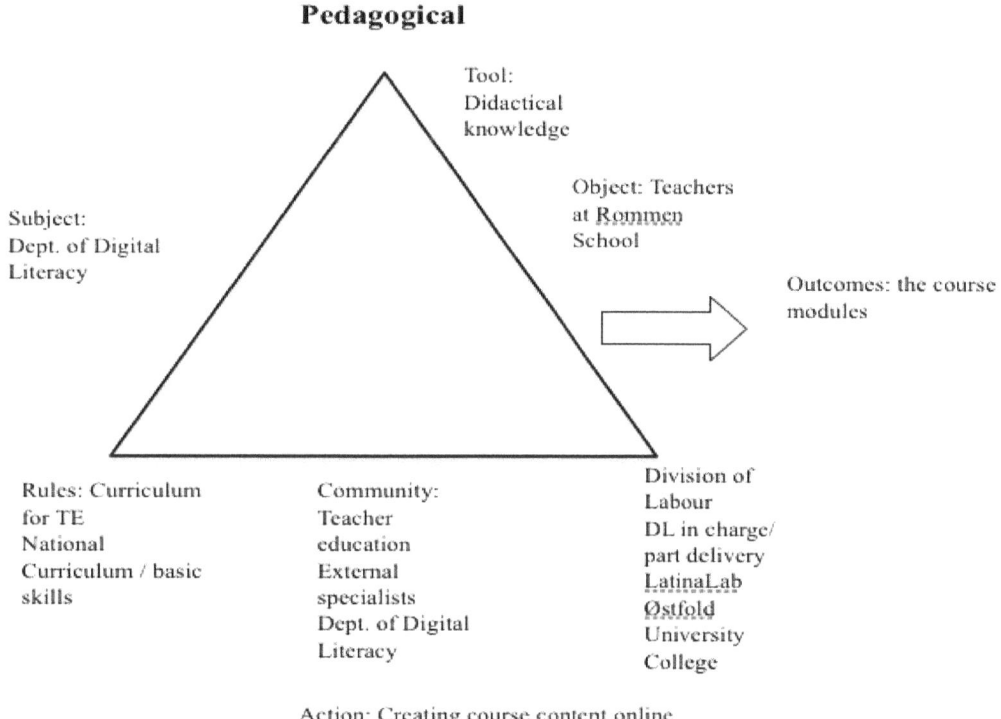

Figure 4: Pedagogical System

Tensions and Challenges

With regard to flexibility, the idea was for teachers to take the modules that were relevant for their classroom practice and therefore not in chronological order. From a pedagogical perspective, we wanted both external and internal students to take the modules in the order that they wanted so that they could reinforce their classroom practices and in this manner create a synergy between the course and their classroom practices and their digital literacy. In this way, they could "practice" their newfound knowledge directly in the classroom. As we pointed out earlier, student teachers in the new teacher education course do not take the same subjects, and being able to take the modules that fit according to the subjects that they are currently studying would have been ideal. In formalizing the course description, the administration body and national laws and directives for the university pointed out that the course could not be as flexible as we wished, and they required that students have to take the modules chronologically if they are to sit for two exams of 15 credits each. Our original course design was for module 1 to be taken first as this builds the theoretical foundations for the rest of the course, and the other five modules to be taken randomly according to the students' needs. The challenge was that to take an exam after 15 credits, the administrative exam body wanted the students to take modules 1–3 first and 4–6 second in a pre-determined plan. The need for flexibility was countered by administrative resistance from the organizational system, as we described in the previous section. This resistance gave way however over to a turning point through negotiation and crossed the boundaries of the two educational systems: the solution was to create one 30 credit exam, as this gives the student the flexibility to choose modules at random and according to their needs.

Designing the course such that teachers in all grades could benefit from it was recognized as a challenge. The in-service teachers pointed out, for example, that several of the assignments were not compatible with a first grade class. The challenge here was in being specific—what can teachers do with a blog or a wiki in social science—at the same time as being general to the point that not only social science teachers can use wikis or blogs in their classroom. In-service teachers' comments were taken heed of, and the course modules adapted according to their suggestions. A similar challenge emerged in designing instructional videos have to be short and to the point as well as pedagogical, giving ideas of how to use a tool in the classroom to both support teaching and impart digital literacy to the pupils at all levels. The latter challenges describe challenges within the system, rather than tensions with the organizational system.

In the next section, we discuss these two systems and juxtapose the issues that we have taken up and how the interaction between the two systems influenced the course design and course description.

Concluding Reflections

Teacher education should reflect society's need; the teacher education of two decades ago is not identical to the one offered today and "what counts as knowledge" (Ludvigsen 2011) for today's schools is not identical with what counted as knowledge two decades ago. Furthermore, teacher education needs to educate teachers to be self-sufficient in gaining new knowledge and literacies after they have qualified. Yet, in defining new knowledge areas or subjects to be studied at the higher education level involves negotiation and crossing boundaries between different activity systems. Designing new areas of knowledge in a different medium, such as an open online course, can present tensions such as financial and technological. However, the influence of technological and financial systems is on a different level from the pedagogical and the organizational systems, which we have described above.

Within the pedagogical system several challenges concerns were revealed in the process of designing the course. Creating content that is specific enough to be meaningful as well as broad enough to cater for the groups within school was one of them. At the same time it was important that content was adaptable in terms of using it in different subjects at school. Another challenge was creating a course that was flexible in the sense that teachers could choose which modules to focus on depending on their current classroom situation.

From the organizational system we argue that the main challenges are the need to collaborate on a system level more than based on personal relations. The timing is also a crucial element that needs to be taken into account. Rules for exams can be experienced as a hindrance to aims of flexibility. Flexibility in terms of approaching the course content in a non-chronological order was also a bone of contention between the two systems. From the pedagogical system, a chronological approach to the course gives the course predictability both in terms of student progression and in terms of facilitating for collaboration between students. In negotiating between these two, crossing boundaries between the two systems, led to a mutually supportive outcome.

In this paper, the negotiations between the two systems can be summed up in Figure 5. This figure illustrates the tensions and challenges between the two systems: the pedagogical and the organizational. While the pedagogical system is concerned with creating an online course for teachers and student teachers that is flexible, where a synergy effect can be drawn from teachers' work in the schools, the organizational system is concerned with upholding the university's rules for course descriptions and examinations. However, it is also obvious that these two systems are mutually dependent, and part of the larger activity system: the teacher education activity system.

The course that we describe in this paper aims at giving students and teachers the necessary tools to increase digital competence to teach their current and future pupils as well as having tools to prepare and evaluate their teaching.
The tensions and challenges described and discussed in this paper raise the issue of the need for different activity systems within a larger system to collaborate through negotiations and boundary crossings on mutual outcomes. Boundary crossings are viewed as necessary in order to achieve collaboration and a successful outcome. The organizational system challenged and conflicted with the aims of the pedagogical system, and it is through boundary crossings that negotiation is achieved to result in a course description that fulfills university requirements with regard to regulations and that is flexible and online and contributes toward renewing knowledge.

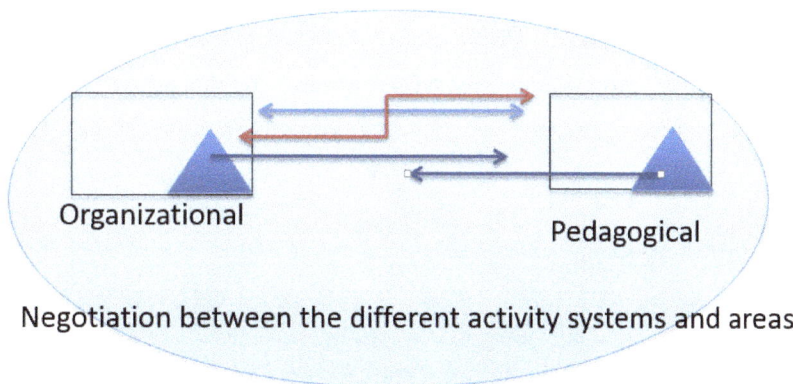

Figure 5: Negotiation and collaboration

Acknowledgements

The resource is financially supported by Norgesuniversitet (http://norgesuniversitetet.no). We would like to thank the anonymous reviewer for constructive comments.

References

Benson, A., Lawler, C., & Whitworth, A. (2008). Rules, roles and tools: Activity theory and the comparative study of e-learning. *British Journal of Educational Technology*, 39 (3), 456-467.

Bjarnø, V. (2008). *Oslomodellen: Integrering av IKT i allmennlærerutdanninga med vekt på flerfagsdidaktikk.* Oslo: HiO-rapport nr. 8.

Digital Skills for Teachers (2013). Course description. Oslo and Akershus University College of Applied Sciences. Retrieved from http://digitalkompetanse.hio.no/larer/emneplan.html (15 May 2014).

Engen, B. K., & Øgrim, L. (2009). Integrating ICT without throwing the baby out with the bathwater. In: *Proceedings of World Conference on E-Learning in Corporate, Government, Healthcare, and Higher Education (E-Learn 2009)*. Association for the Advancement of Computing in Education.

Engeström, Y., Engeström, R., & Kärkkäinen, M. (1995). Polycontextuality and boundary crossing in expert cognition: Learning and problem solving in complex work activities. *Learning and Instruction*, 5, 319-336.

Engström, Y. (1996). Developmental work research as educational research. Looking ten years back and into the zone of proximal development. *Nordisk pedagogikk*, 16 (3).

Engeström, Y., Miettinen, R., & Punamäki-Gitai, R.-L. (Eds.). (1999). *Perspectives on activity theory*. Cambridge: Cambridge University Press.

Framework for Basic Skills. (2012). Directorate of Education. Retrieved from http://www.udir.no/PageFiles/66463/FRAMEWORK_FOR_BASIC_SKILLS.pdf?epslanguage=no. (15 May 2014).

Jahreie, C. F. (2010). *Learning to teach: An activity theoretical study of student teachers' participation trajectories across boundaries.* University of Oslo, Oslo.

Johannesen, M. (2000). Et gløtt inn i klasserommet på IT-seksjonen. Tilrettelegging for åpen og fleksibel læring. *Norsk pedagogisk tidsskrift* Volume 2/3. pp. 185-194.

Kennedy M.M. (1990). *Choosing a goal for professional education.* In Housten, W. R., Haberman, M., Sikula, J. (Eds.) *Handbook of research in teacher education*, 813-825. NY, London: Macmillan Publ. Co.

Kunnskapsdepartementet. (2006). *Kunnskapsløftet [National Curriculum of Norway]*. Retrieved from http://www.udir.no/Lareplaner/. (15 May 2014).

Ludvigsen, S. (2011). What counts as knowledge: Learning to use categories in computer environments. Learning, Media and Technology. DOI:10.1080/17439884.2011.573149.

Tyner, K. (1998). *Literacy in a digital world: Teaching and learning in the age of information.* Mahwah, N.J.: Lawrence Erlbaum.

Wertsch, J. V. (1981). *The concept of activity in Soviet psychology.* Armonk, N.Y.: M.E. Sharpe.

Guiding Preservice Teacher Candidates to Implement Student-Centered Applications of Technology in the Classroom

Christine J. Anderson
Western Illinois University, USA
cj-anderson2@wiu.edu

Laura Kieran
Drake University, USA
Laura.Kieran@drake.edu

Abstract: The problem examined in this study was how to increase teacher candidates' implementation of student-centered technology applications in their lesson planning. Teacher candidates submitted two lesson plans for review. The researchers found a statistically significant difference in scores from the first to the second lesson for candidates in both classes. The areas in which candidates made the greatest gains were collaborative and constructive technology applications.

Introduction

Technology affects how we work, collaborate and communicate; yet the best practices for preparing teachers to meet the ever-changing digital world have not been clearly defined in higher education (Anderson, Beard, & Othman, 2011; Williams, Foulger, & Wetzel, 2009). Tapscott (2009), as quoted by Geist (2011) suggested that the college students of 2025 will be identified as the "mobile generation" stating "these students' fundamental view of learning, communicating and interacting will be very different from their educator's own experience" (Geist, 2011, p. 758). The demand and preference for technological instructional strategies has been increasing, particularly as a scaffold for exceptional learners (Cornell, 1999; Ikpeze, 2007; Rapp, 2005; Smith & Robinson, 2003). Therefore, it has become essential that teacher educators effectively integrate technology into the assignments and instructional practices of future teachers in order to adequately prepare them to teach in the 21st century and serve the growing population of diverse learners (Anderson et al., 2011; Fleming, Motamedi, & May, 2007; Williams, et al., 2009).

Pre-service Teachers

Researchers have suggested that teacher candidates participate in technology-based assignments and use technology in order to enhance their participation and performance (Anderson et al., 2011; Blackbourn et. al., 2008; Fleming, et al., 2007; Honigsfeld, Giouroukakis, Cohan, & Walsh, 2009). According to the International Society for Technology in Education (ISTE) standards teachers must be prepared to effectively and efficiently incorporate technology into daily instructional practice in order to create digital places of learning (ISTE, 2008). Research suggests a positive correlation between pre-service teachers' participation in hands-on computer activities, such as iPad tablets, with the development of their technology skills and perceived comfort level of those skills (Fleming et al., 2007). New teachers must be comfortable with technology (Harmon, n. d.); toward that end, McClanahan, Williams, Kennedy, and Tate (2012) completed a project using the iPad as the vehicle that allowed pre-service teachers to identify issues and concerns, collect data, analyze data, develop an action plan, and implement the plan.

Honigsfeld et al. (2009) outlined steps for the incorporation of technology into a Teachers of English to Speakers of Other Languages (TESOL) teacher preparation program with these major components: electronic assessment (individual and program assessment), technology-based course assignments; and web-based instruction and communication. The technology skills were integrated into the program to build the competency of the pre-service teachers to increase their technology skills in their own classrooms (Honigsfeld et al.). Although colleges do not have control over the level of access to technology at the field site, they can prepare students for the expectation of technology through course experiences (Dexter & Riedel, 2003).

Administrators' expectations of beginning teachers do not match the skills and experiences of the new teachers in the area of technology knowledge and experience (Albee, 2003). Children, K-12, have grown up in a digital world; mobile technology tools have become part of their daily lives in and out of the classroom; hence a need exists for educational systems to keep pace with current learning trends such as m-learning, instruction through mobile technology (Geist, 2011; Nedungadi & Raman, 2012; Peluso, 2012; Shuler 2009a). Rather than monitoring students' covert use of technology in the classroom; teachers should be guiding students to use the tools as a daily part of their learning. Bridging this gap requires that education faculty be adequately prepared to train the pre-service teachers through instruction, assignments and most importantly modeling the use of technology (Albee, 2003; Fleming et al, 2007; Honigsfeld et al., 2009).

Frequently, however, students have reported that they are not prepared to use technology in the classroom and that they have not experienced technology in their courses, yet modeling has been shown as a strong predictor of beginning teacher use of technology (Fleming et al., 2007). New teachers' preparation demands that their instructors practice m-learning, develop course experiences and construct evaluations that incorporate mobile devices (Geist, 2011). Pre-service teachers that used mobile devices reported great potential for increased interaction and engagement (Geist, 2011).

Instruction and Apps

K-12 classrooms use a variety of information and communication technology (ICT) such as web applications, internet connections, blogs, wikis, virtual literature circles, digital mapping, video conferencing and chats (Banister, 2010; McPherson, Wang, Hsue, & Tsuei, 2007). Although most children have been exposed to mobile devices, teachers cannot assume that all students have sufficient training for instructional practice in the classroom (Peluso, 2012). Likewise, pre-service teachers need authentic experiences, respective of diverse abilities, to prepare productive lessons that incorporate ICT resources; technology skills were inextricably connected to content and pedagogy (McPherson et al., 2007; Honigsfeld et al., 2009; Peluso, 2012). Additionally, teachers must be able to design lessons and assess the use of mobile devices with the understanding that technology itself does not have educational benefits (Peluso, 2012).

The educational value of mobile technology, such as cellular phones and tablets has yet to be determined, however their presence cannot be ignored (Melhuish & Falloon, 2010). While over three million iPads were sold in the first three months of production and although hundreds of universities (Rutgers, Georgia State University, University of Kentucky, etc.) have adopted tablets and mobile devices as part of their programs, even developing curriculum around the mobile device; yet rigorous research with peer-reviews have not validated the effectiveness of instruction with iPads and other mobile devices (Geist, 2011; Murphy, 2011). The Abilene Christina University completed a 3-year study with iPads that was uniformly positive, including scores that were 25% higher on questions regarding information than their paper-based peers and graduate students that reported an 85% satisfaction rate for online iPad-based coursework (Rose, 2011). Observations on the use of iPads in the classroom have favorably reviewed classroom interaction, convenience, and use as a teaching tool (Banister, 2010; Geist, 2011; Owen, 2011: Rose, 2011). Conversely, faculty and other teachers, consistently report that iPads have been a distraction during lectures or other similar formats (Geist, 2011). Additional concerns were raised at the 3rd International Conference on Education and Information Systems in 2005 concerning the digital divide due to: poverty, social exclusion, personal factors (age, gender or disability), education/skill gaps, and no access to the Internet (Masullo, Moreno, & Tsantis, 2005). The advantages that the mobile devices offer include such characteristics as: access to content (blending environments, situated learning, individualized, ubiquitous learning, self-publishing), productivity (executive skills), data integration, collaboration (peer-to-peer) and communication (teamwork, community, social interactivity, portability and affordability) (Melhuish & Fallon, 2010; Murphy, 2011). Owen (2011) reported immediate feedback and increased student engagement as specific benefits of instruction with iPads in the classroom.

Over 1 billion apps have been downloaded from the Apple App Store, a review of the characteristics divided by age, subject and price showed that nearly half, 47%, targeted preschool or elementary aged children

(Shuler, 2009b). In fact, 60% of the top 25 apps focus on toddler/preschool children (Shuler, 2009b). Mobile devices offer apps that serve a variety of purposes such as: a media tool for photos, music, movies and you tube; executive skills- notes, clock calculator, maps, weather' web applications and internet connections (Banister, 2010). Because of the impact on student learning, researchers recommend that producers develop Apps that address the potential in children's mobile learning and that parent groups monitor the growth of this industry (Shuler, 2009b).

The iPad has been promoted as an educational tool based on these factors: hands-on applications, ability to be customized, creation of interactive materials, ease of organization and delivery (Apple, n. d.). Researchers report that the iPad is a good multi-modal tool because it meets students at the current level increases motivation, engagement and success (Harmon, n. d.). A review of 25 handheld learning projects in the United States featured five elements: "anywhere, anytime" learning, low cost and accessibility for low-income communities, improved social interactions, match the learning environment, personalize the learning experience (Shuler, 2009a). Shuler (2009a) further reported that over 93% of children 6-9 years old live in a home with a cell phone while over 50% own their own portable video player and 30% have their own phone and the numbers continue to experience rapid growth. Harmon (n. d.) reported that some standardized assessments and students' self-reporting indicated that iPads increased student achievement in literacy. The challenge for educators is to insure that m-learning is integrated into effective, evidence-driven practices that enrich the educational environment (Melhuish & Falloon, 2010).

Assistive technology has long been used to enhance instruction for individuals with disabilities. Boyd (2011) called the iPad an educational 'equalizer' with examples of communication apps used on the iPad by Leuck Lehmann, an 18-year old quadriplegic with multiple disabilities. Similarly other schools have used iPads for individuals with physical limitations, as the touch screen is user friendly Boyd, 2011; Johnson, 2011). Children with ADHD have used the apps for executive skills (Boyd, 2011; Raggi & Chronis, 2006). Teachers have been encouraged to use tablets as an intervention for RTI enabling students to read and hear themselves read, improve comprehension with conspicuous strategies and use electronic graphic organizers (McClanahan et al., 2012). Tablets have also been used to differentiate instruction and apply a one-to-one component as with computer-aided instruction (CAI) (McClanahan et al., 2012). Warren County public schools in Kentucky purchased iPads and tables for students with autism to use for communication (Boyd, 2011). The use of CAI has shown to parallel that of peer and parent tutoring as it provided immediate feedback and necessitates active responding on the part of the student (Raggi & Chronis, 2006).

Even without wide-scale research-based evidence to show that iPads have an impact on students' learning, school districts continue to invest in iPads and other mobile devices for classroom use. Teacher candidates need to be prepared to effectively teach and engage students in learning using mobile devices. The researchers noted that when instructed to incorporate technology into their lessons, their teacher candidates frequently used the technology in teacher-centered means. Technology was most frequently used to provide students with directions or to deliver content to the students; rarely were students actively engaged with learning using technology. Therefore, the problem examined in this study was how to increase teacher candidates' implementation of student-centered technology applications in their lesson planning.

Method

Two classes of special education teacher candidates were provided with instruction on how to use technology in their lesson planning, including explicit explanations and examples of how to incorporate technology to develop their students' higher order thinking skills. The pre-service teachers in these courses were in their junior and senior years of the special education teacher preparation program. All of the teacher candidates in these classes were currently enrolled in a field placement. Candidates in one of the classes were in their fourth and final field placement before student teaching (7 pre-service teachers, 4 of whom participated in the study). Candidates in the other course were in their second field placement; in this placement the candidates' level of involvement shifts from primarily observing in the classroom setting, to planning mini-lessons to implement with the students in their field placement (14 pre-service teachers, all of whom participated in the study).

A variety of websites and apps were explicitly modeled for the teacher candidates over the first month of the course. Candidates had access to iPads in the classroom in 3 of the first 8 sessions of the course so that they could experience different levels of student engagement using the technology. The candidates were provided with a lesson plan format, which was similar to what had been used in their previous courses. As a class they brainstormed how to use technology tools to engage students in learning at different points of the lesson plan.

The teacher candidates in their second field placement were also given 6th grade English Language Arts Common Core standards and an historical fiction selection, *Pink and Say* to write their lessons. Candidates were encouraged to incorporate technology throughout their lessons, and to develop authentic, student-centered uses of technology in their lessons. The pre-service teachers in both courses were free to select the apps and websites they felt applied to their lessons. Although a variety of instructional methods were used to introduce the principles of technology integration, the Technology Integration Matrix (TIM) was intentionally withheld until after the first lesson plan was completed.

After the first lesson was written, students were provided with the TIM as an instructional guide to evaluate the degree of technology integration on multiple levels. The TIM was created by the Florida Center for Instructional Technology at the University of South Florida as a model for teachers to follow when integrating technology in the classroom in meaningful ways. The matrix was used to encourage candidates to consider technology integration across five learning characteristics: active, collaborative, constructive, authentic, and goal directed. The Florida Center for Instructional Technology created an online interactive matrix, through which teachers can view video examples of technology integration at each point the matrix. The Arizona K12 Center at Northern Arizona University adopted the TIM and created a printable version of the matrix; this was designed to help schools evaluate technology integration in the classroom. This PDF version of the Arizona TIM was provided to teacher candidates in both courses as a self-assessment tool to increase their student-centered use of technology in their lesson planning.

Teacher candidates submitted two lesson plans each scored with the TIM; the first lesson plan was created before the students were given the matrix, the second after the students had been given the matrix. Students enrolled in this course were active in their second field experience. In the first lesson plan the students were partnered as a means of scaffolding; lessons written after the initial submissions were developed independently. In both courses students received explicit instruction related to methods of incorporating student-centered technology in their lessons.

Each researcher independently rated the lessons in comparison to the Technology Integration Matrix. In order to quantify students' performance with the assignment, the matrix was treated as a scale of students' strength or weakness with technology integration. Each cell in the matrix was therefore assigned a numeric value, from entry-level technology use (1) to the transformative level of technology use (5). The researchers independently conducted a content analysis of the lesson plans submitted by the teacher candidates. The researchers' scores were then compared for each lesson and each category to establish inter-rater reliability. Students' mean scores were calculated and a paired samples t test was used to determine if there was a significant change in students' scores from lesson 1 to lesson 2.

Results

Teacher candidates submitted two lesson plans for review. The first lesson plan was submitted after 3 in-class sessions of explicit instruction on how to incorporate student-centered uses of technology in the classroom and a student-led in-class discussion of how to incorporate the technology tools that had been modeled for the candidates. The second lesson plan was reviewed after the candidates were introduced to the Technology Integration Matrix. Two raters independently scored the candidates' lesson plans using the Technology Integration Matrix. Scores were compared to evaluate consistency. Inter-reliability was calculated using a Pearson product moment correlation. The correlation coefficient for the independent raters was .860; which indicates a strong correlation between scores and a high degree of agreement between the raters. Fourteen of the 18 students who participated in the study increased their scores from the pre-assessment to the post-assessment conditions as evaluated by one or both raters.

Table 1
Lesson Plan Scores Before and After Introduction to the Technology Integration Matrix

	Rater 1		Rater 2	
	Pre	Post	Pre	Post
Mean	4.33	6.83	4.88	7.22
Standard Deviation	1.64	3.11	1.74	3.35
Paired Samples Test		.007*		.014**

Note: *Significant at $p < 0.01$ **Significant at $p < 0.05$

The researchers found a statistically significant difference in scores from the first to the second lesson, for candidates in both classes. The pre-service teachers were found to move from the entry level of their lesson planning to entry and adoption. In the first evaluated lesson plan, candidates had 48 instances of technology use at the entry level and 22 instances of technology use at the adoption level when evaluated with the Technology Integration Matrix. In their subsequent lessons, candidates had 55 instances of technology use at the entry level, 34 at the adoption level, and 5 at the adaptation level. The areas in which candidates made the greatest gains were collaborative and constructive technology applications.

The researchers also found that candidates in their final course before student teaching were more likely to indicate that technology in their secondary field placements limited their ability to create student-centered lessons because they did not have access to enough devices for students in their special education placement. Two candidates stated that although there was an iPad cart that could be checked out by teachers in their settings, their mentor teachers had informed them that the iPads were more often used by general education teachers, so they should not count on the availability of the technology for their lessons. One candidate was able to bring her class to the computer lab to implement student-centered technology uses in her lessons.

Discussion

Teacher candidates significantly improved in their lesson planning skills when provided with a rubric (TIM) as a guide for technology implementation. As we move forward with this research, we will continue to gather data regarding the impact of scaffolds and interventions with teacher candidates. Pre-service teachers will be prompted to view the video clips for the different levels of technology integration, as well as self-rate their lessons before turning them in. Candidates will also be prompted to set a goal of technology integration based on feedback they receive from their first lesson submission. It is anticipated that these additional requirements will increase students' scores again.

A strength of this study was the agreement between the raters when using the TIM as a rating tool. The matrix is clear and easy to use; thus establishing agreement on how to interpret the students' scores did not involve a lengthy process. A limitation of this study was the small sample size; this limits the generalizability of these results. In addition, as most universities, the population of preservice teachers majoring in special education represented a small number of students, therefore it was not possible to include a control group in the study. The researchers will expand on this study by continuing to examine candidates' lesson plans. Finally, improvements made by candidates in this study may have occurred due to uncontrolled variables such as the continued feedback and experience during the semester courses and practicum experiences. Candidates received feedback on their lessons related to other lesson plan requirements (use of academic language, cohesion between the selected standards, lesson objectives, and lesson assessment; student engagement, clarity of directions and instruction, etc.). However, candidates did not receive specific feedback on their technology integration or see their scores on the matrix until after their second lessons were collected.

Another strength of this study was that candidates in these courses were not currently enrolled in courses for instructional design incorporating technology. This helped to limit outside influences on the candidates levels of technology incorporation. They were concurrently enrolled in an elementary reading methods course in which they were not explicitly taught instructional strategies incorporating technology. Candidates may have been enrolled in other courses in which instruction and student engagement with technology was modeled, but it was not explicitly taught.

One weakness of this current study is that there was not a control group for comparison. Even though candidates did not have other courses in which there was explicit instruction of student-centered technologies, the more advanced use of student-centered technologies in their second lesson could have resulted from exposure to technology use in their other courses.

Researchers have made recommendations and cautions for mobile learning such as: invest in 'mobile kids', learn from other countries, develop learning interventions, plan for educational standards for the industry, eliminate classroom bans, promote situated learning, remove barriers between home, school, afterschool programs, reach out to disadvantaged socioeconomic groups, personalize education (Shuler, 2009a). In keeping with evidence-based practice, the development of instructional strategies based on using mobile devices builds an individualized instructional plan for students, without geographical limitations, and with built in data collection components (Melhuish & Falloon, 2010; Murphy, 2011).

The challenge for teacher education programs is how to best prepare pre-service teachers for professional growth and leadership in the digital age. Mobile devices will continue to exist and increase in number and capacity regardless of the resistance by faculty, preparation then becomes essential. This study examined the development of mobile learning with future special education teachers. Higher education programs must model and provide instruction on the use of modern technology that is an integral part of everyday life as tools for learning. Course instruction develops the knowledge base and provides experiences for mastering skills that will promote a more effective use of technology as an instructional tool.

Additional research is needed to determine the impact of technology instruction in students' methods classes. The researchers plan to examine the impact of 1:1 iPad adoptions at the university level on the incorporation of student-centered applications of technology in teacher candidates' assignments. The study will be expanded to examine additional related artifacts from candidates' assignments and candidates' perceptions of technology-based instruction in their classes.

References

Albee, J. (2003). A study of preservice teachers' technology skill prepardness and examples of how it can be increased. *Journal of Technology and Teacher Education, 11*(1), 53-71.

Anderson, C., Beard, M., & Bergstrand Othman, L. (2011). Pre-Service teacher survey and collaboration between the United States and Jordan. In M. Koehler & P. Mishra (Eds.), *Proceedings of Society for Information Technology & Teacher Education International Conference 2011* (2833-2840). Chesapeake, VA: AACE.

Apple Education-iPad makes the perfect learning companion. (n.d.). *Apple*. Retrieved October 4, 2013, from http://www.apple.com/education/ipad/

Banister, S. (2010). Integrating the iPod Touch in K-12 education: Visions and vices. *Computers in the Schools, 27*(2), 121-131.

Blackbourn, J. M., Fillingim, J. G., McCelland, S., Elrod, G., Franklin Medley, M. B., Kritsonis, M. A., & Ray, J. (2008). The use of warless technology to augment problem-based learning in special education preservice teachers. *Journal of Instructional Psychology, 35*(2), 169-176.

Boyd, A. W. (2011, September 11). Adapting to the iPad, called education's 'equalizer'. *USA Today*. Retrieved October 4, 2013, from http://usatoday30.usatoday.com/news/health/wellness/special-needs/story/2011-09-11/Adapting-to-the-iPad-called-educations-equalizer/50362426/1

Cornell, R. (1999). Paradigms for the new millennium: How professors will certainly change? *Educational Media International, 36*(2), 89-96.

Dexter, S., & Riedel, E. (2003). Why improving preservice teacher educational technology preparation must go beyond the college's walls. *Journal of Teacher Education, 54*(4), 334-346.

Florida Center for Instructional Technology (2011). *Technology Integration Matrix*. Retrieved from http://fcit.usf.edu/matrix/.

Fleming, L., Motamedi, V., & May, L. (2007). Predicting pre-service teacher competence in computer technology: Modeling and application in training environments. *Journal of Technology and Teacher Education, 15*(2), 207-231.

Geist, E. (2011). The game changer: Using iPads in college teacher education classes. *College Student Journal, 45*(4), 758-768.

Harmon, J. (n. d.) Unlocking literacy with iPad. Retrieved May 9, 2014 from http://www.throughstudentseyes.org/ipads/unlocking_literacy_with_ipad/ipads_files/unlocking_literacy_ipad.pdf

Honigsfeld, A. Giouroukakis, V., Cohan, A., & Walsh, M. (2009). Ten ways to incorporate technology into a TESOL teacher preparation program. *Contemporary issues in Technology and Teacher Education, 9*(2). Retrieved April 7, 2010 from http://www.citejournal.org/vol9/iss2/currenpractice/article1.cfm

Ikpeze, C. (2007). Small group collaboration in peer-led electronic discourse: An analysis of group dynamics and interactions involving pre-service and in service teachers. *Journal of Technology and Teacher Education, 15*(3), 383-407.

International Society for Technology in Education (2008). ISTE standards for teachers. Retrieved from http://www.iste.org/docs/pdfs/nets-t-standards.pdf?sfvrsn=2

Johnson, B. (2011, October 31). Teaching and Learning: Using iPads in the Classroom. *Edutopia K-12 Education & Learning Innovations with Proven Strategies that Work.* Retrieved October 4, 2013, from
http://www.edutopia.org/blog/ipad-teaching-learning-apps-ben-johnson

Masullo, M., Moreno, W., & Tsantis, L. (2005, July). *An anatomy of the international ICT divide.* Paper presented at the meeting of the International Conference of Education and Information Systems, Orlando, FL. Retrieved 10/8/2013 from http://www.invivovision.com/library/R-0507b.pdf

McClanahan, B., Williams, K., Kennedy, E., & Tate, S. (2012). A breakthrough for Josh: How use of an iPad facilitated reading improvement. *TechTrends, 56*(3), 20-28.

McPherson, S., Wang, S., Hsu, J., & Tsuei, M. (2007). New literacies instruction in teaching, *TechTrends, 51*(5), 24-31.

Melhuish, K. & Falloon, G. (2010). Looking to the future: M-learning with iPad, *Computers in New Zealand Schools, 22*(3). Retrieved 9/20/2013 from
http://education2x.otago.ac.nz/cinzs/mod/resource/view.php?id=114

Murphy, G. (2011). Post-PC devices: A summary of early iPad technology adoption in tertiary environments. *E-Journal of Business Education & Scholarship of Teaching, 5*, 1, 18-32.

Nedungadi, P. & Raman, R. (2012). A new approach to personalization: integrating e-learning and m-learning, *Education Tech Research Development 60*, 659-678.

Owen, P. (2011). iPads, not chalkboards. Retrieved 9/20/2013 from
http://www.telegram.com/article/20111125/NEWS/111259786/1246

Peluso, D. C. (2012). The fast-paced iPad revolution: Can educators stay up to date and relevant about these ubiquitous devices? *British Journal of Educational Technology, 43*(4), 125-127.

Raggi, V. L. & Chronis, A. M. (2006). Interventions to address the academic impairment of children and adolescents with ADHD. *Clinical Child and Family Psychology Review, 9*(1), 85-111.

Rapp, W. H. (2005). Using assistive technology with students with exceptional learning needs: When does an aid become a crutch? *Reading & Writing Quarterly, 21*(2), 193-196.

Rose, M. (2011, September 18). iPad-enabled students get performance boost, says ACU study | TUAW - the unofficial Apple weblog. *TUAW-The Unofficial Apple Weblog.* Retrieved October 4, 2013, from http://www.tuaw.com/2011/09/18/ipad-enabled-students-get-performance-boost-says-acu-study/

Shuler, C. (2009a). Pockets of potential: Using mobile technologies to promote children's learning, New York: The Joan Ganz Cooney Center at Sesame Workshop. Retrieved 10/8/2013 from
http://www.joanganzcooneycenter.org/wp-content/uploads/2010/03/pockets_of_potential_1_.pdf

Shuler, C. (2009b). iLearn; a content analysis of the iTunes app store's education section, New York: The Joan Ganz Cooney Center at Sesame Workshop. Retrieved 10/8/2013 from
http://www.telegram.com/article/20111125/NEWS/111259786/1246

Smith, S. J. & Robinson, S. (2003). Technology integration through collaborative cohorts: Preparing future teachers to use technology. *Remedial and Special Education, 24*(3), 154-160.

Williams, M. K., Foulger, T. S., & Wetzel, K. (2009). Preparing pre-service teachers for 21st century classrooms: Transforming attitudes and behaviors about innovative technology. *Journal of Technology and Teacher Education, 17*(3), 393-4.

EdITLib

The Leading Digital Library Dedicated to Education and Information Technology

EdITLib.org

DOES YOUR LIBRARY SUBSCRIBE?

The EdITLib digital library is the premier aggregated and multimedia resource for peer-reviewed research on the latest developments and applications in Educational Technologies and E-Learning.

Subscribe today to access 100,000+ articles and 16,000 dissertations written by 200,000+ international authors covering 30+ years of advancements in IT in Education!

Abstracts are available open access so you can try the Digital Library at no cost!

- Special Topic Books
- Conference Papers
- Presentation Slides
- Conference Talks
- Journal Articles
- Webinars
- Videos

Individual subscriptions $19/month or $150/year
Libraries $1895/year

Academic Journals including:

- Journal of Educational Multimedia and Hypermedia
- International Journal on E-Learning (Corporate, Government, Healthcare, & Higher Education)
- Journal of Computers in Mathematics and Science Teaching
- Journal of Interactive Learning Research
- Journal of Technology and Teacher Education
- Contemporary Issues in Technology & Teacher Education (electronic)

Conference proceedings including:

- **EdMedia** – World Conference on Educational Media & Technology
- **E-Learn** – World Conference on E-Learning in Corporate, Healthcare, Government, and Higher Education
- **SITE** – Society for Information Technology and Teacher Education International Conference
- **Global Learn** – Global Conference on Learning and Technology
- **Global TIME** – Global Conference on Technology, Innovation, Media & Education

Newest content additions:

e-Books:
- Handbook of Games and Simulations in Teacher Education
- Adding Some TEC-VARIETY: 100+ Activities for Motivating and Retaining Learners Online

Conference Books:
- Education and Information Technology 2014: A Selection of AACE Award Papers

Journals:
- Journal of Open, Flexible, and Distance Learning

... and many more titles!

NEW!

- Curated ERIC indexed publications on Educational Technology

- Relevant Content from Proquest Dissertations **Just Added**

Like us on Facebook: facebook.com/editlib
Follow us on twitter: twitter.com/editlib

Association for the Advancement of Computing in Education
P.O. Box 719, Waynesville, NC 28786 • Email: info@aace.org • aace.org

www.ingramcontent.com/pod-product-compliance
Lightning Source LLC
Chambersburg PA
CBHW081134170426
43197CB00017B/2854